Theories of Development

THEORIES
OF DEVELOPMENT

Jonas Langer

UNIVERSITY OF CALIFORNIA, BERKELEY

HOLT, RINEHART AND WINSTON, INC.

NEW YORK • CHICAGO • SAN FRANCISCO • ATLANTA
DALLAS • MONTREAL • TORONTO • LONDON • SYDNEY

*to the late Heinz Werner
with affection and appreciation*

Preface

A T BEST, THEORIES OF PSYCHOLOGY, whether developmental or other, are only partial theories or hypotheses about certain types of physiological processes, behaviors, experiences, feelings, personal characteristics, social interactions, cognitions, and so on. Academic debate about whether a complete theory of all psychological phenomena is possible in principle begs the present and immediately forseeable limited status of psychological theories. Consequently, it seems more valuable to order and relate the major hypotheses, or clusters of hypotheses, into what appear to be the three main contemporary streams of thought on psychological development than to present separately the hypotheses of individual developmental theorists who, in any case, have been receiving more individualized exposition than has ever before been accorded to them in the history of psychology. These three general developmental perspectives are what we will call the psychoanalytic, the mechanical mirror, and the organic lamp theories.

Debate about the relative adequacy of the three perspectives, too, is limited because the theories are more tangential than in clear-cut and direct opposition to each other. For example, mechanical mirror theory focuses upon the organism's continuous, quantitative accumulation of response elements that are stimulated by the environment. These elements cumulate to make up the individual's growth of behavior. The primary focus of organic lamp theory is the organism's construction of its own rational systems of action. These systems are transformed from biological to psychological stages of development. Psychoanalytic theory began as a theory of instinctual and pathological phenomena. Its treatment of normal development focuses upon the transformation of arational instincts into rational processes and upon the maturation of psychosexual functions. More recently it has also proposed a theory of psychosocial evolution modeled after psychosexual development.

A consequence of attempting to portray theories, rather than theorists, is that the particular formulation of each perspective is necessarily a result of the writer's construction. It would therefore be wise to know at least my general perspective before "accepting" my formulation and evaluation of developmental problems and theories. While the scope and spatial limits of this book do not permit a direct presentation of my views, it is possible to obtain a fair understanding of them from the last chapter. The reader is therefore urged to take a quick preliminary look at that chapter before reading the text so that the understanding and evaluation that he forms of the issues in, and theories of, developmental psychology may be as objective as possible.

JONAS LANGER

Berkeley, California
September, 1968

Contents

Theories of Development

Chapter 1

Introduction to the Conceptualization
of Change

DEVELOPMENTAL PSYCHOLOGY is generally considered to be the theoretical and empirical investigation of the mental changes that occur in the course of life. The subject of inquiry may be divided into three parts: The first is the genetic origins of functional systems of action, for example, of grasping in hand or in thought. The second is the formal character of the evolving psychological organization. Here, the object is comprehensive description and explanation of consecutive patterns of functional systems of action, such as the various ways of grasping in thought that evolve during a lifetime. The third is the progressive and regressive transformation of systems of action. Here the issues that arise are of the character: Do modes of grasping in thought evolve out of grasping in hand? Do more sophisticated ways of grasping in thought evolve out of more primitive ways? Taken as a whole the inquiry is into how the child comes to have functional systems of action A_1, B_1, C_1, . . .; what these new systems and their pattern of functional and structural organization are; how they change to A_2, B_2, C_2, . . .; what these transformed systems and their organization are; and so on for the origins and development of all subsequent systems of action and their patterns of organization.

It is easy to determine that death has arrested all psychological action and change. It is not as easy to determine the initial, subsequent, and final (in the sense of "most mature") stages of a particular system of action, such as thinking, or even speaking, about which there is still controversy as to whether or not the baby's babbling constitutes the beginning of speech. As a matter of fact, what can be said about the stages of a system of action at this period in the history of developmental psychology is usually more hypothesis than fact.

Of course, different functional systems arise at different times of life. For example, sucking begins shortly after birth, while crawling appears only later in the first year.

Different functional systems also develop at different rates. Consequently, the age at which each achieves its most mature form varies. For example, mathematical reasoning is slower to develop than reading although it begins at about the same time. In a full life-span it is hardly ever the case that the final (most mature) stage of a system occurs just before the system ceases to operate. For that reason it is probably not true that systems evolve simply because we grow older.

The duration of the most mature stage of a system also varies. Some functional systems of action remain stable longer than others. And some systems deteriorate more rapidly than others; for example, memory deteriorates more rapidly than reading. We do not know whether rate of formation, duration of stability, and rate of deterioration are correlated for individual systems.

Insofar as processes of functional deterioration may be assumed to be lawful, it is necessary to formulate principles of regressive change that complement those that are proposed to govern progressive change. A theory of development that hopes to be comprehensive should probably inquire into both progress and regress, even if the laws governing each turn out to be different.

We must recognize, then, that a person has many systems of action and that each may achieve initial, intermediate, most mature, and subsequent functional forms at different times of his life. Consequently, these systems operate at different levels at any given period. For example, the child's eating skills are highly developed by the time he makes his first attempts at reading.

In sum, the type, rate, and duration of change vary for different systems of action, such as walking versus mathematical reasoning. This is typically true of both progressive and regressive change. Normative notions of natural rate of progress are presumably what is behind our suspicion of retarded or precocious development when we assert that a person's social or emotional development is lagging behind his intellectual development or vice versa. Implicit in such assessments are standards of what constitutes fast, retarded, and arrested tempos of change.

CONCEPTS OF CHANGE

The above description of the genetic, organizational, and transformational parts of the developmental inquiry suggests that change and system are theoretical and correlative concepts. They are theoretical notions because pure observation cannot tell us whether the recording of two actions is that of two different systems, A and B, or of the same system that has changed from stage A_1 to A_2. They are correlative conceptions because (*a*) the ascription of change to an observed process over time assumes that two different forms (A_1 and A_2) of the same system of action rather than two different systems (A and B) are being compared, and (*b*) the assignment of continuity to two different stages (1 and 2) assumes that a change took place in one system (A_1 to A_2 or B_1 to B_2) rather than that the actions of two different systems (A and B) have been observed.

The issue of continuity versus discontinuity in development is theoretical, not empirical (see Werner, 1957). It was once argued that a growth curve of behavior without a dip in it, such as

was a clear indication of continuity, while a dip in a growth curve, such as

proved discontinuity. It is now clear that the issue is logical, not statistical. Consider the psychological act of pointing with one's finger in order to indicate something. It is quite clear that the development of this activity is chronologically continuous with manipulatory activity, such as grasping at things. Whether there is psychological continuity or discontinuity between grasping and pointing, such that they belong to the same or two different systems of action, is a logical interpretive issue. It depends upon whether they subserve the same underlying function, such as reference, that is transformed from grasping into indication (A_1 to A_2), or two different functions, such as manipulation and reference (A and B).

Functional continuity of a system of action is observed when the change is only quantitative. For example, an increase in vocabulary may be nothing more than a quantitative change in the speech system of action. Quantitative change was called *growth* by Aristotle. Growth refers only to the increment or decrement in the content of an entity, whatever its state. Functional discontinuity of a system of action is always a qualitative change. Discontinuity is the result of either (*a*) the emergence of a completely new, and at least to some extent preformed, system for which no precursory form was present or (*b*) the degeneration and loss of a system that was once available. Aristotle called the former type of change *coming-to-be* and the latter *passing-away*. Properly speaking, these two kinds of change constitute the genetic or maturational part of the developmental inquiry. Aristotle delineated one more type of change, namely, *alteration*. Alteration is a qualitative change by which the system is conserved, but its mode or structure is transformed. The transformation of crawling into walking may be an example of alteration of the locomotory system of action. This type of qualitative change means both continuity and discontinuity in the system. Properly speaking, alteration and growth constitute the transformational part of the developmental inquiry.

MODELS OF MAN

The type of change and of systems attributed to humans typically hinges upon whether man is conceived of as *active* or *passive*. This distinction, made by Aristotle, is between man as an actor who spontaneously initiates his own actions, which move his surroundings to react, and man as a patient whose behavior is merely a response to external agents, which move him to react in ways that conform to the demands immanent in their stimulation.

Differing conceptions of man and change lead the three major contemporary theories of development to focus upon different types of phenomena, methods of inquiry, and forms of explanation, as will be seen in some detail in the next three chapters. In this chapter, the general outlines of their respective approaches will be sketched.

Mechanical Mirror Theory

The view most closely associated with a passive model of man is that which we shall call the mechanical mirror theory. At the core of this perspective is the thesis that *man grows to be what he is made to be by his environment.*

In the history of philosophical thought this thesis has been based upon two central assumptions. The first is that the content of the mind can be analyzed into constituent elements. Historically, this meant speculating about the building blocks or atoms, such as impressions and images, of which the mind was presumed to be composed. Once the character of the smallest constituent element was decided upon, the task was to posit some principles governing the way in which these atoms connect or associate with each other.

The second assumption is that external forces impinge upon the child's sensorium and leave elementary impressions. Thus Locke maintained that the mind is an empty slate before sensory impressions mark it. Ideas, as Hume put it, are merely the faint images of these impressions. These images are the elements or simple ideas that make up the mind, and complex ideas are the association of elementary or simple ideas. We may therefore characterize the growth of the mind, from this point of view, as the quantitative accumulation and association of elements supplied by the environment.

The contemporary mechanical mirror conception focuses upon behavioral reactions, rather than impressions, that the child can be observed to make in response to environmental stimulation. The methodological advantage that results is clear because it is much easier to observe and record the child's reactions to, rather than his impressions or images of, experimentally controlled conditions.

The search is primarily for the efficient cause of, or antecedent conditions that lead to, the child's behavior. Efficient causality is one of the four types of determination in Aristotle's *Physics*. Aristotle uses examples like the following to illustrate what efficient causality means: "Why did they go to war? Because there had been a raid." The mechanical mirror theory is concerned with behaviors of the child that are motions or responses, that is, the effects of initiating agents. The quest is for (a) the initial antecedent conditions, for example, the motive forces (stimuli or needs) that initiate or inhibit the child's consequent behavioral motions and (b) the secondary determinants, for example, rewards or punishments, that reinforce and shape his responses once they have been initiated.

The developmental, theoretical aim is to formulate the long-term efficient causality of the child's behavior, that is, how earlier events in life are remembered and may influence responses to stimulation later in life. The concern is with what Aristotle called growth, namely, with the accumulation and strengthening of observable behavioral achievements due to initial and secondary causes. The ideal is to create a science of behavioral growth based upon one principle of determination, efficient causality. Efficient causality is an adequate explanatory principle because it is assumed that behavior, however complex, is the effect of, and may therefore be analyzed into, antecedent elements:

> The history of science suggests that the complexities of the child's real world are probably only multiple combinations of pure and simple processes. Hence the complexity of child behavior *in vivo* may result only from the large number of factors involved; yet each factor by itself may operate in a simple manner, readily and completely understandable in a laboratory setting. (Bijou & Baer, 1960, p. 143)

Analysis of the efficient causes of the child's behavior and its growth has generally led proponents of the mechanical mirror view to use some variant of the experimental method as their ideal tool of investigation. In practice, however, it is first necessary to observe formally or informally the growth of some aspects of the child's behavior, such as his social, emotional, and linguistic behavior. Then two major types of technique are employed to determine the efficient cause.

The first is a laboratory experiment of local causality following these general lines: Children of determinate ages (the subjects) are subjected to a stimulus or motivating condition that is hypothesized to be the initial or secondary cause of the behavior in question, that is, of its occurrence, the frequency of its occurrence, and the strength with which it is emitted. The effect of this condition is compared with the results due to counterconditions. All other possibly relevant conditions are kept constant for both the hypothesized cause and the counterconditions. It should be noted at this point that even if positive results are obtained, it is not impossible that other conditions may produce the same or a similar result. Different initial causes may lead to similar effects.

Cross-sectional experiments on the causes of long-term growth usually investigate whether the experimental conditions have the same effect upon the behavior of groups of children at different ages. A clear example of a cross-sectional study is reported by Zaporozhets (1965). The eye movement patterns of different groups of children, aged 3–4, 4–5, 5–6, and 6–7 years, looking at the same stimulus figure, were compared. At this point it is only necessary to remark that in general, when similar results are obtained, the cross-sectional study probably has little relevance to the actual course of the child's growth in behaviors that we know change with age. The converse is obviously true when different results are obtained between age groups.

Although they are often used for the same purpose as the cross-sectional method, longitudinal experiments on the causes of growth are most useful for determining whether the experimental conditions have long-term effects upon the behavior of the same children, who are repeatedly tested as they grow older. Again, different groups of children are subjected to differential experimental conditions. But now the long-term, as well as the immediate short-term, effects of the conditions are measured and compared. The general form of the hypothesis is that at least some of the behavioral effects of the experimental conditions should be observed over time in the same children. (For examples see the Rheingold, 1956, and Rheingold & Bayley, 1959, studies described on pp. 63–64 and the Hicks, 1965, study described on p. 69.)

To find differences between ages is not to determine their relevant causes. They tell us that the effects of the experimental condition vary with the age of the child. But the important causal difference is hidden by the age index because age is hardly an initiator of behavior. The problem is then to interpret what cause is suggested by the age index and to test the interpretation.

The second type of technique used to determine the efficient causes of behavioral growth attempts to take advantage of "natural" experiments. The form of the hypotheses is that particular kinds of stimuli or motives that operated earlier in life are the causes of presently observable behaviors of the child, that is, of their occurrence, frequency, and strength. The method is correlational. The aim is to record differential stimulus and motivating conditions early in the child's life, such as high versus low parental nurturance, and to determine if they differentially correlate with specific behaviors of that child later in life, such as dependence versus independence. If high correlations are obtained, they may be interpreted as indicating a causal linkage. But this interpretation is still purely theoretical because it is clear that many highly correlated things do not cause each other; for example, day and night are perfectly correlated, but they do not cause each other.

Organic Lamp Theory

The perspective that most clearly conceives of man as an active agent and his development as a self-constructive process is that which we shall call the organic lamp theory. At the heart of this view is the autogenetic thesis that *man develops to be what he makes himself by his own actions.*

The contemporary autogenetic thesis derives from the conceptions of earlier organismic theorists. Coleridge, the nineteenth century poet, contended that self-generating growth or creativity is the "first power" of all organic systems. He elaborated upon this notion by asserting that (*a*) the future organization of the organism is inherent in the seed out of which it develops, and (*b*) the organism "must . . . assimilate and digest the food which it . . . receives from without" in order to grow. Thus, inherent potential organization, constructivist power, and the assimilatory function ensure that the organism "shapes as it develops itself from within."

Kant formulated a more complex conception of the autogenetic thesis. He argued that organic systems can only be understood *as if* they were "natural purposes" or functions. The organism is a "self-organizing being": it has self-"*moving* power" and self-"*formative* power." Although the organism is not necessarily conscious of these powers, they permit it to generate or construct its own growth. It is as if the development of organisms represented a directedness toward ends immanent in their organization. This is possible because the most important characteristic of organic structures is that they have functions; that is, they are both agencies (means) for action and the end products (purposes) toward which action is directed.

Contemporary organic lamp theory is particularly concerned with the processes that underlie psychological acts and how these acts generate development (coming-to-be and alteration) through a determined sequence of stages. The central hypothesis is that stages of evolution are like a sequence of geometric theorems, each of which is rendered necessary by the entirety of the preceding ones without being contained by them. Piaget (1967) has formulated the following criteria for the determination of sequential alteration of stages. First, each stage of the child's functioning is a necessary result of the previous one (with the exception of the first, which, as we have seen, must be due to a process of coming-to-be) and prepares the following one (with the exception of the last, which must be considered a process of passing-away). Second, each stage in the child's development must be defined by a unity of organization that characterizes all his new conduct at that stage (and not by a simple dominant property). Third, the organization of the child's functional structures at each stage integrates the structures that prepared for the new stage. Finally, the succession of the stages must be universal, although the tempo may differ from individual to individual.

The organic lamp focus upon autogenetic processes of development means that the explanation of change is not conceived as primarily the determination of efficient causality. Rather, the first step toward explaining development is taxonomic work to determine what Aristotle called formal and material causality. Formal causality is the definition, the figure or form, of an entity. Material causality is the source of the present entity, that is, the original entity out of which it came. The formal task for developmental psychology is to determine the configuration of psychological activity that constitutes an organized stage of the child's life, while its material task is to determine the form of the preceding stage, which was its source. This implies that the first step in explaining development is both descriptive and interpretive.

Consequently, the research method employed must subserve both descriptive and interpretive ends. The ideal technique would be something like the following. The first step is careful and detailed observation of the child's activity in a particular situation. On the basis of these observations and of whatever hypotheses he brings to the situation, the experimenter formulates some tentative description and interpretation of the underlying processes or logical structure of the child's activity. He then tests his formulation by subjecting the child to disruptive, counter, or complementary conditions. Observations of their effects upon the child's activity are used as a means of (*a*) testing previous descriptions and interpretations and (*b*) obtaining new hypotheses and information. This technique is continued as long as it yields relevant results.

When studying the development of the preverbal child the investigator is limited to nonverbal conditions and to the child's consequent sensori-motor actions. Nevertheless, if they are used in this descriptive-interpretive fashion, the results may be very rich. The classical example is Piaget's (1951, 1952, 1954) investigations of the developing cognitive processes underlying the preverbal child's actions, which will be described in some detail in Chapter 4.

When studying the development of the verbal child, the investigator may introduce both nonverbal and verbal manipulations into the testing situation. Moreover, he constantly questions the child about what he is doing or saying. These two tools of investigation are interwoven until the limits (potential) of the child's capacities have been explored. This technique for obtaining descriptive-interpretive data has been used most successfully to study cognitive development; Piaget has called it the clinical method. As we shall see in Chapter 4, the clinical method has yielded much descriptive-interpretive information on the development of the reasoning operations, or the logic, underlying the child's overt actions.

After comprehensive interpretive-descriptive data on each stage of the child's development are obtained, it should be possible to explain the process of development from one stage to another. Only recently have such comprehensive data begun to be available, and organic lamp theorists are just beginning to speculate fruitfully and test assertions about the developmental process.

Two major kinds of theoretical assertions have been made about the process of development. Some theorists (particularly Werner, 1948) characterize development as an orthogenetic process. The central idea is that the initial stage of the child's mental organization is global; that is, it is composed of functional structures that are structurally undifferentiated and functionally unrelated. The orthogenetic process is directed towards increasing differentiation, centralization, and hierarchic integration of the child's mental organization (see pp. 91–93 for a fuller exposition of the orthogenetic process). Other theorists (particularly Piaget, 1967) characterize development as an equilibration process. Here the idea is that development proceeds from relative disequilibrium to increasing equilibrium, such that when the child is in disequilibrium (due to internal imbalance in interaction with external perturbation), he will operate to establish greater equilibrium. As a consequence the child changes himself and develops (see pp. 93–96 for a fuller exposition of the equilibration process).

The research method is therefore to test children who are presumed to be in internal disequilibrium because (*a*) it is known that they are in a transitional phase between two stages or (*b*) they are placed in situations that are supposed to simulate real-life perturbations. The general hypothesis is that an external perturbation is most successful in changing action when the child is in the transitional phase in which the perturbation has particular significance for him. The child's advance is usually expected to be fragile, relatively nontransferable to other similar situations, and easily disruptible.

Psychoanalytic Theory

Whereas both mechanical mirror and organic lamp theories view the child, whether his behavior is passively learned from others or actively self-generated, as basically intellectual and rational, the psychoanalytic theory sees him as basically affective and irrational. Only gradually does he learn to control his impulses and passions, and even then, he is always in a state of conflict between his natural instinctual impulses and the unnatural societal mores imposed upon him. Psychoanalytic theory is therefore primarily concerned with man's affect, and only secondarily with his intellect. For this and other reasons it cannot be definitively located on the active-passive dimension of man's action and development. The psychoanalytic thesis, more precisely, is that *man is a conflicted being who is driven to action and growth both by his own passions or instincts and by external demands.*

Man is constantly responding to and defending against internal (instinctual) urges and external (physical and social) stimuli. It is as if he were under a constant barrage that instigates or triggers his action or development. The nature of the driven person varies with his maturational stage of psychosexual development, for example, oral or anal. One basic theoretical assumption is made about the maturation or coming-to-be of stages. Most recently Erikson (1959, 1963) has expressed this assumption as an epigenetic principle. It asserts that the instinctual energy with which the child is born is invested in different parts of his body in a prescribed sequence and at determinate times of his life cycle. The instinctual stimulation of a bodily part or zone, such as the mouth, causes it to function. That function, such as sucking food or incorporating experience, becomes the child's predominant mode of action during that period of his life. It is therefore said to characterize a stage of the child's sexual and social development. Only the maturationally predetermined shift of instinctual energy to another bodily zone causes a change in the child's functioning and the development of a new stage (see pp. 33–34 for a fuller exposition of the epigenetic process).

The central concern with *healthy* personality formation has led psycho-analytic theory to investigate the role of internal conflicts and disturbing experiences upon the child's development. A different major crisis of a predestined nature is assumed to characterize each stage of the child's sexual and social development. For example, it is hypothesized that conflict between trust and mistrust, of oneself and the environment, necessarily arises in all infants during the first, oral stage. The ways in which the child resolves his crises at each stage determine the character and health of his personality formation at that stage. They also limit the possible types and the health of his character formation later in life. In this way antecedent conflicts are hypothesized to affect subsequent personality development: the child is father of the man. And in this sense, psychoanalytic theory is concerned with conflicts as the efficient causes of both the formation and the health of individual personality.

This focus upon the effects of antecedent conflicts on personality development has led to the unique investigatory tool employed in psychoanalytic research—the situation that Freud first developed as a therapeutic technique for adult patients with mental problems. In general, the focus has been upon the individual's conflicts (dynamics). When it was first used, the method involved free association to events and dreams in a patient's life. Freud attempted to interpret and reconstruct the earlier conflict-producing experiences that were the source of current problems. This work led to the hypothesis of infantile sexuality. The hypothesis was that the child's earliest acts are motivated by primitive and partial sexual instincts which are precursory of later and more mature forms of sexuality. Subsequent work led Freud to conclude that a patient's verbalizations were not true reports of earlier experiences, but primarily fantasies he had created about his early life.

Nevertheless, the major method of psychoanalytic research remains the therapeutic situation in which dynamics or conflicts are explored. However, recent investigators have greatly expanded the technique. In addition to freely associating, the patient is encouraged and directed to discuss the variety of events that he or the therapist believes to be related to his dynamics. The subjects are no longer adults only, but people of all ages. With young children, the therapeutic technique employed is primarily free and directed play. Discussion is used only to the extent that the child is capable of it.

RESEARCH METHODS

Before turning to the meat of our subject, it is necessary to make explicit what we have been saying about the association between theoretical perspective and research method. It is generally true, as we have been suggesting, that certain research methods are typically preferred and used by each perspective, although the correlation is hardly perfect. Strict adherents of the mechanical mirror view restrict research to cross-sectional and longitudinal variants of the experimental and correlational methods. They establish stringent criteria for formulating testable hypotheses and gathering reliable data with these methods. In general, they are loath to accept the results of investigations that use the clinical method or the psychotherapeutic method. Strict adherents of the psychoanalytic view, on the other hand, typically assert that their theoretical propositions can only be tested properly and conclusively by findings obtained with psychotherapeutic techniques. They tend to doubt the validity or relevance of findings contradictory to psychoanalytic propositions when these findings are obtained with any but the psychotherapeutic method. Adherents of the organic lamp view tend to be the most eclectic users of research methods. In addition to observational and clinical methods, they are willing to use any research technique that generates interesting and relevant findings. For example, organic lamp research on perceptual development is composed almost entirely of cross-sectional experiments. Nevertheless, when it comes to cognitive development, strict adherents of the view maintain that the only method that yields consistently valid evidence on the form of reasoning phenomena is the clinical method. All other research methods may generate misleading evidence about the formal character of cognition and its development.

Now it is obvious that many developmental theorists are not strict adherents of any general perspective. There are many shadings and gradations between the three theoretical perspectives formulated here. Theorists who take compromise conceptual positions are also those who are most likely to use research methods in an eclectic and pragmatic fashion.

Basically, however, each theoretical perspective establishes different criteria as to what scientific research is and how it is properly performed. In the ensuing descriptions, criticisms of research generated by a theory will be based only on the criteria that that theory itself accepts.

Chapter 2
The Psychoanalytic Perspective

FREUD'S MODEL OF MAN was of a being whose essential psychological nature is desire rather than reason. His focus of analysis was therefore primarily upon man's passions or affect, and only secondarily upon his intellect. The immediate historical roots of this view are in nineteenth century romantic philosophy, but the idea in its most general form probably can be traced to the Judeo-Christian tradition. The child is born in a state of original sin with irrational appetites and passions, and his development is directed toward overcoming this initial state. This means that development is characterized, at least partly, by the transformation of inherent irrational intentions into socialized rational purposes that are goodly, or that aspire to the godly.

In Freud's hands this conception became pregnant with scientific intuition. First, intentionality is not merely an acquired characteristic. It is part of the child's inherited equipment, embodied in the instincts with which he is born. That is, man is a purposeful animal from birth. And his intentionality need not be conscious. Many of his purposes stem from biological needs and thus antedate consciousness, while others are unconscious. The latter are intentions that once were conscious but that have been forgotten because they are in some way disturbing.

It is perhaps not strictly correct to speak of intentions at the nonconscious stage of life. Wishes are conscious phenomena and the infant is not yet a conscious being. In Freudian terminology wishes are the conscious manifestation of nonconscious instinctive needs. These biological needs provide the initial energy which instigates and provides the fuel for the infant's psychic apparatus. That is, unconscious instincts drive the infant to operate psychologically. This is, at least, as true before the child has conscious wishes as after. It is, however, disturbing formerly conscious intentions which have become unconscious that may have a particularly impelling or motivating force as the child grows up. For example, a boy who has uncomfortable sexual feelings toward his mother may entirely forget them; yet they may influence his behavior toward women when he grows up.

The thesis that man's essence is desire also led Freud to hypothesize developmental continuity between nonconscious prerational intentions and conscious rational processes. Both are energized by the same biological endowment, namely, instincts. The instincts which energize rationality are merely an outgrowth, a displaced (sublimated) part, of the instincts that energize prerationality. For example, the instincts that energize the scientist's research activity are supposedly sublimated prerational instincts.

The development of rational instincts in the child is the result of the interaction between prerational instincts (the id structure of personality) and external reality. That is, when the child's prerational instincts lead to action that is nonadaptive, these instincts are transformed. The consequence is the development of a psychic structure of rationality, called the ego, "that part of the id which has been modified by the direct influence of the external world" (Freud, 1923, p. 29). The child's ego is in large measure devoted to the internal representation of external reality. One of the major functions of his ego is to repress the prerational instinctual appetites; it does so in accordance with reality. The intervention of reason between the instinctual child and his environment causes man, unlike other animals, to hesitate in his interaction with the milieu. This delay in the gratification of, or sublimation of, his immediate instinctual urges is in turn the basis for man's eventual cognitive transformation of external physical reality into the many special realities, such as mythical, scientific, and social realities, that constitute his civilization and culture. Thus, Freud seems to suggest a circular, probably feedback, evolutionary relationship between man and his environment in which the initial genetic cycle is the following: through interaction with external reality, prerational man is transformed into the first form of rational man, and with further development, rational man transforms natural reality into special realities.

There is also a major negative consequence of rationality: man hesitates in his interaction with nature. This is the initial genetic reason for man's state of disease, his constant neurosis. Freud assumed that the prerational instincts keep the human organism, like all other animals, in direct contact with the world. The intervention of reason makes it impossible for man ever to recapture his pristine state of instinctual undifferentiatedness from the world. The child loses this immediate contact when he leaves the nonconscious paradise of the womb, that purely instinctual and affective world, and enters the mediated world of consciousness, volition, and intellect. Since reason is forever bound to interfere with the maintenance of pure affective tranquility or instinctual homeostasis, this state can be totally re-achieved only when the death instinct once more rules supreme and enforces a state of equilibrium.

In more prosaic and practical terms, this metaphysic provided a cogent basis for explaining human mental pathology. Neuroses are the result of conflict between (*a*) the nonconscious or unconscious wishes for gratification or tensionlessness and (*b*) reason, that internal representation of reality or of social norms which produces tension through its conflict with id desires. Freud's application of the notion of conflict between conscious and nonconscious forms of intentionality to the understanding and treatment of mental disturbances was novel. His conception of nonconscious and unconscious intentionality was not; it was a common notion of romantic philosophy.

The primary efficient cause of mental life, then, is instinct. Experience or environmental factors are only secondary, transforming determinants. Two major ways in which instincts might influence development have been postulated. One is Jung's hypothesis of causal *instinctual forms* that are part of the racial heritage of man. These forms are the archetypes of all experience, presumably universal to all minds. Indeed, they constitute the collective unconscious of mankind, whether "of the beginnings of things before the age of man or of the unborn generations of the future." This heritage is made up of symbolic forms that are genetically transmitted and therefore present before birth. Their influence is independent of the particular interactions the individual has with his environment.

Vague references to the influence of "prehistory" upon individual behavior abound in the psychoanalytic literature, including Freud's writings. The central and clearly articulated Freudian hypothesis, however, is of hereditary types of *instinctual energy*, rather than of any instinctual forms that existed before the individual. The type of energy posited, in Freud's case life giving and death seeking, is assumed to determine the general type, for example, oral or anal, but not the specific content, of individual experience. The actual character of experience is determined by an interaction between the person's instinctual energies and the environmental forces acting upon him.

The possibility of transforming nonrational instinctual energy into rational energy has been questioned by a group of neo-Freudians who are usually called "ego psychologists." These men argue that the child is born with rational instincts in addition to the prerational instincts posited by Freud. The rational instincts are presumed to energize the child's conflict-free perception and thinking in his rational interaction with external reality. Hartmann, Erikson, and R. W. White, in particular, have focused upon the role of both rational and nonrational instincts in the developmental unfolding of personal identity.

Finally, Freud maintained that the development of the person is marked by a series of stages that are universal to mankind. Erikson has explicitly hypothesized that the process whereby these stages evolve is governed by an *epigenetic* principle. By this he means that the sequence and tempo of the unfolding of stages are genetically determined (see pp. 33–34 for a fuller discussion). In addition, Erikson has sought to elucidate the role of the social milieu—how it interacts with instinctual aims—in determining adaptive ego functioning at different stages of the life cycle.

THE COLLECTIVE UNCONSCIOUS

As noted above, one factor postulated to determine psychological development is instinctual form. This factor has been dealt with in psychology almost exclusively by Jung (1959), who hypothesized that there is an identical, "impersonal" psychic system in all people. This system owes its existence exclusively to heredity and not at all to individual learning of cultural content, because its form consists of preexistent archetypal symbols or collective representations that "have never been in consciousness." These preformed universal symbols "only become conscious secondarily" by imposing their character upon the content of experience, whether perceptual, imaginary, or contemplative:

> Archetypes are not determined as regards their content, but only as regards their form and then only to a very limited degree. A primordial image is determined as to its content only when it has become conscious and is therefore filled out with the material of conscious experience. . . . The archetype in itself is empty and purely formal, nothing but a *facultas prae-formandi,* a possibility of representation which is given *a priori.* (Jung, 1959, p. 79)

Archetypes result from the constant repetition of typical life situations that has "engraved these experiences into our psychic constitution." The archetypes then are not purely instinctual energy but "unconscious images of the instincts themselves." These unconscious images act as motivating forces that are present "long before there is any conscious-ness" in the individual, and they "pursue their inherent goals" even after consciousness has arisen.

The appropriate archetype becomes "activated" whenever a situation arises that corresponds to it. At such times the archetype imposes its form upon experience "against all reason and will, or else produces a conflict of pathological dimensions . . ." As long as neurosis is a purely idiosyncratic affair, the archetypes play no role in it. However, if a given neurosis is found in many people, then Jung assumes the dominating force of an archetype. An example of Jung's (1959, p. 48) argument which also serves to indicate his contribution to historical analysis is the following:

There is no lunacy people under the domination of an archetype will not fall a prey to. If thirty years ago anyone had dared to predict that our psychological development was tending towards a revival of the medieval persecution of the Jews, that Europe would again tremble before the Roman fasces and the tramp of legions, that people would once more give the Roman salute as two thousand years ago, and that instead of the Christian Cross an archaic swastika would lure onward millions of warriors ready for death—why, that man would have been hooted as a mystical fool. And today? Surprising as it may seem, all this absurdity is a horrible reality. Private life, private aetiologies, and private neuroses have become almost a fiction in the world of today. The man of the past who lived in a world of archaic "représentations collectives" has arisen again into very visible and painfully real life, and this not only in a few unbalanced individuals but in many millions of people.

The method for proving the existence of archetypes and their instinctual influence, according to Jung, consists of finding correspondences between the functioning of the archetype as known from historical sources and the themes of adult and early childhood dreams, active imagination, paranoid delusions, and fantasies produced by individuals in a trance. The object is, of course, to find correspondences with themes that play a function in the psychological production but which the producer "couldn't possibly know." Dreams are therefore particularly important as evidence because they "have the advantage of being involuntary spontaneous products of the unconscious psyche and are therefore pure products of nature not falsified by any conscious purpose."

Jung has catalogued many archetypes in his monumental works but the following is a particularly intriguing example. He describes the religious delusion of a paranoid schizophrenic who—while shaking his head, blinking into the sun, and telling Jung to do the same—claimed he saw "the sun's penis" out of which "the wind comes." Jung cites two historical productions that he asserts to be in thematic correspondence with this delusion and argues that the patient could hardly have been aware of their theme. The first is found in a Mithraic ritual of the Alexandrian school of mysticism. The instructions for the ritual include, "Draw breath from the rays. . . . The path of the visible gods will appear through the disc of the sun, who is God my father. Likewise the so-called tube, the origin of the ministering wind. For you will see hanging down from the disc of the sun something that looks like a tube." Again, in another but different religious context, that of medieval paintings of the Virgin Mary, one finds the depiction of a wind tube that connects God's throne with the body of Mary. A dove or the Christ child is shown flying down the tube into Mary's body. The dove is symbolic of "the fructifying agent, the wind of the Holy Ghost."

ORIGINS OF ID, EGO,
AND SUPEREGO STRUCTURES

Freud (1923) assumed that the infant is born with nothing more than irrational instinctual appetites. For this reason he considered the newborn infant to be an "it" or *id* like other animals whose actions are guided primarily by their instinctual needs. Erikson (1963, pp. 192–193) puts it succinctly:

> The id Freud considered to be the oldest province of the mind, both in individual terms—for he held the young baby to be "all id"—and in phylogenetic terms, for the id is the deposition in us of the whole of evolutionary history. . . . The id . . . [is] the sum of all desire which must be overcome before we can be quite human.

Instincts, according to Freud, are characterized by their source, impetus, aim, and object. The *source* of the child's instinctual energy is any somatic or physiological process that stimulates his mind, that is, serves to initiate psychological activity. However, instincts stimulate the child's mind in a fashion that is quite different from stimulation coming from the external environment. Instinctual energy causes needs that the child cannot avoid and that must be dealt with, whereas external stimulation does not. Instincts provide an *impetus* for the child's motoric activity. The strength of this impetus is defined as "the amount of forces or the measure of the demand upon energy which it represents." The *aim* of the child's instincts is the pleasure or tension reduction that comes about with the gratification of his biological needs, such as hunger and thirst, while the *object* is anything which the child's instincts can achieve as their aim. For the child, objects become associated with an instinct by the experience that they lead to satisfaction. For example, the child comes to love his mother because she is intimately associated with the satisfaction of his needs and the reduction of the tension that these needs cause.

Freud (1915, 1930) posited two conflicting yet complementary classes of instincts that are presumably operative from birth on: *Eros*, the life (sexual-reproductive and self-preservative) instinct, and *Thanatos*, the death (aggressive and self-destructive) instinct. The aim of Eros is to stimulate activity: its energy (called libido) is constructive, life seeking, and life giving. Libidinal instincts are numerous; they have different sources, aims, and objects; and they predominate at different stages of development. The aim of Thanatos, on the other hand, is inhibition and a state of tensionlessness: its energy is destructive and death seeking. A possible developmental interpretation, not expressed by Freud, is that both instincts are required for progressive development. The excitation created by Eros is necessary to initiate change, while the inhibition that is the aim of Thanatos is necessary to stop change. Thanatos is therefore needed if the child is to achieve enough closure with respect to one train of change so that a new course of change may be set into motion.

The primary aim and function, then, of the child's id is to gratify the needs caused by instincts, and thereby to reestablish a tensionless (pleasurable) state. This is why the id is said to operate in keeping with a *pleasure principle:* the child's *primary process* of operation is to fulfill his basic bodily needs so that he becomes tensionless.

Because of their nonrational nature many of the id's instinctual wishes do not accord with "reality," that is, the structure of the external physical and social environment. Therefore, instinctual needs are often not gratified. For example, it has been suggested that the primary processes of the id may lead the infant to wishful imagination (fantasying) of a desired object, such as the breast to suck on, and temporary reduction of tension due to hunger. However, fantasying can hardly lead to the actual reduction of hunger tension in the child, which obviously requires obtaining milk. When the child's needs are not satisfied, two consequences become possible: he remains in a state of tension; or unresolved tension somehow causes part of the id to be transformed into a structure which can at the same time (*a*) cope with or function in accordance with external reality and (*b*) deal with the tension produced by the id's needs that are in conflict with reality. This means that part of the child's nonrational id is changed into a rational structure that is oriented toward reality and can cope with the environment, for example, by activating and controlling the behavior necessary to obtain food. Freud (1923) called this transformed part of the child's id the "I" or *ego*. This new development, which begins during the first year of the child's life, means that his personality is now composed of two structures, an id and an ego, and that the ego is the secondary but dominant structure when development is normal. Thus, a *secondary process*, or operating in keeping with reality, is substituted for the pleasure principle as the major determinant of child behavior and its development. The coping mechanisms of the child's ego are supported by his intellectual system, which permits him to test present conditions and to anticipate future situations and contingencies.

Let us now consider in somewhat greater detail Freud's conception of how the structure of the ego originates and then how its functions develop. The initial structure of the child's ego is the result of perceptions by his id, because those are all the child is capable of at that point:

The ego is that part of the id which has been modified by the direct influence of the external world acting through the Perception-Consciousness. . . . In the ego perception plays the part which in the id devolves upon instinct. The ego represents what we call reason and sanity, in contrast to the id which contains the passions. (Freud, 1923, pp. 29–30)

Freud then sketchily points to the role of bodily sensations in the origins of the structure of the child's ego:

The body itself, and above all its surface, is a place from which both external and internal perceptions may spring. (1923, p. 31)

The ego is first and foremost a body-ego; it is not merely a surface entity, but it is itself the projection of a surface. (1923, p. 31)

The development of the child's ego structure is the result of his replacing attending to (cathexis of) desired objects that are unattainable by identifying with (introjecting) objects he desires. At first, very early in life, the child doesn't differentiate between attending to and possessing the desired persons (object-choices), but when he begins to find that he can't have the desired "sexual object" he also begins to substitute introjecting (identifying with) the lost object for having it. Identifying with the lost object results in "a reinstatement of the object within the ego" such that the child's ego accords with or reflects the object of identification. Freud admitted that "the exact nature of this substitution is as yet unknown to us," but he argued that

the process, especially in the early phases of development, is a very frequent one, and it points to the conclusion that the character of the ego is a precipitate of abandoned object-cathexes and it contains a record of past object-choices. (1923, p. 36)

The instincts that energize the newly developed ego structure are erotic instincts that have been displaced from the id and neutralized. Freud hypothesized that the child's erotic, more than his destructive, instincts are transformable. They can be "readily diverted and displaced" into a reservoir of neutral energy that is at the disposal of his ego. There is developmental continuity in the source and the aim of the child's neutral displaceable energy:

If this displaceable energy is desexualized libido, it might also be described as sublimated energy; for it would still retain the main purpose of Eros— that of uniting and binding—in so far as it helped toward establishing that unity, or tendency to unity, which is particularly characteristic of the ego. If the intellectual processes in the wider sense are to be classed among these displacements, then the energy for the work of thought itself must be supplied from sublimated erotic sources. (1923, p. 64)

But there is also developmental discontinuity in the aim and object of the child's neutral displaceable energy:

> The transformation of erotic libido into ego-libido of course involves an abandonment of sexual aims, a desexualization. By thus obtaining possession of the libido from the object-cathexes . . . and desexualizing or sublimating the libido of the id, the ego is working in opposition to the purposes of Eros and placing itself at the service of the opposing instinctual trends. (1923, p. 65)

How the child's instinctual energy becomes displaced and neutralized, thereby activating ego functioning, is not clear. As we shall see in the next section, the entire problem of how the child's ego could develop out of (in the sense of being an alteration of part of) his id is an issue that has led some psychoanalytic theorists to extend but also to modify Freud's hypotheses on the origins of the ego.

Once the child's ego structure has arisen, the functional relationship between it and the id structure

> is like a man on horseback, who has to hold in check the superior strength of the horse; with this difference, that the rider seeks to do so with his own strength while the ego uses borrowed forces. The illustration may be carried further. Often a rider, if he is not to be parted from his horse, is obliged to guide it where it wants to go; so in the same way the ego constantly carries into action the wishes of the id as if they were its own. (1923, p. 30)

The ego develops several mechanisms of defense against the wishes of the id (A. Freud, 1946). The major mechanism is that of *repressing*, or not permitting the aims of the primary instinctual process to become conscious. (Repression is an unconscious mechanism of defense against frustration.) Thus, the child's ego comes to include not only conscious perceptible aspects of mental life but also unconscious repressed aspects.

The *unconscious* aspects of the child's mental life are ideas and wishes that are unrecognized because he has repressed instincts that have never been conscious or suppressed desires that have become conscious. Suppression is the conscious equivalent of repression. Repressed and suppressed mental content is said to be in a state of latency; that is, it retains the potential capacity to cause the child mental conflict and to affect his behavior because it consists of traces of ideas and desires that have not really disappeared. Rather, they are stored in the unconscious. Consequently, they may fester and grow like a sore until they erupt into consciousness, causing pathology.

Consciousness is the outer layer of the child's mental apparatus because it is closest to, or in the most direct contact with, the external world. Its content is perceptions and feelings coming from outside (external reality) and from inside (instincts). Just like external perceptions and feelings, the child's internal images (dreams and thoughts) can only become conscious by the perceptual apparatus. Sometimes the child's internal processes are invested with excessive energy, which causes internal images to be perceived as if they came from the external world and therefore to be accepted as real. When this happens while the child is asleep it is nothing more than the normal process of dreaming, but if it occurs when he is awake it indicates that he cannot yet differentiate between appearance and reality. If it happens when he becomes an adult, it is an abnormal hallucinatory process indicating a breakdown in the ability to distinguish between reality and appearance.

The transitional layer between the child's conscious and the unconscious is his *preconscious.* The child's unconscious (unrecognized) ideas become preconscious by being connected with verbal images that correspond to them. (Verbal images are "memory-residues" which were once percepts.) This notion of the preconscious is the basis for the psychoanalytic therapeutic technique of verbalization, which attempts to enable the patient to represent unconscious material in verbal forms so that it may become conscious and be dealt with more directly and rationally.

The child's ego controls all of his voluntary activity. Freud (1923) defines activity as the "discharge of excitation into the external world." For example, even though the child's ego "goes to sleep at night," it still functions. It censors dreams by not permitting certain unconscious id-derived material to become manifest aspects of the dream content. It does this by disguising the intended, latent content. This is why manifest content does not represent the true significance of the dream.

Trying to repress the id instincts that are in conflict with reality is only one major function of the child's ego. Another is to *sublimate,* or divert and channel, instinctual energy into creative and culture-building activity. According to Anna Freud,

> the ego was evolved out of the id as a helpmate, to locate the best possibilities for need satisfaction and object attachment, and to safeguard wish fulfillment amid the hazards and dangers of the environment. The ego's role as an ally of the id precedes that of an agent designed to slow up and obstruct satisfaction. (1952, p. 45)

The child's ego also has several coping mechanisms for dealing with the social environment, particularly with adults who have expectations about how he should behave, so that they encourage some behaviors and prohibit others. The major adaptive mechanism is to conform to adult expectations by identifying with adult attitudes and normative demands and adopting them by *introjection*. In this way, when he is about two or three years old, part of the child's ego begins to be transformed into a conscience, or what Freud called a *superego* because it is a differentiated and surrogate part of the ego. This alteration of part of the ego results in the third and final structure of the child's personality.

Itself the result of cultural pressures, the child's superego serves to perpetuate culture by identifying with its ideals and demanding that the operations of the rest of the psychic apparatus conform to these ideals. These rigorous demands cause conflict between the instinctive urges of the child's id and the restrictive attitude of his superego. Consequently, the role of mediator between his id and his superego becomes another major function of the ego:

> Consistently balancing and warding off the extreme ways of the other two, the ego keeps tuned to the reality of the historical day, testing perceptions, selecting memories, governing action, and otherwise integrating the individual's capacities of orientation and planning. To safeguard itself, the ego employs "defense mechanisms." These . . . are unconscious arrangements which permit the individual to postpone satisfaction, to find substitutions, and otherwise to arrive at compromises between id impulses and superego compulsions. (Erikson, 1963, p. 193)

INTELLECTUAL FUNCTIONAL AUTONOMY AND THE DEVELOPMENT OF THE EGO

The aim of a recent group of psychoanalytic theorists, often called ego psychologists, is to clarify how (*a*) the structure of the ego originates and develops, and (*b*) the adaptive, rational forms of the child's ego functioning develop. These theorists accept Freud's conceptualization of the child's personality as composed of id, ego, and superego. Unlike Freud, however, they do not assume that the child's ego was ever part of his id; rather, both id and ego are personality structures that are present from birth and that gradually differentiate from each other. Consequently, the focus of analysis for ego psychologists has shifted from the defensive mechanisms to the adaptive, coping ones (White, 1960).

To the extent that adequate differentiation between id and ego is accomplished, the child develops an ego identity that is coherent and independent. This ego is his "specialized organ of adaptation" which mediates the adjustment of his id instincts to the demands made upon him by external reality (Hartmann, 1939). By interposing itself in this way, the ego progressively removes the child's instincts from the relatively direct contact they had with the external milieu early in his life.

Ego psychologists maintain that there are three major steps in the child's relationship with his environment which are of utmost importance for the healthy development of (*a*) the differentiation between his id and his ego and (*b*) his ego or rational functioning.

The first and most important step is the development, during infancy, of the capacity to distinguish between the self and the surrounding world. Three conditions are necessary before this first step can take place: the normal physiological maturation of perceptual organs and skills; the transformation ("neutralization") of prerational instinctual energy focused upon the self ("primary narcissistic cathexis") into rational energy for attending to and recognizing other things ("object cathexis"); and partial deprivation, which will be described shortly in discussing Klein and Riviere. If all the child's needs and wishes are totally gratified from birth onward he will be in a constant state of equilibrium and will remain *fixated* at the undifferentiated level. No change can occur and the initial state of fusion (egocentricity) between self and environment will be maintained. If this state is continued over a substantial period of life the result must be the arrest of development, a form of pathology. Thus, some deprivation, while at times uncomfortable, is a necessary condition for change and development.

The second important step is the development of means of communication between the child and his mother, for example, such facial expressions as smiling. Deprivation of social contact, particularly communicative contact, may well result in abnormal personal and intellectual development. To support this contention, ego psychologists point to findings about children raised from infancy in institutions, particularly to the celebrated and controversial results reported by Spitz (1949). Among other indications of abnormal development, Spitz reports that institutionally reared children die at a young age, manifest anaclitic depression (lie apathetically in their cribs, don't respond to attempts by adults to interact with them, and weep for hours on end), and are retarded in their motor, perceptual, and intellectual functioning.

The third step is the achievement of adequate control over voluntary functions. This involves progressive mastery of the bodily musculature used in locomotion and manipulation of inanimate objects in the environment.

Once the child's ego is formed, "it disposes of independent psychic energy" (Hartmann, 1939). Many ego functions develop out of the originally present conflict-free ego processes, "that ensemble of functions which at any given time exert their effects outside the region of mental conflicts." These intellectual functions could not possibly be the result of conflict between the child's ego and his id or "love-objects." Rather, they are the *"prerequisites* of our conception of these [personality structures] and their development." In other words, the ego psychologists maintain that rational ego processes could not be alterations of nonrational id processes. The basic argument is that it is logically absurd to assume, as Freud did, that the child's rational processes are transformations of his nonrational processes. Consequently, the material source of the ego's rational processes must be innate intellectual functions that are activated by conflict-free instinctual energy.

The child's rational processes determine, in relationship with other factors, which mechanisms of defense he will utilize and to what effect, or what goals he will substitute for his id desires. Hartmann (1939) mentions three intellectual functions which especially modify the child's instinctual goals, but he does not analyze their effect. These are social action and ethical values, artistic activity and esthetic values (which presumably have their origin in magic but have undergone a shift of function in the course of history), and religious actions and values.

The inner processes of the child's intelligence serve to organize, rather than to replace, all his other functions: rationality is the integrative function of the child's psychological organization. Ideally, his intellectual processes lead the child to progressive mastery over the external environment and control of himself. In this logical sense the integrative and regulatory functions of the child's ego are prior to his id; historically or ontogenetically the ego and the id are contemporaneous.

By focusing upon the development of rational functioning and adaptive coping, rather than upon instinctual wishes, ego psychologists have become particularly concerned with two theoretical issues. One is the determination of the major forces that influence ego development, and the other is the determination of the course of ego development. These two issues will be the subject of the next two sections.

Causes of Ego Development

Ego psychologists assert that there are three major causes of ego development. Two are inherited and internal; these are the rational instincts and the nonrational instincts. The third is external and acquired; this is the environment, which is assumed to constitute reality.

Among the major influences of *external reality* upon the child's ego development is delay of gratification, which is partially dependent upon internal influences as well. Voluntary delay substitutes future for immediate gratification. It leads to progressive ability to inhibit impulses, defer immediate action, and substitute other means of behavior and desired ends. Two further influences are associated with the child's development of voluntary control. The first consists of restrictions (interruption, restraint, and prevention) placed upon the child's actions, and the second, which is often related to the first, is the formation of habits of behavior in accordance with parental training.

Among the major influences of the *nonrational instinctual drives* upon ego formation is the child's ambivalence toward his first loved objects, particularly his mother. This ambivalence is attendant upon the mother's normal variation in her behavior from indulgence to deprivation.

Melanie Klein and Joan Riviere (1937), who are not ordinarily counted among the ego psychologists, have provided a theoretical account of this primordial developmental occurrence and its influence upon how the child differentiates himself from others. Their basic proposition is that the child's consciousness of his dependency is always associated with the fear that support will be withdrawn. The newborn infant, although he is totally dependent, experiences no anxiety because he is not aware of his dependency. He cannot yet differentiate between himself and others, so that in essence he believes that support, such as food, comes from himself. He therefore expects that it will always be forthcoming.

In the normal course of bringing up the child, however, the mother must eventually fail to fulfill immediately and completely the infant's wants. The result is that the infant becomes increasingly aware of his dependence:

> He discovers that he cannot supply all his own wants—and he cries and screams. He becomes aggressive. He automatically explodes, as it were, with hate and aggressive craving. (p. 8)

This is the primordial and universal

> experience of something like death, a recognition of the *non*-existence of something, of an overwhelming loss, both in ourselves and in others . . . And this experience brings an *awareness of love* (in the form of desire) and a *recognition of dependence* (in the form of need), at the same moment as, and inextricably bound up with, feelings and uncontrollable sensations of pain and threatened destruction within and without. (p. 9)

On this basis, it is assumed that the infant's "first object of love and hate is his mother;" his feeling toward her varies according to whether she is or is not satisfying his needs. This conflict also provides the tension for that type of mental activity necessary for the child to imagine an object that is separate from himself or that he is not in immediate contact with:

> The baby who feels a craving for his mother's breast when it is not there may imagine it to be there. . . . Such primitive phantasying is the earliest

form of the capacity which later develops into the more elaborate workings of the imagination. (p. 60)

The ego psychologists particularly stress the *hereditary rational* factor in the development of the child's ego. The ego functions of controlling and regulating the intellectual equipment for perception, memory, action, experience, and learning are not created by either instinctual needs or environmental demands, although they develop subject to their influence. According to Hartmann (1939), the newborn infant "is not wholly a creature of drives; he has inborn apparatuses (perceptual and protective mechanisms) that appropriately perform a part of those functions which, after the differentiation of ego and id, we attribute to the ego." The ego's material independence of the id and the environment is what gives it functional autonomy, that is, permits it to operate as an independent source of experience and behavior.

Every stimulus is assumed to disrupt the equilibrium between the infant and the environment; but only certain stimuli cause a conflict with the id, that is, disrupt the balance between instinctual desires and environmental conditions. When the latter occur, the child's autonomous ego functions for adaptation are directed toward establishing a new balance which is "favorable for survival." This equilibrium is not always normal; it may be abnormal.

The immediate tendency to set adaptive processes into motion when disequilibrium arises is guaranteed by the child's genetically endowed intellectual equipment, which is part of his ego. Many forms of adaptation may result from the possession of intellectual skills. One type is to seek out new environments which are particularly suitable. In addition, man, like other animals, actively and purposefully changes his environment. Only man, however, has the intelligence necessary to make the environment suitable to human functions and then secondarily to adapt to the new environment which he has been, at least partially, instrumental in creating.

Human adaptation is characterized by a long period of infancy during which the child is helpless and dependent. The infant's instinctual equipment that is ready for use in adapting to environmental stimulation is relatively meager. However, because the child is born into the social and cultural history of man, he does not have to "come to terms with his environment anew in every generation" (Hartmann, 1939). A long tradition of problem solving is used by his parents to aid him in adapting. In actuality, much of the child's adaptation is not to the natural environment but to the human environment that has been reconstituted by historical human adaptation. It is the competence with which the child adapts to or copes with the social environment, his "social compliance," that determines whether his development is normal. Inadequate adaptation is a source of unhealthy development.

Stages of Ego Development

The complete course of healthy ego development has been sketched out by Loevinger (1966), who divides the process into a sequence of seven stages that are not age specific; that is, there is no certainty about the exact age at which any given stage will come about. Loevinger does not spell out the theoretical relationship between her description of ego development and that of the ego psychologists just described. In the main, however, there would seem to be fundamental agreement. The stages are:

1. *Presocial and Symbiotic.* Ego development initially centers upon differentiating "self from nonself." This stage is made up of two substages. During the first, the presocial substage, the infant does not differentiate between "animate and inanimate parts of the environment." During the second, the symbiotic substage, the child becomes strongly attached to his mother and cannot clearly differentiate himself from her, although he does differentiate her from the rest of the environment.

2. *Impulse Ridden.* The child begins to exercise his own will, thereby confirming his separate existence from his mother. However, he lacks voluntary control over his impulses and he does not yet know shame. Although he is not aware of it, the child is exploitive and dependent upon others, who are perceived as "sources of supply." He does not understand rules of conduct, and he believes that "an action is bad because it is punished." A major conscious concern is with sexual and aggressive drives.

3. *Opportunistic.* Rules are understood but are followed only for "immediate advantage." The child is much more independent and in control of his impulses. His

> interpersonal relations are manipulative and exploitive. . . . Conscious preoccupation is with control and advantage, domination, deception, getting the better of, and so on. Life is a zero-sum game; what you win I lose. (p. 199)

4. *Conformist.* The child begins to internalize rules and to obey them "just because they are rules." He conceives interpersonal relations "primarily in terms of actions rather than of feelings and motives." A positive aspect of this is that

genuine interpersonal reciprocity is possible now; reciprocity is, after all, the Golden Rule. (p. 199)

A less positive, if not negative, aspect of this is that

conscious preoccupation is with material things, with reputation and status, with appearance, and with adjustment. References to inner feelings are typically stereotyped, banal and often moralistic. (p. 199)

5. Conscientious.   The adolescent becomes introspective, self-conscious, and self-critical. Interpersonal relations become more important and "are seen in terms of feelings and traits rather than actions." Two positive developments are associated with this stage. First, morality is internalized in such a way that the adolescent's own moral principles and feelings of guilt when he transgresses them "take precedence over group-sanctioned rules." Second, his conscious concerns shift to "obligations, ideals, traits, and achievement as measured by inner standards rather than by recognition alone."

6. Autonomous.   The person's conscious concerns focus upon "role differentiation, individuality, and self-fulfillment." In his interpersonal relations he now recognizes "inevitable mutual interdependence . . . and other people's need for autonomy." He becomes more tolerant of the attitudes and conflicts of others and is more conscious and direct about coping with his own conflicts. His conflicts are largely moral and internal, for example, the conflict between duties and needs.

7. Integrated.   Few people achieve this highest stage because not many realize their full potential. The person who comes this far

proceeds beyond coping with conflict to reconciliation of conflicting demands, and, where necessary, renunciation of the unattainable, beyond toleration to the cherishing of individual differences, beyond role differentiation to the achievement of a sense of integrated identity. (p. 200)

Although to do so is to anticipate Chapter 4, it is worth pointing out that Loevinger's formulation of ego development has much in common with Werner's (1948) conception of personal-social development. The main difference between them is not in content, but in scope and depth. Loevinger attempts to sketch the entire sequence of ego development from the most primitive (and first) stage to the final (most mature but not necessarily last) stage. Her description of each stage, however, is limited in scope. Werner's analysis, on the other hand, is limited to the most primitive and the final stage, but for these two stages his characterization is much more extensive.

DEVELOPMENT OF PERSONAL IDENTITY

Like Freud and other psychoanalytic theorists, Erikson (1959a) is concerned with the development of personal identity. He accepts the two types of analysis usually attempted by psychoanalytic theory. The first is dynamic; that is, it deals with the interaction and conflict of forces within the person and with his reaction to the external environment—for example, his defense against danger—at a given time, or during short periods of time. The second is a historical analysis of how present identity grew out of the person's past. It is based on a description of childhood sources of current dynamic and ego states, and it includes a determination of the specific solutions adopted to past conflict situations, of the reasons why some modes of solution have been retained while others have not, and of the causal relation between these solutions and later development.

Freud's dynamic and historical analysis of the identification process is generally accepted by psychoanalytic theorists. In his initial egocentric state the infant does not differentiate between his acts (that will mediate identification) and the objects of his attention, namely, the persons with whom he will come to identify. Initially, then, the instinctual objects of the child's libidinal energy (loving attention) are both parents. Eventually, after he differentiates between his parents, the child invests his libidinal energy primarily in the same-sex parent. (Why this happens is not clear.) Then, owing to the Oedipus situation, which Freud assumed to develop universally during the phallic stage (described in detail, pp. 41–44), the child comes to suffer a "real injury" from, and a "disappointment" in the same-sex parent. The result is at least a partial break in the investment of libidinal energy in that parent. The freed id energy is "withdrawn into the ego," where it establishes "an identification of the ego with the abandoned object" (Freud, 1917). That is, the child introjects a fantasy of the lost love object and thereby identifies with the same-sex parent. He does this by interiorizing an image and a feeling that copy the loved object. Thus, not being able to have his father as an object of his loving attention, the boy would like to be (and in this secondary way, to have) his father.

Insofar as this analysis is dependent upon the assumption that the Oedipal situation is universal, it is open to serious question. Indeed, Malinowski (1927) reports that Oedipal situations do not seem to arise in societies where the social family unit is not composed of the biological parents, but only of the biological mother and an uncle acting as guardian. Nevertheless, sex-role development is not radically different in these societies.

Mutuality

Erikson (1959a) argues that the historical investigation of the dynamic relationship between the id, on the one hand, and the demands and inhibitions imposed by external reality, on the other hand, is not sufficient to the study of personality development. He maintains that in order to perform both historical and dynamic analyses adequately, it is necessary to study the origins of the self in organized social activity. This addition is predicated upon Erikson's working assumption that the development of identity is not only a "dynamic fact," "a subject for clinical investigation," and "a subjective experience," but also "a group-psychological phenomenon." A complete description of personality development must therefore include an investigation of what the social environment gives to the infant in order to keep him alive. It must also determine in what ways the social norms dictate that his needs be ministered to so that the milieu "seduces him to its particular life style." Thus, the research focus of psychoanalysis must shift from its one-sided historical concern with the intrapsychic dynamics of the person to a historical analysis of (1) the structure of the social organization in which the child finds himself and (2) the interpsychic relationship between the child and the milieu, its structure and dynamics.

For example, Erikson (1959a) believes that the growing child gets a sense of himself and "a vitalizing sense of reality" from becoming aware that his own way of dealing with experience is in accord with his group's mores, institutions, and social modes of functioning. When the child begins to be able to walk, he

> also becomes aware of the new status and stature of "he who can walk," with whatever connotations this happens to have in the coordinates of his culture's life plan,—be it "he who will go far," or "he who will be upright," or "he who might go too far." (pp. 22–23)

To become "one who can walk" is only one of the many events in the child's development which contribute to the formation of his identity and a realistic sense of himself.

The basic life condition which supports such developments of personal identity is the positive correlation or mutuality among (a) the maturation of the child's physical mastery, for example, the ability to walk, (b) the functional pleasure obtained in exercising the new-found power, for example, walking and the other activities that only then become possible, and (c) the fact that he exercises this capacity at a time and place which evoke social recognition of his action and the expression, overt or covert, of the cultural meaning attributed to it, such as approval and status.

Erikson's mutuality thesis of social evolution is based upon the assumption that instinctual modes of functioning have been transformed (in the course of evolution) into psychosocial modes of functioning. Psychosocial development is expressed in human life in eight stages, which are described in the next section.

Not only does the child change; the significant persons in his environment also change, and they perceive that the child is developing. Together these events cause the significant persons to alter their behavior toward the child. These intersecting but different types of development of the individual and society have an interactive effect, causing the universal sequence of crises and phases that have to be faced by both children and adults in their respective life cycles. Erikson (1963) has generalized this mutuality thesis of social evolution as follows:

> Each successive stage and crisis has a special relation to one of the basic elements of society, and this for the simple reason that the human life cycle and man's institutions have evolved together. (p. 250)

Development, then, is characterized by a succession of interactional imbalances (crises) within the child's personality structures and between the child and his milieu. Crises cause the child's ego to try to adjust the relationship between internal personality structures and to manipulate the external environment so that an adequate balance between it and the ego is restored. Readjustment has two primary consequences for healthy development. First, personality structures are changed so that the child will interact with the environment differently in the future, although new imbalances and crises will occur. Second, a "feeling" of having changed and successfully coped with the environment strengthens the child's capacity and willingness to meet new challenges. If these two consequences do not regularly occur, then the conditions for pathological development, for arrest or regression, are present.

Mutuality between the child and his social environment supports the development of personal identity. Identity formation is the child's growing capacity for simultaneous perception, awareness, and belief that he is continuous in time, that is, his recognition that although he has changed he remains identical with himself in his previous state and that others have the same view of him, that he is the same person in their eyes. The subjective feeling of personal identity lies precisely in the child's awareness of his continuous "selfsameness," or conservation in which the ego capacities master experience, and in the belief that his ego capacities will effectively maintain his identity for others.

In order to achieve such personal synthesis, the child's ego utilizes two types of models (Erikson, 1959*a*). The first is based upon historical prototypes that represent the social milieu's "ideal" concept of personality. The other is the actual and idiosyncratic representations of the contemporary, collective prototypes of the child's milieu. The ego's organizational function is to integrate the fragmentary identifications, developed at each stage of growth, that are based upon these models by subsuming them under coherently structured "images and personified Gestalten."

An interesting example of this process, described by Erikson (1959), is the development of personal identity by the American Negro. Black infants are often given unusually large amounts of oral and sensual gratification. The enforced symbiosis with the feudal South built the identity of the slave upon this storehouse of sensory gratification to form the servile and dependent individual with "childlike wisdom." Underneath this a "dangerous split" developed because of the "humiliating symbiosis" and the need of the white "master race" to ward off the "sensual and oral temptations" of the black slave race. Historically, therefore, "white" became associated with being light, clean, and clever, and "black" with being dark, dirty, and dumb—for both groups. The result, particularly in the black individual who has left the South, is the formation of three different identity fragments:

> (1) mammy's oral-sensual honey-child; tender, expressive, rythmical; (2) the clean anal-compulsive, restrained, friendly, but always sad "white man's Negro"; and (3) the evil identity of the dirty, anal-sadistic, phallic-rapist "nigger." (p. 38)

One of these fragments will become dominant if the individual is presented with only partial opportunities and not with the real freedom necessary for the healthy integration of these identity fragments. For example, when he becomes tired of this caricature, the individual may retreat to

> hypochondriac invalidism as a condition which represents an analogy to the ego-space-time of defined restriction in the South: a neurotic regression to the ego identity of the slave. (p. 38)

Epigenesis

All developmental processes, and particularly that of identity formation, are governed by an epigenetic principle of maturation. By this Erikson (1963, p. 66) means that "anything that grows has a *ground plan*" out of which parts (organs) emerge. Each part has its *"decisive and critical time"* of origin and "special ascendancy" until all have arisen and been synthesized into a functionally integrated whole. Pathological development occurs when a part "misses its time of ascendancy." The consequences are twofold: not only is that part "doomed as an entity," but "it endangers at the same time the whole hierarchy of organs." Normal personality development is governed by a "proper rate and a proper sequence" of stages with respect to the succession of (*a*) the instinctual energy invested in different bodily zones, and (*b*) the psychosocial functions of "potentialities for significant interaction" with the social and physical environment, which is modeled after the inherent psychosexual functioning of the bodily zones.

The basic determinant of *which* part (organ) is invested with instinctual energy in the course of normal development is the maturational code with which the child is born. (Although Erikson does not assert it, when development is not normal the basic determinant is probably a product of interaction between the forces of maturation and environment.) Likewise, the ontogenetic *sequence* in which and the time *when* different parts are invested with energy is predetermined by the maturational code.

This means that stages of development do not grow out of each other. For example, the stage when anal-type functioning is dominant does not result from the child-environment interaction necessary to successful passage through the oral stage. Rather, adequate resolution of the crises met in the oral stage, as we shall see more fully later, is presumed to be a necessary condition for the child's healthy transition to the anal stage. It is not, however, the primary condition for his entrance into the anal stage. The primary condition for this development is his maturational code, which determines when the locus of instinctual investment will be shifted from the oral to the anal zone.

The cause of discontinuity between stages is the fact that the primary zonal focus of instinctual energy changes in accordance with the epigenetic principle of development; that is, each part of the ground plan has its special time of ascendancy. But continuity between stages is also implied by the epigenetic principle insofar as each organ must already be a potential part of the ground plan in order for it to grow out of it and mature at the proper time. Even though one mode of functioning dominates at a given stage, all other modes are present in an auxiliary fashion. Functions that belong to later stages, that is, that are yet to be the central focus of instinctual energy, operate in a rudimentary but unintegrated fashion before their period of ascendancy. Functions that were once focal become an integral but less important mode of later functioning when development has been healthy.

UNIVERSAL SEQUENCE OF STAGES
IN THE LIFE CYCLE

The developmental thesis of psychoanalysis is that personality development in general, and identity formation in particular, is based upon the physiological maturation of bodily zones and their modes of functioning. Each stage of personality development is the consequence of the investment of libidinal energy in a particular bodily zone; this instinctual energy activates that zone's mode of functioning. The zone and mode of functioning that mature during a given period of development determine the form of the person's adaptive activity at that stage of his life. The nature of the zone's operation therefore constrains, or provides the limits, within which the person's identity will be formed and his social interaction may take place.

Freud (1930) provided the initial conception of this psychosexual thesis that the maturational investment of sexual energy in different bodily zones is the basis of psychological activity and personality development. He maintained that the source, impetus, aim, and object of the sexual instincts are different during successive periods of life, as will be described more fully below. As a consequence, the inevitable conflicts that arise between the id, ego, and superego change in the course of psychosexual development. The way in which early conflicts are dealt with and the adequacy with which they are resolved determine whether later personality development will be relatively healthy or not. This idea is based upon the hypothesis that "traces" of early experience may causally determine the health of later states and behavior. As previously noted, aspects of early childhood conflicts which have been repressed into the unconscious are hypothesized to be particularly important in determining the health of later personality organization and adjustment.

It was Freud's collateral, and at the time of its conception radical, hypothesis that the first phase of psychosexual activity occurs during infancy. Infantile sexuality has three essential characteristics. Its aim is controlled by the *erogenous* bodily zone in which libidinal energy is invested. An erogenous zone is a part of the skin or a mucous membrane which can feel pleasure when stimulated. The first erogenous zone activated in the child is his oral (mouth) zone. The origin of infantile sexuality is tied to the *function* of that bodily zone. The child's first psychosexual function is therefore that of sucking for pleasure or the reduction of tension. This function is *autoerotic* because the aim of the function is not to know and engage another sexual object, but rather to obtain gratification by operating upon one's own body.

Thus, sexuality originates as an expression of an instinctual, bodily urge. Infantile sexuality is an imitation of pleasure felt in association with other gratifying bodily functions, such as sucking. The major source of pleasure is mechanical stimulation of the erogenous zone. The bodily functions become separate sources of gratification when the child stops sucking and begins to chew in order to obtain nourishment.

It should be noted that Freud assumed that other bodily parts besides those naturally invested with instinctual energy could take on the function of erogenous zones. Moreover, there are at least three other sources of sexuality: exercise of the musculature, intense affective feelings, and intellectual activity.

Although a high degree of unity is attributed to personal identity at each stage of psychosexual development, Freud recognized that the organization of personality at each stage is not totally discontinuous from those that preceded it. As a matter of fact, ideal personality development would seem to involve some integration of earlier aspects into the personality organization of the sexually mature adult. The interaction or lack of interaction between stages is actually most evident when the course of personality development is not healthy. Freud indicated two such abnormal conditions. The interaction between stages is clear when the individual *regresses* (goes back) to forms of behavior that are more characteristic of an earlier stage of his psychosexual development than the one he has achieved at the time of his retreat. Lack of interaction occurs when the individual *fixates* (holds on) to the stage of functioning he is at so that his development is arrested.

Erikson (1963) has elaborated most comprehensively upon this psychosexual thesis. His overall aim is to chart the stages of personality development that are universal among men, and he hypothesizes eight stages. These stages are the result of the epigenetic unfolding of the "ground plan" of personality that is genetically transmitted. Associated with these stages are eight major crises that each person faces in the course of his lifetime. The person must adequately resolve each crisis in order to progress to the next stage of his development in an adaptive and healthy fashion. Early in life these crises are primarily due to conflict between the child's instinctual desires and reality, for example, the Oedipal conflict to be described. Later the source of conflict increasingly shifts to ambivalent social ambitions, for example, what kind of person to be, whom to interact with, and what to do.

Five major categories are used to describe and analyze the first six stages. They are psychosexual zone and mode of functioning, psychosocial mode of functioning (the social homologue of sexual functioning), related elements of the social order, radius of significant relations, and psychosocial crisis. Erikson does not use the psychosexual category to characterize the last two stages of development, those of adulthood and senescence, presumably because little change takes place in the instinctual genital investment from young adulthood to adulthood, while senescence is a period of abating sexual concern so that the psychosexual category is usually of little importance.

Oral Stage.   The child's first maturational stage of psychosexuality (about the first year of life) is the result of libidinal investment in the oral (mouth) zone of his body, which serves the primary self-preservative functions of breathing, drinking, and eating. The first and dominant mode of psychosexual functioning that is attached to this zone is *incorporation* or taking in. The child's radius of significant relations is very much, though not completely, restricted to a maternal figure, usually his mother, who is at that stage of her own life cycle where she wants "to take care of" her infant by giving to him. The infant's

> inborn and more or less coordinated ability to take in by mouth meets the breast's and the mother's and the society's more or less coordinated ability and intention to feed and to welcome him. (Erikson, 1963, p. 72)

According to Freud (1930), the peculiar significance of the oral stage for the later personality development of the child lies in its aim, namely, to "incorporate" its object. Taking-in by the infant is the precursory form of his later modes of introjection (the mechanism whereby the child identifies with the character of significant persons in his milieu, particularly his parents).

Since Erikson assumes that psychosocial evolution is modeled on psychosexual development, he hypothesizes that the child's first psychosocial mode of functioning is inherently modeled on incorporation. It is the developing ability "to get," to receive and accept.

> In thus *getting what is given,* and in learning to *get somebody to do* for him what he wishes to have done, the baby also develops the necessary ego groundwork to *get to be* the giver. (1963, p. 76)

This stage of functioning is therefore the basis of all human trust, that is, all social communality with its associated sharing of a common cultural world.

Among the auxiliary modes of functioning that emerge later in this stage is a secondary means of incorporation, that of biting.

> The teeth develop, and with them the pleasure in biting *on* hard things, in biting *through* things, and in biting pieces *off* things. (Erikson, 1963, pp. 76–77)

This is the bodily instinctual source of the psychosocial crisis that inevitably arises at this stage.

Life's first major crisis for the child is a *crisis of trust* in the person upon whom he is most dependent for his very sustenance (Erikson, 1963). It is predicated upon the intersection of three major developments. The first, which we have already alluded to, is the physiological maturation of the infant. His waking periods are longer and more frequent. At the same time, there is "a more violent drive to incorporate, appropriate, and observe more actively," to which is added the discomfiture of teething. The second development is more psychological. It is the child's increasing awareness of himself as a distinct person, and it is accompanied by the feeling that only biting provides some, if unsatisfactory, relief from the pains of teething. The third development is social. It is the weaning process, whereby the mother gradually turns away from the child in order to pursue concerns she gave up during late pregnancy and postnatal care, particularly her husband, and to avoid the pain of being bitten if she is breast-feeding the child.

Weaning occurs just when the child is becoming more aware of himself as "I am what I am given." Not being given to therefore implies being destroyed, and it occurs when the painful tensions caused by teething are strongest. Together these two factors form the basis for the split in the child's feelings between the images of the good and the bad mother (see the discussion of Klein and Riviere above) and the inevitable crisis between the formation of a "basic sense of trust," of "primal hope" and goodness, and a "basic sense of mistrust," of primal "doom," anxiety, and evil.

For this reason, two of the child's ego mechanisms of defense, projection and introjection, are assumed to have their origins in this crisis. Projection begins as the infant's attempt to attribute all negative feelings to agents in the external world, whereas introjection takes the form of crediting himself with the good aspects of the external world as if they had become "an inner certainty."

Adequate resolution of the crisis of confidence is the first major adaptive problem for the child, and it has major consequences for the future development of his personality. Erikson points to two major factors that determine the type of resolution the child may achieve. The first is the degree to which his ego and his sense of self-trustworthiness have developed. If the child's increasing experience gives him the feeling that things are familiar and continuous with what has come before, then he begins to recognize that correspondences exist between internal anticipatory images and external objects. This is the basis for the child's formation of a "rudimentary sense of ego identity" composed of three aspects of trustworthiness that are necessary to deal adequately with the crisis of trust. These three aspects are the child's increasing confidence in the general consistency of the external provider; a growing feeling of his own competence to deal with instinctual needs of getting, so that he feels less dependent; and a growing feeling that he himself is "trustworthy enough" not to cause his mother so much pain that she will not continue to give to him.

The second factor in determining how the crisis of confidence is resolved is the fact that the mother actually does continue giving to the child, albeit in modified ways and in reduced amounts. Of course, the degree to which this second factor plays a positive role depends upon the quality of the mother's behavior, that is, the sensitivity with which she cares for the child's needs during this crisis and her sense of trustworthiness.

Erikson seems to imply that a third factor may play a role in the resolution of the crisis of confidence. He hypothesizes that attached to each psychosexual zone are secondary functions, which are precursors of future dominant modes of functioning. At the oral stage, these secondary functions are the retentive and eliminative modes (of the future anal stage) and the intrusive mode (of the phallic stage). These modes function in an auxiliary fashion to incorporation: oral retentivity is the child's tendency to close his lips upon things that have entered his mouth; elimination is his tendency to spit things "up and out"; and intrusiveness is his tendency to fasten upon things, particularly his mother's nipple, and not let go. Auxilliary and primary modes of oral functioning are attached not only to the mouth, but to all other bodily zones as well, such as the sense organs and the skin since they are also "receptive and increasingly hungry for proper stimulation." All this activity provides increased functional bases for the child's recognition of the continuity between different parts of himself; for example, the same object is grasped with his mouth, held with his hand, fixed upon with his eyes, and bent toward with his body. It may also provide the functional continuity between the oral and anal stages that draws the child's attention (cathexis) to new vistas of experience and away from single-minded preoccupations with oral needs, the trauma of weaning, and problems of trust. This shift of attention, itself probably helpful if only as a distraction, is of course furthered by the shift of instinctual investment from the oral into another bodily zone in accordance with the epigenetic, maturational code governing the child's development.

White (1960) takes issue with what he considers to be a theoretical exaggeration of one of the infant's needs after the first few months of life. He argues that the child's need for oral satisfaction declines toward the end of the first year and is replaced by a concern with achieving motor and social competence. By competence, White means the child's

> fitness or ability to carry on those transactions with the environment which result in its maintaining itself, growing, and flourishing. (p. 100)

He does not mean to overestimate the importance of competence:

> A person developed wholly along lines of competence, with no dimensions of passion, love, or friendliness, would never qualify for maturity. . . . The competence model must always be used in conjunction with other

models that do full justice to such things as hunger, sexuality, and aggression. (p. 136)

Nevertheless, White believes that the psychoanalytic conception of weaning as "an unmitigated evil and a potential trauma" is one-sided. According to him, weaning is

> aided by the infant's inherent satisfaction in mastering the cup and spoon, in bringing these parts of the environment under the governance of his own effort and initiative. He does not have to do it wholly for mother; as an active living being he has his own stake in growing up. (p. 114)

In his conception of the child as an active agent striving to develop competence, White leans heavily upon, and seems to be in essential agreement, with the organic lamp theory. As a matter of fact, it is probably along the lines of White's conceptual efforts that an integration of psychoanalytic and organic lamp theories of development is most likely to be effected.

Anal Stage.   Freud (1930) maintained that in the second psychosexual stage (from about one to three years of age) the child's instinctual urges shift to the anal erogenous zone and its functions of retention and evacuation. These modes of functioning require the child to attempt actively to master his own impulses. They also presumably occasion the first direct parental attempts to teach the child to inhibit his natural tendencies by toilet training. The importance of this stage for later development lies particularly in the fact that it marks the initial appearance of precursory forms of ambivalence between impulsive and inhibitory (superego) tendencies. At the anal stage the primary observable ambivalence is the child's indecision whether to be active (outgoing, intruding upon the world and exploring it) or to remain passive.

Accordingly, Erikson (1959) hypothesizes that the child's primary concern at this stage is with exercising his anal-urethral musculature by flexion and extension. These bodily modes of functioning provide the prototype for the conflicting psychosexual modes of deriving autoerotic pleasure from retention and elimination ("the particular pleasurableness and willfulness which is often attached to the eliminative organs") and the conflicting psychosocial modes of holding on (or withholding) and letting go (or expelling).

The child's determination to exercise all his musculature and the pleasure he derives from its functioning are the basis for the development of a sense of personal "autonomy," of feeling that he is no longer a totally dependent being but rather that "I am what I will." In the normal course of events this striving for ego identity is met, at least in part, by attempts at control, inhibition, and regulation on the part of both parents. The general aim of parents is to introduce the child to the idea that social interaction is based upon "law and order." They train the child to control his muscular activity with the aim of instilling proper habits, but their training leads to what Erikson (1963) calls the "battle for autonomy."

This battle is a conflict between the child's natural tendencies to assert himself and the parents' just as natural inclinations to restrict his activity, to teach him the limits of his own capacities, and to introduce him to physical reality and social propriety. The ensuing crisis is, then, whether the child will develop a feeling of autonomy or one of shame or doubtfulness about what he has done and about himself and his capacity to behave in an independent yet proper fashion.

This crisis must be satisfactorily resolved if the child is to acquire an adequate feeling of independent identity. His equanimity at this stage is dependent upon the sensitivity with which his parents impose rules. He should not feel omnipotent in the exercise of his capacities, and at the same time he should not feel so much doubt or shame in his own behavior that he becomes unable to act autonomously.

Although White (1960) agrees with Erikson that the child's major crisis at this stage centers upon the battle for autonomy, his emphasis is somewhat different. White believes that

> bowel training is not a correct prototype for the problem of autonomy. It is not the right model for those tryings and testings of the sense of competence that would have to go on anyway, even if bowel training were of no consequence at all. (p. 118)

White's emphasis is again upon the child's motor and social activities that lead him to the development of self-assertiveness and willfulness. He considers an episode reported by Stern (cited in White, 1960) as a paradigm of what really happens in this stage. During a meal Stern's little girl ordered her father to "pick up the spoon." Her father told her to say "please," but she obstinately refused and ended up not having her meal. White explains that the child's activity during this stage is not "a surrender to cultural pressure," but rather, the

> true adaptive significance is that of resisting external influence. If behavior were allowed to be governed wholly from outside, there would be no scope for inner needs and no way to develop inner controls. (p. 119)

Inner needs and controls, particularly of stubbornness, parsimony, and neatness, characterize the child's growing assertiveness and willfulness.

Phallic Stage.   The first major shift in the kind of object the child selects for sexual identification and gratification appears in the next, the phallic, stage (Freud, 1930). The shift is from himself to another person (who is a member of the child's family). It is during this period, between the ages of three and five years, that the presumably universal Oedipus situation takes place. This situation originates "in the prehistory of every person" and is reinforced by his life history. The child identifies with the same-sex parent in such a way that his instinctual urge is to usurp that parent's role vis à vis the parent of the opposite sex.

Erikson (1963) also maintains that when the child's instinctual energy is concentrated in the genital zone his basic mode of psychosexual functioning becomes that of "intrusion" and "inclusion." The consequent analogous psychosocial functions are "to make" or go after desired objects and "to make like" those one would like to be by "playing" their role. In general, a future-time perspective reflected by the development of initiative, an active, industrious, and planning quality, begins to augment the ego quality of autonomy that was developed in the previous stage. The child's ego identity becomes "I am what I will be."

The child derives gratification from his new-found locomotive, linguistic, and imaginative powers to experiment physically, socially, and mentally.

> If we consider the bearing of these developments on social competence, it is clear that the child has reached a point of understanding where for the first time he can contemplate his place in the family and his relation to other people in general. . . . It is at this time that he learns his culture's definition of sex roles, and he experiments with a variety of adult roles. (White, 1960, p. 123)

Inherent in his initiative (in playing make-believe roles), however, is the danger of competing with his parent of the same sex, whom he identifies with. This is the significance of the Oedipal situation, which psychoanalytic theory takes to be the prototypic occurrence leading to the major crisis during this stage. The Oedipal situation represents both the child's wish to become a member of his family and his parents' intentions to integrate him into the basic family of parents and children. The child's primary mechanism is that of identification ("making like" a parent); boys primarily play at the role of father-husband and girls at the role of mother-wife. This is the core of the Oedipal situation: the temptations of forbidden fruit, the desire to usurp powers and perform acts which are not rightfully the child's. Associated with initiative and drive for personal autonomy is therefore a feeling of having transgressed and a consequent sense of guilt and fear of punishment.

Depending upon the relative strength of masculine and feminine dispositions (due to both constitutional differences and differential experiences in the oral and anal phases), the consequences of the Oedipus situation are primary identification with mother or father, and relatively normal or abnormal personality development. The organic and psychological bisexuality of the child makes the Oedipus situation and normal identity formation very complex:

> A boy has not merely an ambivalent attitude toward his father and an affectionate object-relation towards his mother, but at the same time he also behaves like a girl and displays an affectionate feminine attitude to his father and a corresponding hostility and jealousy towards his mother. (Freud, 1923, pp. 42–43)

Usually the child forms an ego identification based upon some combination of the two parental figures. However, the constitutional endowment of masculine or feminine characteristics will ordinarily ensure that the child adopts the appropriate sex role. The primary cause of sexual identification is genetic endowment; environmental factors are only secondary determinants.

A major development of the child's personality structure that is the direct result of resolving the Oedipal crisis is the transformation of part of his ego into his ego ideal or *superego*. According to Erikson (1963), the resolution of the conflict between the child's initiative and his consequent guilt is his acquiring "a sense of moral responsibility." The child begins to understand, and to operate in accordance with, the rules and regulations of his social milieu. This is the condition for "responsible participation" in his environment, which allows him to know and get pleasure from performing appropriate roles and functions. Responsible participation becomes possible because the superego is in part an "energetic reaction-formation" against the choices made in resolving the Oedipal conflict (Freud, 1923). That is, in addition to identifying with the same-sex parent, the child accepts the precept that he may not do certain things that his parent may and does do. In sum, the superego functions so as to repress his Oedipal desires and resolve his conflict.

Erikson (1963, p. 257) is fully cognizant of the difficulties in resolving this crisis. If an adequate resolution is not found, the child's conscience will remain "primitive, cruel, and uncompromising." "The fact that human conscience remains partially infantile throughout life is the core of human tragedy." An optimistic note is struck here, however:

> According to the wisdom of the ground plan the child is at no time more ready to learn quickly and avidly than during this period of his development. (1963, p. 258)

The child is interested in work, in trying out new things, and in taking on the responsibilities available in the society around him. Freud, it should be noted, remained more pessimistic about the outcome of the conflict between the child's ego and superego because the superego

> is a memorial of the former weakness and dependence of the ego and the mature ego remains subject to its domination. (1923, p. 69)

The reasons for the superego's dominance are twofold:

> the fact that on the one hand it was the first identification and one which took place while the ego was still feeble, and that on the other hand it was the heir to the Oedipus complex and thus incorporated into the ego objects of far greater significance than any others. (1923, pp. 68–69)

Latency Stage.   The primary cause for the child's resolution of the crisis between initiative and guilt is the reduction of libidinal energy invested in the genital zone. The result is the onset of the latency stage, a period of sexual retrogression or quiescence. Freud (1930) maintained that this retrogression is reinforced by a reduction in biologically sexual drives from about the age of six until puberty.

White (1960) disagrees with Freud:

> His assumption about the quiescence of sexual energies seems to be simply wrong. Anthropological evidence and better observation in our society have combined to cast grave doubt on the hypothesis of a biologically determined sexual latency. For once we can almost say that Freud underestimated the importance of sex. (p. 127)

White claims that the child's sexual interests are maintained during this period. Only if he has adequate interactions with children of the opposite sex will he develop self-confidence. According to White, self-confidence during this period is necessary in order for the child to rid himself of residues of the Oedipus complex. Without it, the child will be relatively passive and, as an adolescent, in the case of a boy, may show an "inability to be interested in girls other than mother-surrogates."

Erikson's (1963) position is between those of Freud and White. He characterizes latency as the stage during which the child tends to sublimate sexual intrusiveness and re-route social initiative into work that requires skillful activity. His psychosocial mode of functioning centers upon making and completing things, by himself and with others. Such activity is supported and fostered by people in his neighborhood and school, who introduce him to the "technological elements" of the social order by teaching him and working with him. In this way he comes to identify himself as "I am what I learn."

The psychosocial crisis that arises during this stage of identity formation centers around the problem of whether the child will become adequately industrious, in his own and others' eyes, or will feel inferior and inadequate. If the child feels unable to master the basic tools of his society, he is likely to develop a lasting feeling of inferiority. As a consequence he will restrict his activities and goals to solitary work on things he is sure of. There is the further danger that he may develop a "conformist" identity and become subject to technological enslavement. Again, the child's struggle is to develop positive features of industriousness, that is, feelings of competence and adequacy, that will foster the development of ego autonomy.

Adolescent Stage. If the child develops a sense of personal adequacy and is comfortable in working with others, he is ready to deal healthily with the problems that will face him in the next psychosexual stage, that of puberty. This stage unquestionably determines the form of the child's adult sexual behavior. His sexual impulses shift to "a strange sexual object," that is, a person of the opposite sex outside his family. This period of physiological upheaval, of tremendous bodily, particularly sexual, maturation comes at the same time that interpersonal dealings require interaction with various peer groups, of both the same and opposite sex, and with leader figures. The type of interaction the adolescent will engage in is determined by the major modes of psychosocial functioning he develops at this stage of his life, namely, "to be oneself (or not to be)" and "to share being oneself" (Erikson, 1963).

Interactions with others introduce the adolescent to the perplexities of adopting a coherent view of life. They introduce the first "ideological perspectives" he will be trying out and rejecting or accepting. The problem for the adolescent is to find himself, to adopt and maintain a coherent and integrated sense of himself and his purpose. Thus the crisis now is identity adoption and repudiation versus "identity diffusion." The danger is that the adolescent will not further develop his ego autonomy or sense of integrity with a hierarchy of values that make certain things in life particularly meaningful to him, that is, that he will feel lost and unable, because unmotivated, to invest himself in anything. The result may be a disabling purposelessness and inability to "take hold."

Genital Stage. Adequate adolescent ego integration is a necessary condition for the next stage of identity formation, when the young adult's instinctual energy and sexual gratification fully center upon the genital erogenous zone (Freud, 1930). The partial sexual impulses of the previous stages are now coordinated under the control of the genital zone. This integration is directed by the aim of obtaining full sexual gratification in another person.

The young adult's dominant psychosocial mode of functioning becomes "to lose and find oneself in another" (Erikson, 1963). His psychosocial interaction focuses upon becoming "partners in friendship, sex, competition, (and) cooperation," where the elements of the social order that are related to him have become various "patterns of cooperation and competition."

The major crisis that the young adult must face is that of achieving and obtaining gratification from "intimacy and solidarity" with others versus "isolation" and withdrawal from partnerships. This has particular significance for the adoption of a husband or wife role and the occurrence of the next stage of personal development, that of being an adult.

Here, too, White (1963) is in partial disagreement with Freud and Erikson. He argues that the main concern during this and the adult period of life is work.

> Unfortunately the climactic turmoil of the orgasm is completely the wrong model for work. . . . The orgastic model has virtue for certain human activities requiring a temporary submergence of self, such as inspiration, creative imagination, and thoroughly relaxed play. But it will never do for the serious, stable, lasting concerns of human life, the realm that I am trying to designate as work. (p. 135)

The individual must develop skills that permit him to work competently. These skills include "a certain constancy of effort," responsibility, directed attention and endeavor, persistence in the face of the inevitable dull aspects of work, and technical proficiency.

Adulthood and Senescence.   Freud (1923) maintained that adulthood is the ultimate goal of sexual development; it is characterized by the utilization of sexual pleasure for purposes of propagation. The primary personal aim is to establish a family, to create one's radius of significant relations, that is, according to Erikson (1963), of "divided labor and a shared household." Analogously, the aim of the adult may also be to become part of and to help construct the social order, particularly those aspects having to do with "education and tradition." The general crisis then is one of "generativity," "to make be," and "to take care of" versus "self-absorption" and a "pervading sense of stagnation and interpersonal impoverishment."

The adult who has achieved gratification from creating and from helping others to grow is equipped with the personal integrity necessary to face the final crisis of life, that of his own disintegration and death (Erikson, 1963). At this stage of senescence, lack of "ego integration" is likely to lead to despair, whereas adequate ego integrity provides purpose and the feeling of oneness with "mankind" and "my kind." The dominant psychosocial mode is "to be through having been" and "to face not being." This requires "wisdom," which is also what the individual may now impart to the social order.

SUMMARY AND CRITIQUE

The Freudian view is that the child is born with an id structure that is energized by libidinal and aggressive instincts. The child uses arational primary processes in the satisfactions of his passions, but since they aren't always successful, part of the id structure is transformed by its interaction with the environment into an ego structure. The child's ego structure has available to it a number of organs or instruments that aid the ego in its interaction with the environment; these are primarily the perceptual and intellectual systems. It is not clear whether Freud conceived of these systems as part of the ego or as organismic systems that the ego employs. In any case, the idea is that at first the primary processes of the id are autoerotic. Only gradually does the child begin to interact with other objects or to adapt to reality. It is then that he develops an ego that is differentiated from the environment and that begins to operate rationally (in terms of secondary processes). Eventually part of the child's ego identifies with the demands and the morality of the social environment and becomes his superego or conscience.

At the same time, the child is developing both psychosexually and psychosocially. At first, during the oral stage, both psychosexual and psychosocial modes of functioning are also turned inward and are autoerotic, according to Erikson. The child's activity is directed toward incorporating and getting. In short, he is still primarily an id. Only as he begins to operate muscularly upon the world, during the anal stage, can he be said to begin to be also an ego and a superego. The ego and superego achieve their essential form during the phallic stage, when the psychosexual and psychosocial modes of functioning shift to intrusion upon the environment with its attendant guilt.

The ego psychologists do not completely accept this formulation for two reasons. First, they cannot understand how an id structure that operates in terms of affective and arational processes can be partially transformed into a totally different structure that operates in terms of rational processes, just because it has not obtained satisfaction in its interaction with the environment. To them, this is as unlikely as that an organism without a brain structure should develop one simply because it does not obtain satisfaction in its interaction with an environment. Second, they point to the fact that much of the infant's earliest activity, even sucking, is directed outward (for adaptive, coping purposes) as well as inward (for purposes of incorporation).

The ego psychologists assume that the child is born with both an ego and an id structure. The child's perceptual and intellectual systems are instruments of his ego that permit his initial rational interaction with, and differentiation from, the environment. Loevinger has tried to describe the development of the child's ego as an operator that functions rationally in an environment, but she does not seem to make the distinction between the development of ego and superego structures that is more typical of psychoanalytic theory.

As we have seen, psychoanalytic categories for the conceptualization of ontogenesis are strikingly rich with empirical intuition. They are in close correspondence with some important aspects of the events that make up the personal development of the child. But they are sparse in logical structure. There are many reasons, good and bad, for this. Among the best is their aim to capture the real flavor of the child's development, his conflicts, and his defensive and coping activity. This aim has meant, however, that the categories developed reflect the most striking features of behavior (based upon observation of children and interpretation of clinical data) at a given period of life, for example, oral and anal activity. They are not attempts to conceptualize the logical structure of the total psychological configuration that comprises a stage in a developmental sequence. Among the worst reasons, then, is an apparent identification of historical (chronological) categories with developmental (logical) categories. What is most interesting is the consequent paradox: categories that are not well abstracted from real life seem, so far, to be poor conceptual tools for empirical work on real-life development. They remain what they are—rich portrayals concretely bound to, or at best inductively abstracted from, their particular referents. Thus, the limited character of psychoanalytic research as compared with the richness of its historical descriptive categories. This has been recognized by some contemporary psychoanalytic theorists themselves. Indeed, an author with theoretical insight, like Loevinger, is led to conclude, for example, that

> psychosexual development has not yet been conceived in terms of a model that lends itself well to any measurement. There is indeed a postulated sequence of stages, and undoubtedly there is some influence on later stages of the outcome of early stages, but there is no clear model for the nature of this influence. (1966, p. 197)

Moreover, the data most often used in psychoanalytic research are the therapist's descriptions of the patient's verbalizations and actions. The actual nature of the data is the result of the therapist's organization, usually intuitive, of the complex material that makes up a clinical case. The attempt is to portray consistent phenomena that occur with convincing regularity and that may be diagnosed as critically related to past experience during a particular stage of development. For example, Freud-ians attempt to trace symptoms of and dispositions toward exaggerated behaviors, such as obsessiveness, compulsiveness, or miserliness, to con-flicts during the anal stage. Indeed, the typical strategy is to trace present problems to previous, particularly oral, anal, or phallic, conflicts that were not adequately resolved. Such tracing is not easy to verify convincingly, as Freud was the first to agree with respect to infantile sexuality. Yet the therapeutic method of examination probably yields a more thorough and comprehensive tracing of symptoms than any other currently available method. For this important reason, psychoanalytic theorists consider all data obtained by other methods as auxiliary evidence.

The primary findings obtained by the therapeutic method are rich verbal characterizations of the individual's uniqueness. Nevertheless, one is struck by how little such data have served either to test the validity of psychoanalytic assertions or to lead to revision within the theory as to the nature of psychosexual, psychosocial, and ego development. There are at least two reasons for this. The first is that the theoretical assertions are hardly ever stated in a fashion that is subject to empirical investigation with presently available techniques. The second is that the data are uniquely confounded with the therapist's interpretation, and therapists tend to interpret the same observations differently, that is, in accordance with different theoretical assumptions. Thus, not only are the data not reliable, but it is also not always certain which theoretical assertions they are relevant to.

The use of the therapeutic situation as the major source of data is indicative of an important feature of psychoanalytic theory. This is that the content of development with which the theory deals is primarily that of psychopathological behavior. In comparison, little is done to examine average or normally expectable psychological development directly. Rather, the initial and fundamental conceptualization of normal behavior is based upon extrapolations from abnormal behavior. It should be re-membered, however, that the characterization of normal development is only a secondary and recent endeavor of psychoanalysis.

A number of auxiliary sources of evidence are available to psychoan-alytic theory. One source is in the analysis of the type of character and behavior that results from particular parental patterns of dealing with psychosexual and psychosocial conflicts in different sociocultural and historical contexts. An example already described is Erikson's analysis of the development of identity by the American Negro (see p. 33). A second source of confirming evidence is the therapeutic efficacy of psychoanalytic interpretations to the patient of his behavior (for excel-lent developmental examples see the case studies reported by Erikson,

1963). A third source comes from play therapy with children. In their play children often act out and work through the conflicts or problems that psychoanalytic theory expects them to encounter at their stage of development (see, for example, Erikson, 1951; Klein, 1959). A fourth source of evidence is the biographical analysis of famous people (see, for example, Freud, 1910; Erikson, 1959*b*). Here the aim is to show how the most important features of adult personality can be understood, and possibly predicted, from a thorough analysis of the childhood. A fifth source of evidence is some experimental-correlational investigations. For example, the findings of several studies indicate a positive correlation during adolescence between the need for social conformity and ego diffusion (Block, 1961; Cartwright, 1961; Heilburn, 1964).

None of these five auxiliary sources are without their obvious methodological flaws, as critics of psychoanalytic theory have been quick to point out. What seems more damning, however, is that the information compiled from these sources has had relatively little success in extending or modifying the theoretical concepts of psychoanalysis.

At the purely theoretical level, the major developmental weakness of psychoanalysis is the lack of precision as to what the natures of the id, ego, and superego are at each stage of development. The theory does not definitively articulate the organizational parameters that characterize the configuration of the ego at each stage. On the one hand, it is therefore not clear what characteristic functional differences and causal or interactive functional relationships exist between the personality structures and psychosexual, psychosocial, perceptual, coping, and intellectual activity at each stage. The need for theoretical clarification here has been partially recognized and attempted by Loevinger, who states,

> To distinguish ego level from intellectual level, from psychosexual level, and from adjustment is to ask for a clear conceptual distinction without in any way prejudging the question of correlations or of complex triggering or facilitating effects. (1966, p. 198)

On the other hand, it is therefore not clear what the characteristic structural relationships are between the ego and the id and superego at each stage of development.

Chapter 3
The Mechanical Mirror

THE CHILD IS BORN EMPTY of psychological content into a world of coherently organized content. Like a mirror, however, the child comes to reflect his environment; like an empty slate he is written upon by external stimuli; like a wax tablet he stores the impressions left by these stimuli; and like a machine he may be made to react in response to stimulating agents. The contemporary mechanical mirror formulation adheres closely to Plato's analogy between sense perception and the reflection of images in a mirror or painting, between memory and the writing of characters in a book, and between thought and the stamping of impressions upon a waxed tablet; yet it does not adhere to other aspects of Plato's thinking, such as the notion if innate ideas. As a consequence of the propensities attributed to it, the child's behavior increasingly reflects the coherence of external reality as he grows up. His responses become less random and more consistent with the expectations explicit and implicit in the stimuli and signals issuing from the physical and social environment.

Insofar as the mechanical mirror theory has a model of mind, it is patterned after a mirror that reflects sensations from the environment. As we shall see, however, the mechanical mirror theory conceives of psychological phenomena as behaviors, not as mental experiences. The most generally accepted mechanical mirror model of behavior is that of a machine triggered off by an external agent, a stimulus. Behavior merely articulates that action which is already suggested in and by the environment, but three mechanical and reflective processes of transmitting organized external content to the child and causing him to behave have been posited. These are the mechanisms of (1) direct, overt unconditioned and conditioned association of stimuli and responses, (2) imitation, and (3) mediated, covert association of stimuli and responses. These mechanisms are presumed to account for all the observable, quantitative growth of the child's behavior or acquisition of content.

Central to the mechanical mirror conception of growth is the *environ-mentalistic* assumption that the source of all psychological phenomena is stimulation from the external world. Locke clearly stated this assumption in the seventeenth century. He asserted that there is nothing in the mind that does not come from the senses. External and internal sensory organs are "windows" opening on the environment. Plato's expression of this same idea is still quite contemporary in character. Plato argued that the source of sensation is the motion of atomistic particles coming from external objects. Sensations are small, possibly atomistic, but literal copies of the objects from which they emanate, and they impress themselves upon the individual's senses. The sensory organs, which are particularly susceptible to these external forces, transmit them to the mind.

Hull's more recent (1942) conceptualization of environmental emana-tions is the same in all essential aspects, but it is presented in more modern, physicalistic terminology and is concerned with the stimulatory cause of behavior in general, rather than of ideas only. We shall see more clearly that the pre-Socratic hypothesis that environmental stimulation is the material cause of internal images is still a central concept when we discuss perceptual learning.

A stimulus, according to Hull, is always physical. Objects in the external environment produce a variety of potential stimuli. For example, a table gives off light waves in all directions; smells emanate from a cooked dish; and the behavior of others acts as a social stimulus. Modern mechanical mirror theorists add that the child's own behavioral responses may be immediate (Bijou and Baer, 1961) or mediate (Kendler and Kendler, 1962) stimuli for himself. "Self-produced stimuli" are all physi-cal in nature since their source is muscular activity; even speech is considered to be nothing but stimuli produced by the fine striped muscles (Bijou and Baer, 1961). Bijou and Baer give as an example of self-stimulation verbally "reminding oneself of the late hour," which is a fine striped muscle stimulus that "leads to leaving the party."

The environmentalistic assumption derives its plausibility from the collateral assumption that psychological phenomena, like all other natural occurrences, are really physical in quality or, at least, reducible to characterization in *physicalistic* terms. Stimuli emanating from the envi-ronment may be transmitted to a living organism because both they and the person's so-called mental acts are really nothing but physical occur-rences. It is obvious that the substance of external stimuli is physical. With respect to mental acts, it is assumed that they are reducible to responses of or traces in the nervous system, or secretions of the hormonal system, or movements of the musculature, or some combination of these.

This is the basic feature of the theoretical physicalism posited by Pavlov (1957) in order to resolve the major philosophical issue of his day, namely: What is the relationship between the physical body and the psychological mind or, more generally, between nonconscious matter and conscious processes? His solution assumes that both are physical in nature. Consequently, the elements of which they are composed must be the same. The common unit posited by Pavlov was the *reflex* or automatic, overt response to a stimulus. This unit is the basic element of all behavior, whether it be muscular or nervous (so-called mental) behavior.

Pavlov also formulated a methodological physicalism. If all psychological phenomena are really physical, it follows that they are open to objective investigation by the same scientific methods used to study all other physical events. This methodological physicalism was the basis for Watson's (1913) inconoclastic "behavioristic" message that psychologists should concern themselves with observable behavior and not with introspective reports of conscious experience. Any reference to mental activity that could not be reduced to a statement of physical responses to stimuli was dismissed as mystical.

If psychological processes are in fact physical, the stimulus-response laws of behavior should apply equally well to animals other than humans. Therefore, to many contemporary adherents of this view, it makes no difference in what species a behavior is observed. In addition, practical and ethical reasons make it easier and neater to study the behavior of other animals. Nonhuman animals, particularly rats and pigeons, therefore became the major subject of investigation for most strict adherents of physicalism.

Less strict adherents see it as a theoretical and methodological ideal that requires a technological sophistication of measurement not now available. Consequently, they feel justified in studying phenomena like sympathy, for example, for which the primary referent may be more a mental characteristic or state than a physical stimulus and response. Insofar as mechanical mirror theorists assume this compromise position, they are at least temporarily reintroducing the notions of mentalistic phenomena, such as emotions and thoughts, for purposes of research.

Given the assumption that all psychological phenomena are really physical, it follows that mental activity must operate according to mechanical principles analogous to those presumed to govern its material sources. Pavlov (1906) therefore coupled his physicalism with a *mechanistic* assumption. He adapted Descarte's idea that the body works like a machine to the assumption that all behavior, bodily or mental, operates according to mechanical principles.

Descartes had argued that bodily movements need not be considered voluntary or due to a will-to-move, as they were believed to be in his time. He came to this conclusion because he knew that decapitated animals make movements; thus, bodily movements are possible even when no conscious intent can possibly be involved. Descartes thought of involuntary movements as reflex reactions of the bodily musculature to a force he called animal spirits.

The concept of the reflex arc in the description of behavior is a metaphor based upon the way in which light is reflected by a mirror. A stimulus is said to make an impression upon a sensory receiver that causes the receptor to send an impulse, some sort of image or impression, up a neural pathway to the spinal cord. There it is reflected down another pathway to a motor organ, which it causes to move. Behaviorally, this means that the initial cause of a response is always a stimulus. It also means that a response is always a *passive* movement because it reflects the kind of impression made upon the person by the stimulus.

Stimuli may further condition (modify) the child's native repertoire of reflexes so that his responses increasingly reflect the external environment. His innate reflexes may be very gradually conditioned (a) to respond in the same way to other than the original stimulus for that type of reaction and (b) to respond in different ways than they originally did to the same kind of stimulus. That is, by presenting the child with stimuli which are slightly different from the original stimulus for a given response, the environment may modify his behavior so that he generalizes his responses. Alternatively, environmental stimulation may teach the child to discriminate between stimuli in responding and to inhibit a reaction (not react), or to react differently, to similar yet different stimuli.

This assertion has two corollaries. First, the external environment can shape the perception and behavior of the child in accordance with any desiderata. Second, all that is required to predict the child's behavior and to shape it is adequate knowledge of past responses and present conditions of environmental stimulation (Skinner, 1953).

The physicalistic perspective not only determines the way in which so-called psychological phenomena are said to operate, that is, mechanistically; it also determines how they are organized, namely, according to the same associative principles that relate the elements of their material source, the environment. In his *Inquiry into Human Understanding*, Hume asserted that elements are organized into larger complexes by *association*, that "gentle force" which creates a "bond of union" between them. Various characteristics have been posited as prerequisites of association, for example, similarity or dissimilarity and contiguity (Aristotle); and resemblance, contiguity in space or time, or cause and effect (Hume).

Association is the principle assumed by contemporary mechanical mirror theorists to govern not only the organization of (a) stimuli in the external environment and (b) the impressions left by these stimuli upon the person, but also (c) the responses of the person to these impressions and (d) the response habits (tendencies) acquired by the person. Elements in the external environment are presumed to be there in a state of natural association. The newborn child enters this coherently organized world. As a result of progressive association between the stimuli of the external world and his own responses, external coherence is increasingly transmitted to the child and his responses are increasingly controlled by external stimuli. Numerous stimulus-response associative bonds may be conditioned at the same time. Thus, the child may acquire a variety of habits or response tendencies in any situation. New habits may be associatively linked to each other and to previously acquired habits to form long chains of association. Progressive association among the child's own responses causes them to be increasingly unified into a well-organized behavior system in which certain responses, such as speaking, are consistently accompanied by others, such as gesturing, and may possibly come to act as self-stimulation for these other responses.

Associations are cumulative. With time the child acquires a huge number of associations which are added to each other to form a large repertoire of habitual modes of response. This behavioral repertoire is continuously changing as a consequence of (a) the acquisition of new links, (b) the use of already acquired links (the degree to which a response is practiced or repeated determines its current strength), and (c) the disuse of links, which results in their extinction or decay.

This cumulation and strengthening of associations with time constitutes both the growth and the memory of the child. It appears, then, that memory and growth are equivalent concepts in the mechanical mirror theory of development: the storage and strengthening of associations constitutes psychological growth. Stored associations influence the child's responses to environmental stimulation. The major mechanical mirror developmental hypothesis is therefore that early conditioned associations affect the child's behavior later in life.

To sum up, the aim of the theoretical concepts to be discussed in this chapter is to elucidate the general conditioning, imitative, and mediational mechanisms that govern the child's acquisition of associations of stimuli, of responses, and between stimuli and responses at any age. These three mechanisms define the domain of scientific inquiry. The ultimate goal is to find those general "psychological, physiological, and ultimately physicochemical laws" that determine all behavior (Berlyne, 1965). Development is defined as the continuous, quantitative accumulation of behavior. Pursuit of the major theoretical aim—the elucidation of the mechanisms for the acquisition (learning) and cumulation (memory) of conditioned associations—is therefore influenced by the general hypothesis that earlier associations and behavior affect later associations and behavior. The roles of heredity and physiological maturation in the growth of the child's behavior are often alluded to, but little real theoretical or empirical attention is given them.

REFLEXIVE BEHAVIOR

Pavlov (1906) clearly states that there is only one psychological phenomenon to be studied in higher animals: "the response of the animal to external impressions." Man, like all other animals, works like a machine. He naturally, that is reflexively, responds to external agents (stimuli) in a determinable fashion. The aim of psychology, according to Skinner (1953), should therefore be to predict and control behavior by relating it to "the external causes of which the behavior is a function." By determining the "machine-like properties" of man we will be able to specify how he works. The human, like all other animals, has three kinds of machine-like reflexes: one kind is unconditioned reflexes, and the other two are two kinds of conditioned reflexes.

Unconditioned Reflexes

Pavlov described unconditioned reflexes as innate responses to stimuli, for example, salivation when food is put in the mouth. These reflexes are specific and *permanent* involuntary mechanisms of response to certain stimuli. Here, there is a direct connection between the stimulus and the response. As Skinner (1953) puts it, according to the theory of reflexes "the disturbance caused by the stimulus passed to the central nervous system and was 'reflected' back to the muscles."

Conditioned Reflexes

The most basic and general mechanism that governs the transmission of environmental content to the child, shapes his growth, and determines his behavior is conditioning (Watson, 1916). There are two types of conditioning: respondent and operant conditioning.

Respondent Conditioning. Respondent conditioning is a mechanism of stimulus substitution. It elicits the same response to the conditioned as to the unconditioned stimulus and thereby leads to the establishment of those *temporary associations* in the child that make up what Pavlov called the first signal system. These conditioned associations are composed of links between (*a*) concrete and overt conditioned stimuli, which act as substitutes for or signals of the original, natural unconditioned stimuli that cause behavior, and (*b*) the responses, or parts of responses, that the child reflexively makes to the unconditioned stimuli but that he is now also conditioned to make whenever associated conditioned stimuli appear.

Respondent conditioning was first demonstrated experimentally by Pavlov, who found that salivation in dogs occurs not only as an unconditioned response to food but also as a response to signals for food. For example, a bell can become a temporary signal, a conditioned stimulus, for food and can then elicit a conditioned salivary response. The dog's conditioned response, salivation, will be "stamped in" or reinforced if the signal is followed by the unconditioned stimulus for that response, food. Of course, many environmental stimuli may act as alternate signals for the few unconditioned signals which stimulate any animal to respond.

Since Pavlov's original work on respondent conditioning, two major and opposing hypotheses have arisen with respect to the way in which this mechanism operates. Guthrie (1942) hypothesized that conditioned associations are the result of spatio-temporal contiguity between stimuli and responses. Consequently, the necessary and sufficient condition for acquisition by a neutral stimulus of the signal power to elicit a response is that it be followed by that response. Thorndike (1940) and Hull (1942), on the other hand, paid greater attention to the role of motivation in conditioning and insisted that the conditioned stimulus and response must be followed by the effective unconditioned stimulus if the conditioned association is to be reinforced (strengthened) and maintained. The conditioned response will be extinguished after a while if it is not reinforced, for example, if the dog salivates upon hearing a bell but is never given any food.

Miller and Dollard (1941) elaborated upon Hull's view of the role of motivation in respondent conditioning by distinguishing between primary and secondary drive motivation. Primary or innate drives, such as hunger or thirst, are the initial causes or stimuli for the infant's readiness or threshold for a response, such as sucking. When the infant is rewarded with milk the drive is presumably reduced owing to fulfillment. (It is clear that this is not always true, even though it is assumed theoretically.) Secondary drives are acquired social motives. For example, certain characteristics of the feeding situation, such as the mother's picking up the infant, may become associated with the sucking response. The result is that these environmental characteristics become conditioned substitutes for the primary drive. They stimulate the child to suck as if he were hungry. As the child grows older an increasing proportion of his behavior becomes motivated by acquired, social motives.

An early demonstration of how a young infant's behavior may be conditioned by means of association was reported by Watson and Raynor (1920). An eleven-month-old infant, Albert, was presented with a white rat. At first Albert showed no fear of the rat, but as he was about to touch it the experimenter made a loud noise behind the child. This evoked a fear response, crying. Repetition of the association between the unconditioned stimulus, the noise, and the conditioned stimulus, the rat, conditioned Albert to respond by crying whenever he was presented with the rat alone. The fear reaction was then generalized to other objects similar to the rat, such as dogs, human hair, and wool.

This is, of course, only an example of short-term or local conditioning. It demonstrates how an emotional response may be evoked in the child by an appropriate association at a specific time of his life. It does not demonstrate developmental conditioning, that is, conditioning that changes the course of the child's development so that his emotional behavior at a later period of his life is modified as a consequence.

Bijou and Baer (1961) have attempted to describe the role of respondent conditioning in the long-term growth of emotional behavior. The core of their description is a hypothetical example of how the "biological response" of blushing, "the dilation of the blood vessels in the face," is "elicited by shameful situations":

> A young child may be punished by his parents for being naked, past a certain age of tolerance. In particular, the parents are liable to punish a boy for exposing his genitals in public. Thus, they associate a certain culturally defined situation, exposure of the genitals, with a certain biologically powerful stimulus, physical punishment, which (among other things) elicits blushing. Later in life, the man may discover that he has been walking about with his trousers unzipped. He is very liable to blush. He has not been presented with punishment; he has been presented with a stimulus associated with punishment in his past history. Clearly, this is a *conditioned* power. Without his particular history of punishment for this kind of exposure, the discovery that his pants have been open for some time would not elicit blushing. (pp. 27–28)

We cannot simply accept this hypothetical formulation because two different hypothetical results seem equally plausible. One is that an adult would blush even if he had not had the early punishing experience described by Bijou and Baer. The other is that an adult would not blush even if he had had the early punishing experience described by Bijou and Baer.

Associative hypotheses on the acquisition of cognitive behavior were formulated at least as early as the seventeenth and eighteenth centuries. Hull's (1920) description of the way in which verbal concepts are learned may serve to illustrate the contemporary respondent conditioning formulation of the associationist hypothesis. The external factors conditioning concept attainment may be illustrated by a situation in which a young child reacts by some movement response as he hears something in the situation called "dog." The "dog" experience is completely unanticipated. It occurs at irregular intervals, and there is no obvious index of its essential nature. Moreover, the time intervals between the child's "dog" experiences are occupied with all sorts of other experiences leading to the acquisition of other concepts. This makes adequate reaction and acquisition of the concept of "dog" as a label attached to a certain class of objects very problematic for the child.

In the child's first "dog" situation, associative bonds, with strengths that vary with the attention value of their objects, are established between *dog* and each object in the situation. If the situation allows the dog object to have the highest attention value, then the next time *dog* occurs the major associative link between *dog* and the dog object will function and the bond will be strengthened.

If the dog object has the least attention value in the original situation then the bond between *dog* and it is below the threshold of awareness. However, the attention value of the object in future situations will nevertheless be greater because of the bond between the word *dog* and the dog object from the first situation. This process must repeat itself until "the subliminal bonds accumulate and become liminal" before the label *dog* and the dog object become a functional associative link, that is, before the child is aware of the bond between them.

Hull asserted that this was the "standard" way in which children learn concepts. However, his hypothesis is as yet untested. The same may be said of the Bijou and Baer hypothetical example of conditioned emotional behavior. The general notion that experience is a necessary condition for the child's acquisition of some kinds of behavior is obviously true, but this notion is not identical with the specific theoretical hypothesis that respondent conditioned association is a necessary and sufficient condition for the acquisition and growth of behavior. When this specific hypothesis is stated imprecisely, as it is by Hull and by Bijou and Baer, it may be confused with the general notion and be easily demonstrated. However, it is no longer a testable hypothesis because nothing is stated precisely about (*a*) the stimuli, (*b*) the associative conditioning mechanism or situation, and (*c*) the responses that would have to be observed as a consequence, so that in principle it is not confirmable. The tenacity with which this hypothesis is maintained by mechanical mirror theorists is all the more striking in view of the fact that these theorists vehemently defend the principle that hypotheses which are untestable or not disconfirmable are not scientific hypotheses.

Testability is the absolute essential characteristic of any scientifically useful hypothesis. A conjecture which cannot be tested in some way is of no immediate use to science, attractive as it may be for forensic and similar purposes. Moreover, the hypothesis must be so constructed as to be clearly *disconfirmable*—that is, it must be precise enough so that not all possible outcomes can be incorporated within its framework. (Marx, 1963, p. 12)

Operant Conditioning.   Only a small part of behavior consists of unconditioned reflexes, according to Skinner (1953). In addition, respondent conditioning explains only how new stimuli may become controlling signals for old responses. It does not explain how new responses are acquired and, consequently, does not provide the basis for control and prediction of behaviors that are not responses to unconditioned stimuli.

Skinner therefore asserts that a third type of mechanism—instrumental or operant conditioning—must be added to the two already described—unconditioned and conditioned respondent reflexes—if one wishes to account for all types of acquired behavior. Operant behavior is conditioned by reinforcement of the child's response operations, whereas respondent behavior is conditioned by the mere appearance of a stimulus. An operant response is similar to but not identical with a previously elicited response, but it "*operates* upon the environment to generate consequences." When these consequences appear, they reinforce the behavior that preceded them. As such, external manipulation of the consequences or schedules of reinforcement may be used to control, predict, and shape operant behavior.

In an amusing example in a film produced by Skinner (1959), two pigeons are conditioned to play "ping-pong." The two animals are in a four-walled container, and they are separated by a "table top" with no net. A ping-pong ball is dropped on the table. When the ball drops off the table on the side of one of the pigeons, the opposing pigeon is given a pellet of food. As Skinner describes the scene, what happens is that the pigeons naturally peck at the ball. When one of them accidentally makes it fall on the other side, the pigeon is rewarded. Pecking behavior is thus gradually shaped until each pigeon pecks at the ball so that it will not fall on its side (defense) and will fall on the other side (offense).

At least two central aspects of this situation need to be considered in assessing the relevance of such examples and the presumed underlying mechanism of operant conditioning for the understanding of human behavior. The first concerns the actual behavior of the animals in this and other demonstrations of operant conditioning, and the second deals with the comparability of animal and human behavior.

A careful view of the total behavior of pigeons playing ping-pong will show that, whereas one might expect each pigeon always to try to stop the ball from going over its side and to "bat" it to the opposite side once it has been conditioned, this is not what actually happens. Rather, it sometimes makes no effort to stop the ball from going over its own side. It either watches the ball or does something different, as if something other than the reinforcement was determining its behavior. These uncalled for behaviors may be due to what Breland and Breland (1961) termed "instinctive drift."

After many years of training a variety of species by operant conditioning, Breland and Breland found that conditioning mechanisms are not the primary determinants of behavior. For example, they wished to make pigs pick up coins and place them in a "piggy bank" several feet away; when the pigs performed correctly, they were given food. Since pigs naturally have huge appetites, it is easy to reinforce them in this way. At first, they would "rapidly and neatly" pick up the coins, run to the bank, and deposit. Several weeks after conditioning, however, they consistently began to behave differently; for example, one would pick up a coin, then "drop it, root it, drop it again, root it along the way, pick it up, toss it up in the air, drop it, root it some more, and so on" (Breland and Breland, 1961, p. 683). The result was that the pigs would end up hungry since it took them about 2½ minutes to carry a coin 6 feet. Their behavior was therefore certainly not due to satiation or lack of motivation. Rather, Breland and Breland (1961) conclude that

> Whenever an animal has strong instinctive behaviors in the area of the conditioned response, after continued running the organism will drift toward the instinctive behavior to the detriment of the conditioned behavior and even to the delay or preclusion of the reinforcement. (p. 684)

In addition to the question of what actually happens in attempts at operant conditioning, there remains the question of whether description of operant conditioning of animals has any utility for the conceptualization of human growth. The answer depends upon whether animal behavior and human behavior are comparable. Two people playing the same "ping-pong" game played by the pigeons would quickly come to the mutual understanding that if each always let the ball drop over his side, both would get the highest payoff possible. In short, their best strategy would be to play "to lose." This is an alternative that pigeons would not spontaneously arrive at. Human beings might choose to follow many other behavioral routes, such as to stop playing such a silly game altogether. It is quite obvious, then, that many processes that determine behavior, and even that aspects of a particular behavior, differ widely between human beings and other animals.

Nevertheless, operant conditioning theorists claim that what the child learns—that is, the response he is conditioned to make—is gradually shaped by contingent environmental situations. It is as if each situation were naturally programed, as a computer is. That is, the environment is responsive to the child's behavior so that if the child makes the response (or combinations of responses) desired, it reinforces the response with some reward and withholds reinforcement if the child makes any other responses. In time the situation, like all environments, changes slightly and its program of reinforcement changes accordingly, so that it now reinforces a response which is slightly different from the previously reinforced one. It is assumed that the child will eventually emit a modified response which will be reinforced and that this process goes on gradually but continuously throughout life. It should be noted in passing that this hypothesis is the rationale for the construction of so-called teaching machines.

Consequently, all the child's responses are *continuous* with each other, whether one is concerned with the growth of behavior at different times in development, or with contemporaneous responses; separation of responses into "acts" is an artificial strategy that is necessary in order to establish the functional behavioral unit under investigation. (Since different responses are continuous with each other, it is erroneous to speak of processes such as transfer of training, response generalization, or response induction.) Theoretically, what is happening is that reinforcement of one operation, which Skinner calls an operant, causes reinforcement, to some degree, of all other operants.

Applying this formulation of continuity to child development, Skinner maintains that at no point do behaviors appear which are very different from preceding ones. The child's operants never emerge fully formed; rather, they are continuously and gradually shaped by reinforcement. Behavior, even when it is highly complex, may be shaped in any direction one wishes by differential reinforcement of successive approximations to the desired operant.

Skinner acknowledges that he does not know why reinforcers are able to strengthen conditioned or unconditioned responses, but he supposes that the evolutionary concept of survival must play some part here. Inherent reflexes and inherited potential for modification by conditioning processes are both biologically advantageous. Organisms having these adaptive characteristics are more likely to survive and are also more likely to pass them on to their offspring.

As an example of the role of operant conditioning in the growth of behavior, the development of social dependency in the child is particularly instructive. Dependency also serves as a good example because it reveals much about the mechanical mirror conception of man.

Social dependency is defined by Bandura and Walters (1963, p. 139) as "responses that are capable of eliciting positive attending and ministering responses from others." The infant is born dependent upon other people and will become increasingly dependent throughout life. The changes are in the direction of increasing and strengthening his dependency and of improving the child's skill at performing operants which will be instrumental in evoking reinforcement, that is, attentive and helping responses from others. Such dependency behaviors are expected from people at all ages and are therefore reinforced by appropriate reactions. Moreover, it is the cultural expectation that when the individual becomes an adult, he will become dependent upon a person of the opposite sex. The "husband and wife will engage in physical manifestations of dependency that do not differ greatly from those that occur in the parent-child relationship" (p. 138). Inappropriate dependency constitutes a major behavior disorder.

Bandura and Walters maintain that a number of studies directly support the notion that adult nurturance (reinforcement) is a crucial factor in conditioning the child to make increasing numbers of dependency responses in the course of his growth. In particular, they point to correlational studies, their own and others, in which highly nurturent behavior on the part of the parents is associated with a high frequency of dependency responses by the children.

Several remarks need to be made about the significance of such studies: (1) The correlations reported are invariably small, even when they meet statistical requirements for significance. (2) As indicated in Chapter 1, correlation is not causation. (3) The correlation may be mediated; that is, it may be the result of factors that are not all apparent in the correlated behaviors. Many factors are correlated with both nurturance and dependency; and at least some of these factors are probably correlated with each other. (4) Most of the findings are based upon parents', or children's, reports of their own and their children's, or parents', behavior rather than on direct observation by the investigators. This factor introduces all sorts of biases, such as the reporter's wish to impress the investigator.

Bandura and Walters argue that studies like Rheingold's (1956) are further, though indirect, evidence for their contention that positive reinforcement or nurturance leads to dependency. Rheingold reports that infants in institutions for whom an experimenter performed eight weeks of intensive caretaking duties were more socially responsive to the experimenter and to others than a control group of children for whom the experimenter did not perform these duties.

Bandura and Walters do not, however, cite the follow-up study by

Rheingold and Bayley (1959), which is a crucial investigation of whether positive reinforcement influences the development of dependent behavior. When the same children were examined about a year later, no difference was found in their social dependency behavior from that of a control group. The relevant results, then, clearly refute the hypothesis that reinforcement has long-term effects.

To conclude, the assumption is that the child is born dependent upon the environment, which provides the necessary stimulation to provoke him to respond if he is to survive and adapt. In this the child is like a machine which must be set in motion by an outside force. In this sense, the environment does not constitute the scene of (occasion for) the child's behavior. Rather, it is the dominant actor in the drama of his life.

Growth ensures the increasing dependency of the child. The scene gradually shapes his responses to conform with the demands of its stimulation in predictable ways. It reinforces (stamps in) certain reactions and not others so that some responses result in essentially pleasurable (rewarding) consequences and others in nothing or painful (punishing) consequences. The theoretical result, then, is a "patient" who increasingly conforms to and is dependent upon the environment, rather than an "actor" who exploits the scene as an occasion for significant action.

Some mechanical mirror theorists (for example, Skinner) believe that conditioned and unconditioned reflexes make up the fundamental mechanisms for the acquisition or growth of behavior. Indeed, they argue that all other mechanisms are merely derivatives of this fundamental class of mechanisms. Other mechanical mirror theorists (for example, Bandura and Walters) maintain that there are mechanisms for the acquisition of behavior which may or may not be derivative reflex mechanisms even though they seem to appear later in life. One such class of mechanisms is imitation.

IMITATION

The assumption that imitation is a mechanism of learning is at least as old as the formulation of Aristotle, whose conception of imitation, however, was quite different from the mechanical mirror view:

> Imitation is natural to man from childhood, one of his advantages over the lower animals being this, that he is the most imitative creature in the world, and learns at first by imitation.

Contemporary mechanical mirror theorists maintain that imitation is a particularly important mechanism for the child's perceptual and social learning. Yet hypotheses of perceptual and social learning consider imitation in opposite ways. Hypotheses of social learning emphasize the fact that the child's percepts are the basis for his social behavior. He observes the behavior of others and uses it as a model. As a consequence, his own responses come to conform increasingly to social reality. Hypotheses of perceptual learning emphasize the role that motoric responses of exploring and modeling external objects play in mediating the perception of these objects and internalizing correct images or copies of physical reality. For this reason we shall treat the concept of imitation in social learning and perceptual learning separately.

Social Learning

Skinner's contention that there is continuity between all operants is typically accepted by contemporary social learning theorists as a general law of the growth of social and personal behavior. Novel responses do not suddenly emerge in the child. Rather, they are the result of long periods of operant conditioning which reinforce his successive approximations to the new pattern of behavior that is desired. However, social learning theorists add that the mechanism of learning social responses involves a further aspect, namely, that of first observing and then imitating a social model. Whether or not the child will imitate the model that he has observed depends upon whether his own mimicking responses (or the behavior of the model) are rewarded. The maintenance or extinction of the child's responses that successively approximate and imitate those of models is controlled by the contingent environmental schedules of reinforcement for these mimetic responses.

The contemporary origins of this view are the hypotheses by Allport (1924) and Markey (1928) on the child's acquisition of social communicative behavior. The child's learning of language starts with his own babbling behavior, which stimulates his auditory receptors. Auditory responses are the inevitable and invariable concomitants of the baby's motor-vocal behavior that produce specific patterns of sound stimuli. Hearing these sounds stimulates the baby to make the vocal movements with which they are associated. Thus, a circular reaction presumably develops whereby the baby's own vocal behavior stimulates his audition, which in turn stimulates him to make a vocal response. These circular reactions become evident when the child begins to react to the sounds made by others with his own vocal response. The total hypothesis, then, is that vocal imitation by the child depends upon (a) the previous establishment of circular reactions and (b) the coincidence that, at first, the sounds made by others are similar to his own babbling sounds, and possibly also (c) reward for his mimicking responses.

More recently, Miller and Dollard (1941) have suggested that the child's tendency to copy is an acquired secondary drive that can account for much of the identification process described by psychoanalytic theory. For reasons they do not explain, the young child may spontaneously (perhaps coincidentally) imitate the behavior of others. When he does this, his social environment rewards him and thereby reinforces his tendency to imitate. Thus, mimicking becomes a social or secondary motive for the child to copy responses of others that he himself has not previously made. Reinforcement of imitative behavior is the basis of most socialization, according to Bandura and Walters.

> Imitation is likely to bring the rewards the child is seeking. The child learns early to reproduce the parents' affectionate behavior and thus reward himself by expressions of self-love and self-approval. Through the repeated association of imitative behavior with reward, the child becomes motivated to behave like the parent. In other words, imitative behavior becomes rewarding in itself. (1959, pp. 253–254)

Borrowing directly from psychoanalytic theory, Sears (1957) hypothesizes that the child's initial tendency to imitate is motivated by his desire to secure his mother's nurturance of his primary drives, such as the drive for food. When food is not forthcoming, the child imitates the affectionate and gestural behaviors that accompanied or were part of his mother's nurturent behavior. His imitative behavior thereby substitutes for her nurturent behavior and the child secures "at least partial gratification." This is the genetic basis for the secondary drive to imitate.

A similar yet somewhat different view is provided by Whiting (1960) and Kagan (1958), who hypothesize that the child identifies with his parents because he observes that they have the power to control and consume the resources for nurturance and other goals. He therefore envies their status and tries to emulate them in the belief that he will thereby acquire their power and possessions. As a consequence, the child will covertly or in fantasy play the role of the envied persons, particularly parental figures, who control and consume the desired resources. Thus, it will be easier for him to overtly enact the role he has identified with and played in fantasy when he grows up and the conditions are appropriate.

Mowrer (1950), like many other social learning theorists, has attempted to integrate social learning hypotheses on imitation with psychoanalytic hypotheses on identification. According to Mowrer, the basic paradigm of identification is illustrated by the learning of words by mynah birds. These birds are rewarded (primary reinforcement) when they make sounds. In the process, the other stimulus characteristics of the trainer, including his verbalizations, also become rewarding (secondary reinforcers) for the birds' vocalization. If the birds make sounds that approximate (imitate) those of the trainer, they essentially reward themselves or give themselves secondary reinforcement for vocalization that imitates speech. As a result, these birds tend to repeat words that their trainers utter.

It is Mowrer's contention that this process is paradigmatic of the child's learning of language and other social behavior. His parents provide for his primary drives, such as those for food and affection. Since the parents perform other behaviors at the same time, these behaviors also become rewarding (secondary reinforcers). If the child performs behaviors that approximate (imitate) those of his parents, he is essentially rewarding himself for these imitative behaviors. That is, by imitating his parents' behavior he administers secondary rewards to himself and reinforces the imitative behavior. Thus, he comes to identify with his parents.

The general development view of social learning theorists seems to be that the child is selectively rewarded for imitative responses that the social environment deems appropriate. Identification is the gradual learning of many imitative responses that somehow become associated into a coherent personality. For example, the environment tends to reinforce a boy for imitating the behavior of his father and a girl for imitating her mother. In this way children gradually and continuously acquire normal sexual identification. If the child adopts a deviant sexual role, it must be due to reinforcement of socially inappropriate sexual behavior. The method of treatment prescribed is therefore counterconditioning, that is, punishment of deviant behavior and reward of socially appropriate sexual behavior.

Sears (1957) argues that the child is not really reinforced by the parents to imitate specific responses. Rather, he is reinforced to pattern himself after or generally identify with the behavior of his parents. Bandura and Walters (1963) add that reward is not necessary for reinforcement of imitative behavior. It is sufficient for the child to perceive that the model is rewarded for his behavior in order for his mimicking behavior to be vicariously reinforced.

Bandura and Walters (1963), like Skinner, contend that the developmental problem which respondent and operant conditioning principles have been least successful in dealing with is the acquisition of novel responses, particularly new social responses. According to Bandura and Walters, the solution, at least for social behavior, lies in the mechanism of imitation. Children imitate new behaviors that they have observed in a model. For example, in one experiment on aggressive behavior, children observed a model who used a particular way of beating up a doll (jumping on and pounding the doll). The children imitated the model's type of aggressive behavior even though they had not been given any direct verbal instructions to do so. From this and other experiments, Bandura and Walters (1963, p. 67) conclude that *learning* novel responses is a consequence of observing the behavior of others whom the children accept as models: "The acquisition of imitative responses results primarily from the contiguity of sensory events." *Performing* novel responses is determined by reinforcement: "Response consequences to the model or to the observer have a major influence only on the *performance* of imitatively learned responses."

It should be clear that Bandura and Walters are speaking about a novel response that belongs to a class of operants that is already part of the child's behavioral repertoire. The assumption is that the child has never before produced that particular pattern of aggressive responses; it could hardly be assumed that the child had never learned or performed aggressive behavior before participating in the experiments they describe. Moreover it is not at all clear that a child would learn and imitate, particularly in a nonexperimental real-life situation, all the behaviors of a model if they really were novel. It is questionable, for example, that a child who had never swum before would, if he put on a bathing suit and went into the water, attempt to imitate an adult just because the adult is swimming. As Bandura and Walters themselves try to demonstrate, one could easily multiply the contingencies which would influence the probability of the child's learning anything from simply observing a model and then performing behaviors that he has learned by observation.

The problem, then, seems to come down to the following: When a child is told, whether explicitly (verbally) by the instruction of a model or implicitly (nonverbally) by the performance of a model, to behave in a new fashion, will he? It is Bandura and Walters' contention that he will, if the schedule of reinforcement is appropriate. However, the response sought will occur only if it is little different from and of the same kind as previous responses the child has performed. In this way the child's behavior may be gradually and continuously shaped into what might be called new classes of responses. In actuality the responses are not novel since the change brought about is not a qualitative change. In fact, we may more justifiably hypothesize that the child is likely to imitate a response *only* if he has made a response of that kind before, and *not* if he has not. If this is true, then Bandura and Walters have no more accounted for the development of new responses than the conditioning theorists they criticize have.

Growth, according to social learning theorists, is continuous. Logically, therefore, what appear in the child to be novel social responses are not really qualitative changes in his behavior; nor do they imply that new ways of functioning have emerged which make for progressive stages in development. All that one may assert is that a certain type of social behavior has been shaped to look different, to increase or decrease quantitatively, and to be strengthened or weakened. Consequently, social learning theorists need not give descriptions of the child at different ages but rather experiments with children at any one age that demonstrate modification of a behavior that is already available. This is actually what they usually do. They attempt to demonstrate that the subject, whatever his age, may be reinforced to imitate a response that is already in his behavioral repertoire but that he is presumed to have never or very infrequently made in exactly the same fashion before entering the experimental situation. Indeed, some social learning theorists assert that they could just as well have performed their modeling experiments on behavior modification with animals, such as birds and dogs, as with children.

Social learning concepts of the imitational mechanism are also limited in their empirical implications for the understanding of development because imitation does not have demonstrable long-term effects. In fact, as with conditioning, little research is available on the long-term effects of imitation in normal children. What is available are studies such as that by Hicks (1965) on aggressive behavior. Hicks reports that children were exposed to a model who was physically and verbally aggressive toward toys. After witnessing the aggressive behavior the children were mildly frustrated. Then they were placed in a room with toys and their behavior was observed. Six months later they were retested. The result was a general decrease in imitative aggressive behavior after six months. This decrease was significant when the model was an adult female, a peer female, or a peer male, but it was small when the model was an adult male. In general, then, these results provide little evidence of long-term effects upon aggressive behavior. If anything, they suggest the opposite. Unfortunately, they are further confounded as evidence for the long-term effects of imitation by the fact that the children were mildly frustrated before each experimental session. Whatever results were obtained may therefore be due to frustration or to imitation, or both. Yet, it should be noted that the author of this study concludes that long-term effects have been demonstrated—a rather dubious conclusion considering the results and the confused method of investigation.

What is perhaps the most significant demonstration of the effects of imitation upon long-term growth also involves positive or negative reinforcement. In his attempts to shape the primitive behavior of autistic children, Lovaas (1966) reports that some aspects of these children's behavior, such as hurting themselves, can be extinguished by removing the positive rewards that reinforce such self-destructive behavior or by punishment. Other, more normal, but still mechanical or robot-like, behavior can be shaped by modifying present, sometimes autistic behavior by reinforcing imitation. For example, the echolalic behavior (imitating the verbalizations of others in a garbled fashion) of some autistic children has been modified to somewhat approximate normal speech by rewarding the children with candy for appropriate imitations. Both the extinction of autistic behavior and the acquisition of more normal behavior seem to have lasting effects for at least a year when they are accompanied by constant prompting and reinforcement. The necessity for constant prompting and reinforcement means that these are short-term effects that require continuous support rather than long-term growth effects. They are, then, only more short-term effects of imitation, but effects occurring in a special population of children. They may have little relevance to the long-term growth of normal children, whose responses do not usually require constant prompting and reinforcement.

Perceptual Learning

Whereas the social learning hypotheses focus upon the role that observing and imitating models plays in the growth (acquisition and performance) of social behavior, the perceptual learning hypotheses are concerned with how overt modeling responses to stimulation from the external world mediate the acquisition of perceptual images that correctly copy this stimulation. The basic assumption is that there is a *real* world external to the perceiving organism. According to Zaporozhets (1965), this world presents itself to the child in a coherently organized fashion, and adults teach the child "methods of learning the environment." The goal of this training is the child's acquisition of percepts that are accurate photograph-like copies of the world. The result is that the child's perception increasingly mirrors reality with exact and comprehensive copies as he grows up. In this way he comes into increasingly closer and more comprehensive contact with what is really there. This view, then, is a direct translation of philosophical realism into what we may call developmental realism.

Developmental realism adds one more mechanistic assumption to philosophical realism. This is its acceptance of the various unconditioned reflexes, which emerge at different times in ontogenesis and are presumed necessary for the child's acquisition of exact percepts of external reality. Unlike some of the social learning theorists, perceptual learning theorists are clearest in their conception of the relationship between reflexes and imitation as behavioral growth mechanisms. They assume that imitation is originally a set of unconditioned reflex mechanisms.

Indeed, Zaporozhets has attempted to delineate four ontogenetic reflex stages in the acquisition of percepts that correctly copy external reality. The child is born with *executive* or orienting-set unconditioned reflexes. This means that stimulation elicits a working reaction of movement by the child's peripheral receptor apparatus, such as his eyes, in the direction of the stimulus so that he fixes upon it and follows its shifts of direction. A presumed demonstration of the executive reflex is the fact that three-month-old babies fix their attention upon new objects more than twice as long as on familiar ones. Zaporozhets interprets this fixing response as serving an executive function, namely, to make the sensory receptors most capable of responding to the novel incoming stimuli.

The most important unconditioned reflexes in the formation of images appear next. These are the orienting-*exploratory* reflex responses of the child's receptor organs toward stimuli, for example, looking over a visual display. The function of these unconditioned responses is to acquaint or orient the child with the stimulus object by exploring it.

The next stage involves not only fixing and exploring reflexes but also the unconditioned reflexes of *modeling* the stimulus object. Now the child begins to trace the characteristics of the stimulus objects by movements of his peripheral receptor organs, for example, by looking at the outlines of an object. These modeling responses lead to the acquisition of simple and synthetic perceptual images, such as visual or tactile images, which copy the stimulus objects the modeling responses trace.

The final stage delineated by Zaporozhets involves the unconditioned reflex of *correcting* one's percepts. Now the child repeatedly compares his model with the stimulus object and corrects his image until it becomes "more and more precise, finally leading to an adequate perceptive image" and thereby "reproducing and depicting the reality."

Zaporozhets (1965) cites an experiment performed in his laboratory that illustrates these stages. Children's eye movements were filmed while they looked for twenty seconds at an irregular black figure, 30 by 40 cm, on a white background. The children were instructed to inspect the figure carefully and were told they would be asked to recognize it later on. The three- to four-year-old child's eye movements were always within the figure and never upon its outline; he made relatively few eye movements and fixed for long periods upon particular spots. The four- to five-year-old made twice as many eye movements, but the movements were still within the figure and not upon its outline. The eye movements appeared to be orienting-exploratory responses toward the size and length of the figures. From five to six years of age, the child made some modeling responses; he traced the outline of specific portions but not the entire figure. The frequency of eye movements was about the same as that of the four- to five-year-old. From six to seven years the child's eye movements traced the outline of the figure. This developmental sequence was accompanied by an increase, with age, in the child's visual recognition of the object after the experiment.

Although the experiment is supposed to illustrate the theoretical sequence in which these reflex stages develop in the child, two critical difficulties still remain. First, it is difficult to determine what the theoretical boundaries between the different stages of unconditioned reflexes are supposed to be, and this empirical study does not help. Second, but of lesser theoretical importance, is the lack of specification of the correspondences between the empirical results obtained at different ages and the reflexes that are assumed to emerge at successive stages.

It is relatively easy to see that these four types of unconditioned reflexes might play a necessary role in the child's acquisition of visual and tactual images. It is more difficult, however, to understand how the world is mirrored by the child's other perceptual modalities, such as his olfactory and auditory modalities. A further problem is how images from one sensory modality may be "translated" into another at different stages of development so that, for example, the child may come to visually recognize an object with which he has only had tactual acquaintance. Research in the laboratories of Leontiev and Zaporozhets has attempted to deal with aspects of these problems.

Leontiev's hypothesis is that the child may acquire auditory images because they are mediated by vocal-motoric responses. In the course of development the child is assumed to focus on a sound first with his auditory receptors, then to orient himself toward it by exploring it, then to model the sound by vocal imitation, and finally to compare his copy with the real stimulus object and to modify his product until it is a correct copy. This vocal copy is the basis for his internalized auditory image.

Leontiev provides the following type of experiment with adults in support of his vocal mediation hypothesis. The ordinarily experienced correspondence between the pitch and timbre of a sound was disrupted so that adults heard sounds with low pitch and high timbre, and vice versa. The result was a large increment in pitch discrimination thresholds for 35 percent of the subjects. But when the subjects were told to vocalize both tones before making a judgment, the discrimination thresholds were greatly reduced. When the subjects stopped vocally reproducing the tones, their discrimination thresholds were again raised. It should be noted that Leontiev's developmental hypothesis of how auditory images are acquired has not been directly demonstrated by ontogenetic research and that his results hold for only 35 percent of his adult subjects.

The problem of translating images from one perceptual modality into another has led to the following type of ontogenetic study in Zaporozhet's laboratory. A flat, irregularly shaped object was presented to children for tactual examination. After 60 seconds of examination, the child's task was to find the object visually among a number of other objects. Three-year-olds appeared to be playing with the figure (for example, pushing it around) rather than examining it. The children's activity looked more like catching the object than touching it. The four- to five-year-old children used the palm and surface of the fingers more, but not the fingertips; usually they used only one hand. The five- to six-year-olds used both hands moving toward each other. They examined some specific features of the object but did not systematically trace the outline of the entire figure. After six years of age, the children systematically traced the entire outline with their fingertips as if they were modeling it. Along with this developmental sequence, the investigators found a corresponding increase with age in accuracy of visual recognition of the object.

It should be noted that the description of tactual development in this experiment is very similar to the description of eye movement development in the previously mentioned experiment. This descriptive correspondence and the improvement in recognition is used as evidence to support the argument that the growth of the responses involved in the two modalities is parallel and mediates the translation from one perceptual modality to another. In actuality this still remains a supposition rather than a demonstrated fact.

The general question of how the child internalizes overt reflexive responses and transforms them into mental images still remains open. Executive, orienting-exploratory, modeling, and correcting reflexes may be necessary behaviors in the process, but they only explain how overt responses come about. They do not explain how covert mental images are formed and what their character is, nor do they explain how overt responses may mediate the translation from one type of mental image to another.

Finally, it should be added that this conception of perceptual learning diverges in one important respect from the typical mechanical mirror approach, although in all other major respects it conforms to that approach. The divergence is in the hypothesis that qualitatively new unconditioned reflexes emerge in the course of the child's development. This presumes that there is discontinuity between stages of perceptual functioning that influences what the child can acquire from the environment. It should be recognized, however, that these reflexes are physiological. Consequently, the discontinuity between stages may be due merely to physiological maturation.

MEDIATION

In the previous section we discussed the mechanical mirror conception of how the child's observable, overt modeling mediates his acquisition of social behavior and perceptual imagery. Here we shall be primarily concerned with how hypothetical but nonobservable covert responses that are attributed to the child mediate his production of other overt responses. This hypothesis of covert responses is at the heart of the mechanical mirror reduction of man's higher mental processes, such as thinking, to primarily physical responses, their physical association with other responses, and their physical cause—stimuli.

A rudimentary and restricted developmental conception of mediation has been presented by the Kendlers and by Berlyne, who assume that, as a growth mechanism, mediation is merely a derivative of the reflexive mechanism. Vygotsky and Luria present a much more comprehensive developmental analysis and, in some instances, seem to argue that mediation is an independent growth mechanism, although their formulation is not always consistent.

According to Kendler and Kendler (1962), mediating responses may be overt or covert. However, it is the child's covert mediating responses that constitute the mechanism whereby simple responses are built into larger, complex behavior. Covert mediators are inferred, but not observed, responses of the child; they are probably silent verbalizations. These inferred responses are called mediators because they are presumed to link external stimulation with the external responses to which they eventually lead. The mediational mechanism may be described as follows. Overt stimuli evoke overt bodily responses, which may function just like external stimuli. Not only may they act as stimuli upon others, but they may leave sensory impressions upon the responder himself. Traces of these impressions are somehow stored in memory. By association these traces may be linked together into chains. Thus, these traces may cause the child to make another overt response, or they may activate the stored associated trace of another response. In the latter case, the activated trace itself acts as a covert stimulus or cue for a response, which could be another covert response, and the chain could go on for some time. It is clear, however, that the end result will always be an overt response. The mechanical mirror notion that an external stimulus will always be reflected by an external response, if it was truly a stimulus for a response in the receiving organism's repertoire, is thereby maintained, even if only in a tautological form.

The Kendlers are led to the mediation hypothesis because they find that adult learning of concepts cannot be adequately accounted for by the conditioning hypothesis that overt stimuli are directly connected with overt responses, or what they call "a single unit S–R theory." They therefore hypothesize that some stimuli elicit covert responses which constitute implicit stimuli or cues for overt responses. Nevertheless, they and Berlyne maintain, in apparent disagreement with Vygotsky and Luria, that the same principles which govern immediate or single-unit stimulus-response relationships apply to mediate connections between covert stimuli and responses. For this reason they believe it unnecessary to resort to a conceptualization like Vygotsky's, where, as we shall see, internal conscious mediating processes are posited to account for much of mature human cognitive behavior. Thus, for example, Berlyne (1965, p. 19) asserts that "reasoning must be defined as something manifested in behavior rather than as a kind of conscious process." Reasoning is a phenomenon of covert association in which a "class of stimulus situations" is linked to a "class of responses." The only difference from overt associations, which constitute all observable behavior, is that the link may be between stimuli and covert or implicit responses; this has nothing to do with consciousness.

On this basis the Kendlers assert that the child's acquisition of covert mediating links is developmentally continuous with, and grows out of, his acquisition of overt single-unit links: they are based upon the same conditioning mechanisms. Rats and young children "respond in a manner consistent with a single-unit S–R theory. With age, they [children] develop a tendency to respond in a mediational manner."

The empirical basis for this assertion is the following kind of experiment. Subjects are presented with a task that can be dealt with best by double alteration or changing the response every third trial, that is, by making one response twice, then its opposite response twice, then the first response twice, and so on. For example, the subjects are presented with a right and a left door. A prize placed behind the right door the first two trials, then behind the left door the next two trials, then behind the right door the next two trials, and so on, is the only clue to the rule of behavior which is most rewarding. Animals and young children have difficulty in consistently finding the reward; older children do not. On the basis of such results it is concluded that the success of the older children is due to the mediation of covert verbal behavior that is not available to the young children and animals. The validity of this conclusion has been seriously questioned by Furth (1966), insofar as he and others have found that illiterate deaf children are about as successful in solving this kind of problem, particularly the double alteration problems, as literate children.

Finally, it should be added that, unlike Vygotsky and Luria, the Kendlers make no attempt to specify the principles governing the growth of this hypothetical mediational mechanism. Mediators are simply conditioned associations that we can no longer observe.

Vygotsky's view is a hybrid that stands midway between (*a*) the mechanical mirror conception, which reduces all development to the growth of immediate and mediate conditioned associations among stimuli, among responses, and between stimuli and responses and (*b*) the organic lamp conception, which considers development as a self-evolving psychological process that cannot be reduced to the acquisition of stimulus-response associations. On the one hand, some of Vygotsky's concepts naturally lent themselves to reformulation by disciples like Luria into relatively typical mechanical mirror characterizations of mediated behavior. On other hand, Vygotsky's own formulation rejected any reduction of higher mental processes to reflex processes. His formulation is similar to organic lamp concepts in some important respects, which cannot, of course, become completely clear until we reach the discussion of organic lamp theory itself in the next chapter. Nevertheless, Vygotsky's hypotheses will serve as a conceptual bridge between these two opposing theoretical approaches to development.

Growth of Voluntary Behavior

Vygotsky's (1966) contention is that man is not only acted upon by stimulation from the environment, but he also acts upon his milieu to create new external stimuli. One set of stimuli that man constructs are signs that cause modification of his own and others' responses to environmental stimulation. Signs are external mediators that communicate between individuals and, at least to some extent, control behavior.

> The mastery of one's own behavior presupposes . . . the main laws which govern these phenomena. . . . But we know that the main law of behavior is the stimulus-response law, for which reason we cannot master our own behavior other than through corresponding stimulation. Mastery of the stimuli offers the key to mastering the behavior. Thus, mastering the behavior is a mediational process which is always carried into effect through certain auxiliary stimuli. (p. 35)

In the course of development, these external communicative signs are internalized by the child and become what Luria (1961) calls the "highest self-regulatory system" for the voluntary control of behavior. This second signal system, as Pavlov called it, is composed of verbal thoughts that become the primary mediators of human behavior.

Speech passes through many stages before it becomes "the main mechanism of conscious voluntary behavior" (Luria, 1961). At first it plays an impellant function; it may initiate behavior but it cannot inhibit it or change activity from one kind to another. As early as the second year of life the child is able to respond to verbal statements, such as "give me your hands." However, the function is weak. It cannot overcome behavior that the child is already performing. For example, Luria reports that it is difficult to bring a child to take off his stockings by verbal instructions if he is in the process of pulling them on.

The initial and simplest level of voluntary behavior occurs when the child's movements produce an external signal that controls these very same movements. Luria (1961) reports an experiment performed by Yakoleva. A child was told to press a ball when a light went on in front of him, but not when it was off. The apparatus was rigged so that as soon as the child pressed the ball the light went off. Thus, the child's own pressing resulted in an external "conditioned signal," the light going out, for "don't press any more," and the child stopped pressing. Under these circumstances, on-going behavior that cannot ordinarily be inhibited by verbal instructions at the age of one and a half to two years can be brought under voluntary control.

By the time the child is three to four years old he begins to develop real voluntary control of his own behavior when it is reinforced by consistent verbalization. For example, the instruction to say "Go!" as the child presses effectively takes the place of the external conditioned light signal in the bulb-pressing situation, so that when the child says "Go!" as he squeezes he will only do it once. However, the control function is still weak because if the instructions are changed so that the child is supposed to squeeze twice, verbalization of "Go!" will no longer control his move- ments and he will squeeze the bulb many times. If, on the other hand, the child is told to say "Go! Go!" as he squeezes twice, he regains voluntary control and does not squeeze more often than instructed. The child who is able to effectively control his movements by the external verbalization of "Go! Go!" is not able to do so when he verbalizes "I shall press twice!" Rather, he presses once for a long time. Moreover, if the child says "Don't press!" when he is supposed to stop, he accelerates his squeezing reactions rather than inhibiting them.

According to Luria, all these findings indicate that it is the intonational or impulsive, motoric qualities of speech, and not the significative or semantic aspects, that act as the voluntary signals for regulation. The next stage appears between the ages of four and a half to five years, when the semantic qualities of speech replace the intonational qualities as signals for voluntary control. An example is a situation in which the child is instructed to press twice when a brief signal appears and not to press at all on a long signal. The child responds appropriately as long as he repeats the instructions aloud, thereby reinforcing the internal sequence of active and inhibitory reactions. The five-year-old is not able to perform the task if he does not make the external verbal reactions.

The final stage appears when the child no longer needs to make external verbal reactions in order to control his own behavior voluntarily, that is, when the shift from external to inner control has become effective. Luria argues that this internal system of complex, temporary links and the indirect way in which they function is what radically changes the child because it "leads to a new, specifically human, stage of development."

This stage has four major characteristics. First, the child's inner verbal analysis becomes the major mediator of his behavior. It regulates the formation of novel associative connections. Environmental stimuli or signals are immediately incorporated into his existing system of stimulus-response associations as new temporary links, or they are immediately excluded. Second, once the child formulates a verbal "behavior rule" he uses it to orient himself with respect to new environmental signals. He no longer requires constant external reinforcement in order to maintain the new signal-response link. The reinforcement becomes the fact that his response was congruent with the rule. Third, reshaping of behavior is no longer gradual. Reinforcement of a stimulus need be changed only once in order to modify the behavior rule. For example, the instruction not to press upon the presentation of a red light after a previous instruction to do so will immediately inhibit and change the response. Fourth, the child develops verbal mediational systems of regulating his reactions to abstract stimuli, such as sequences of signals and alternate signals, in situations that require him to make opposite responses to the same stimulus depending upon its position in a complex set of different stimuli.

This, then, is the developmental course whereby "the process of elaboration of temporary connections" between stimuli and responses, which is characteristic of the conditioning mechanisms of the child's first signal system, is transformed into the new "information" and "self-regulating" system that comprises the second signal system. The child's mediational system (a) affects the way in which new stimuli act upon him and the way in which he orients himself to these stimuli, (b) controls the responses he makes, and (c) regulates his consequent formation of new internal links between signals and reactions.

Growth of Consciousness

As we have just seen, Vygotsky's and Luria's approach to the study of language and thought is rooted in the Pavlovian tradition that rejected idealism and the subjective character of psychological phenomena. Unlike Pavlov and later mediational theorists like Berlyne, however, Vygotsky (1962) did not renounce the study of consciousness as a legitimate endeavor for objective science. Although like Pavlov he rejected spiritualistic theories of consciousness, he probably saw in the organic lamp conception of egocentricity a formulation that permitted objective consideration of it. As we shall see more fully in the next chapter, organic lamp theorists like Piaget and Werner characterize the developing subject-object relationships (the child's interactions with his environment) along an egocentric-perspectivistic dimension, rather than along the specifically nonconscious-conscious dimension of some philosophical theories, such as those of William James, Sartre, and Merleau-Ponty (see Gurwitsch, 1964). Briefly, egocentricity is the child's cognitive state early in development when he doesn't differentiate between himself, his action, other things, and their action in an event. Perspectivism is the child's progressive capacity to differentiate cognitively between these aspects of an event and between his own and others' points of view, then to reflect upon these differences, and eventually to integrate his reflections into a personal "theory" of the relationship of himself to other things and people in a given event.

In his early work, Piaget (1926) thought he had found some forms that were transitional between egocentric and perspectivistic cognition in children's linguistic expressions of their thought. Now, if we substitute the words *nonconscious* for *egocentric* and *conscious* for *perspectivistic* in the previous sentence, a scientifically objective basis for studying the evolution of consciousness has been found, namely, the way in which the child communicates his thoughts in language.

Although Vygotsky (1962) did not completely agree with Piaget's formulation, it was this type of reasoning that led him to reject both the view that consciousness consists of purely private, subjective acts and the view that consciousness must be considered a mystical concept with no scientific referent. He asserted that consciousness develops and that this development has a material embodiment in the forms of language. In Vygotsky's words, "Life reveals itself in consciousness," and language is man's "real consciousness." All the more sophisticated forms of symbolization, such as mathematics, develop out of the primordial conscious form of language.

The better to study consciousness, Vygotsky sought to place it in its proper biological-evolutionary and sociohistorical context. Man develops material means or "tools" which take on socially mediated forms. This development causes a "sudden change" or discontinuity in psychological development between man and other animals. Vygotsky viewed this change as an evolutionary step that "is not determined primarily by the laws of the historical development of society." It constitutes a stage of phylogenesis which stands apart from all previous stages. Its form is social and linguistic; its function is communication; and its consequence is the emergence of consciousness. It should be noted that this hypothesis of discontinuity between man and other animals is a radical departure from a mechanical mirror view in the direction of an organic lamp perspective.

Language is characterized by the fact that all its functional forms, namely, words, have meaning. The proper unit for the analysis of verbal thought is therefore "word meaning," according to Vygotsky. The meaning of a word is a "generalization of a concept." Generalizations and concepts are acts of thought. There is, then, a very close relationship between language and thought. This is not to say that there may not be thought which is embodied in forms other than speech or that speech may not have other functions than the communication of meaning. Nevertheless, the major problem for developmental psychology is to determine the laws governing the evolution of thought *and* of language.

Growth of Thought

Vygotsky (1962, p. 55) recognized that it was not enough to characterize the process of acquiring thought as the ability to understand and communicate existing concepts. The reason for this is that although the young child is capable of acquiring simplified functional equivalents of adult concepts, his "forms of thought . . . differ profoundly from the adult's in their composition, structure, and mode of operation." Unlike most mediation theorists, Vygotsky did not assume that concepts are merely conditioned associations:

> A concept is more than the sum of certain associative bonds formed by memory, more than a mere mental habit; it is a complex and genuine act of thought that cannot be taught by drilling but can be accomplished only when the child's mental development itself has reached the requisite level . . . [of] deliberate attention, logical memory, abstraction, the ability to compare and to differentiate. (1962, pp. 82–83)

It is therefore necessary to study the concepts formed by children in their own right. In order to do this, Vygotsky adapted a procedure devised by Ach (1921) in which the subject is asked to sort twenty-two blocks varying in color, shape, and volume into four classes. There are five different colors and six different shapes but only four different volumes. The situation is such that all objects belonging to the same class have the same volume and the same, artificially constructed, name printed on their underside.

The first major stage of concept formation evidenced is the formation of "heaps" of blocks for which there is no basis except that they are "linked by chance in the child's perception." At the same time, a name means only a vaguely, and highly unstably, related conglomeration of individual objects. For example, the child may string some blocks out into a line and say that the result is a train.

The second stage is characterized by "thinking in complexes." The child's basis for putting things together is not only subjective impressions but actual similarities between the blocks. Moreover, the child begins to distinguish his subjective impressions from the objective character of things. He may sort the blocks by the five colors—even though he is instructed to sort them into only four groups. However, the bonds he forms between things are still based upon his direct experience. They are "concrete and factual rather than abstract and logical." He uses words as names for such concrete complexes. That is, he uses words as if they were proper names, much as he uses family names on the basis of his experience that certain people belong to a given family although he is not at all aware of their relationship, that is, the logic of why they are all called by that name.

The third and last major stage of concept formation is characterized by both synthesis and analysis. The adolescent abstracts elements out of the totality of concrete experience. By naming an abstract element, he gives it the privileged status that it must have to be used as the basis for synthesizing objects in a new fashion. The process is one of constant movement in thought from the particular to the general and the general to the particular, where names are used as a means of focusing attention upon particular elements. The adolescent is ready to sort the blocks into the correct classes according to their appropriate names.

Scientific concepts taught in school are a major source of consciousness:

> School instruction induces the generalizing kind of perception and thus plays a decisive role in making the child conscious of his own mental processes. Scientific concepts . . . seem to be the medium within which awareness and mastery first develop, to be transferred later to other concepts and other areas of thought. Reflective consciousness comes to the child through the portals of scientific concepts. (Vygotsky, 1962, p. 92)

We can only wonder in passing whether Vygotsky thought that consciousness can arise in societies that have no science.

Scientific (nonspontaneous) concepts, such as the social science concept of planned economy, are acquired through opposite but complementary processes from those through which everyday (spontaneous) concepts, such as the concept of family, are acquired, according to Vygotsky.

The child does not know or understand scientific concepts until they are taught to him in school. Therefore, scientific concepts are taught from the top (abstract generalizations) downward (toward concrete experience). The teacher instructs, questions, and corrects the child in his acquisition of the systematic network of abstract and general concepts that make up science. The child is thus forced to become conscious of scientific concepts at an earlier age than he is of the everyday concepts that he himself spontaneously generates. Everyday concepts develop from the bottom (concrete familiar experience) upward (toward more abstract notions like those of science).

The reason why scientific concepts can be passed downward is that the child has everyday concepts which help him make concrete sense out of the ideas he is being taught. And the reason why spontaneous concepts can develop upward is that the child applies the more abstract ways of thinking taught to him in science to the formulation and generalization of everyday concepts. Thus, scientific and everyday concepts develop in opposite directions, but their development is mutually dependent.

Growth of Language

Paralleling his argument that two basic conceptual processes evolve in opposite but complementary directions, Vygotsky hypothesized two basic linguistic processes that also follow opposite but complementary structural and functional developmental paths. The two processes that compose linguistic behavior are inner and external speech.

Structurally, the development of external speech proceeds from the part to the whole. At first the child utters single words, then phrases of two or more words, and so on. On the other hand, when the child uses inner speech he starts with meaningful wholes or complexes. Eventually, he begins to master the meaning of words and to divide his formerly undifferentiated thought into separate semantic units. Moreover, the child has the capacity to produce syntactically correct sentences in external speech before he has internal understanding of their meaning. Thus, for example, he uses the term *because* correctly in sentences before he understands its logical implication.

At first the child is not conscious of the difference between the external phonetic and the internal semantic character of words. The word is fused with the object to which it refers (word realism). The child will deny, for example, that it is possible to call a dog a "cow." If he is told that he is going to play a game in which a dog will be called a "cow," he may assert that that kind of a dog must have horns.

Functionally, inner speech is communication for oneself, whereas external speech is communication for others. Consequently, the child's external speech is directed toward putting thoughts into material and objective forms, namely, words. The child's inner speech turns into internal thought. The syntax of his inner speech is "disconnected and incomplete." Its form is abbreviated: the subject and the words connected with it are omitted, while the predicate is maintained. The child conveys to himself the implicit sense of the situation rather than any explicit meaning.

Language and Thought

In order to get the proper view of the child's cognitive development, it is necessary to take a unified look at the parallel evolution of his language and thought, since Vygotsky maintained that the structure of consciousness is primarily the connections and mutual relationships between particular mental functions, such as language and thought. The total structure of consciousness determines the significance of individual functions. For example, perception loses its quality of immediacy of experience when the child acquires the capacity to speak. At that time his perception becomes more closely related to his thought. Such secondary connections may be the occasion for the formation of new systems of mental processes in the child, but Vygotsky did not specify their nature.

Analysis, then, must proceed from an understanding of the entire character of consciousness in order to determine the qualities peculiar to individual functions, rather than the reverse. This holistic approach is, of course, a basic rejection of the analytic method that attempts to understand psychological functions by breaking them up into their component elements or atoms and then determining how they fit together. In this, too, Vygotsky stands apart from, and in direct opposition to, the theorists described previously in this chapter and is actually allied with the organismic perspective to be described in the next chapter.

Now, if we take Vygotsky's conceptualization of language and thought together, the following picture emerges: there must be a motive or reason for the child to think and try to formulate thought. First he embodies thought in inner speech, then in the "meaning of words, and finally in words."

According to Vygotsky, two principles of mental development govern the evolution of inner speech and thought. The first is that the primordial mechanism of creating consciousness and meaningful forms is totally *external*. Only after he has used language as a means of communicating with others does the child use it with respect to his own mental processes. Thus, words first evolve as a means of external communication.

The second principle is concerned with the transformation of external into inner mediational tools. In general, the course of mental development is characterized by the *internalization* of initially external, linguistic and conceptual, forms and acts. Only after a long period of external use of mediational means for social interaction are these overt forms interiorized as means of organizing individual mental processes. This long process of internalization is manifested by a transitional stage in the child's development between interpsychic functioning (external speech and nonspontaneous conceptualizing) and intrapsychic functioning (inner speech and spontaneous conceptualizing). Vygotsky called this transition egocentric speech.

The function of egocentric speech, like inner speech, is to help the child to orient himself in his conscious understanding and behavioral activity. The volume of egocentric speech decreases between the ages of three and seven, and the quality of the egocentric speech becomes increasingly inscrutable; that is, the meaning of the speech is decreasingly understandable to another person. This change denotes "the child's new faculty to 'think words' instead of pronouncing them."

The hypothesis that egocentric speech grows out of social, external speech is supported by three facts. First, egocentric speech occurs only when the child is with other people and not when he is alone; it is a type of collective monologue. Second, the child believes that his egocentric speech is understood by those around him, even though it isn't directed toward them. Third, egocentric speech has the material character of external speech; it is audible rather than silent or whispered.

There is one plane of thought that is "still more inward than inner speech." This is "thought itself," which underlies any medium, such as speech, that is used to convey thought. In order to describe thought itself, Vygotsky borrowed Stanislavsky's conception that there is a "subtext" beneath the lines of a play. The subtext of all linguistic forms is thought. Thought does not even have the structure of inner speech since, unlike speech, it is not composed of separate units. The whole thought is present as one unit in the mind. When it is externalized, it must be developed into a string of successive speech units. A very short thought sometimes requires elaborate verbalization in order to be communicated. Vygotsky did not, however, specify how "thought itself," which is "more inward than inner speech," develops in the child.

SUMMARY

The mechanical mirror approach is more concerned with establishing a systematic research program than a comprehensive theoretical position.

Consequently, any attempt to determine the mechanical mirror view of development, such as the attempt made here, must virtually construct the theoretical position because there is little systematization to work with.

The assumption is that the full picture of growth will eventually be synthesized from analytic data on the observable elements of behavior. The aim is to show that reflex mechanisms govern the acquisition of behavioral elements, and the aim explains why mechanical mirror theorists rely almost exclusively on the experimental and correlational methods.

The search for the mechanisms that govern the acquisition and modification of behavior is an important part of psychology. The question that arises with respect to the mechanical mirror view is whether it actually looks for mechanisms of acquisition and modification or whether it merely applies the preconceived notion that the growth of all behavior is caused by conditioning and thereby overlooks the actual mechanisms governing acquisition and modification. A less biased investigation might well reveal that the mechanisms are different for different species and for humans of different ages.

Within the mechanical mirror perspective, there is a wide spectrum of approaches to development. At the fundamentalist end there is the view, represented by such theorists as Skinner or Bijou and Baer, that the underlying mechanism is the conditioned reflex. The attempt is to demonstrate that the acquisition and modification of all behaviors, whether motoric, social, linguistic, or logical, can be attributed to respondent and operant conditioning.

In the middle ground is the social learning view, which is heavily influenced by psychoanalytic hypotheses. This view is most concerned with the mechanism of identification in the acquisition and modification of social behavior. The most general formulation of identification postulates four factors (but there is disagreement as to the theoretical sequence in which these factors operate): (1) The child observes possessions that others (particularly parental figures) have and that he desires. (2) The child believes that having the attributes of these others leads to possession of the desiderata. (3) The child notices and attempts to copy some of the attributes of these others. (4) The environment selectively reinforces his efforts to copy some, but not other, attributes, depending upon what it considers socially appropriate. If they are accepted, the first three factors require much more complex mechanisms than the conditioned reflex. They require an explanation of how the child is capable of observing and imitating certain behaviors and of why he comes to want specific things. The least that is required is a conception of a machine with complex programs for observation, storage, desire, conceptualization, and performance. Such a conception would lead to a rich program of systematic research into the mechanisms of behavior, and the merest hint of such a program is beginning to appear (see, for example, White, 1967).

At the revisionist end of the mechanical mirror perspective, we have primarily the views of Soviet theorists, particularly Vygotsky and Luria. These theorists make fewer assumptions about the nature of the mechanisms of acquisition (even though they seem usually to have the peculiar need to call them reflex mechanisms regardless of their descriptions of them). They are more concerned with determining what mechanisms the child uses to acquire complex programs for interacting with the environment. In this sense, the revisionist position is more allied with the organic lamp view, which we will discuss next. If the revisionist position had a more comprehensive formulation, it would be more appropriate to discuss it separately under the label "mechanical lamp."

Chapter 4
The Organic Lamp

T HE VIEW THAT MAN is like an organic lamp has its source in the Hellenic spirit. It found its true expression in the Platonic ideal that man's essence is contemplation. According to Aristotle, contemplation is the final determination, the actualization, toward which man's potential as an actor is directed, and according to Descartes, it is his defining characteristic—"I think, therefore I am."

Because humans spontaneously initiate their actions, they play a constructive role in their own psychological experience and development. Formally, they are organizations of organs or systems of action that operate (1) to interact with their environment and (2) to construct their own experience and knowledge of themselves and the world. Genetically, they are endowed with (a) the necessary systems for initial interaction with the milieu in personally meaningful ways and (b) the self-generative characteristics that ensure their own development and self-actualization. Of course, the various systems emerge at different times of life. Developmentally, humans are actors or operators who function to keep themselves adaptively interacting with the environment, thereby conserving their own organization at the same time as they transform it, so that they can live and develop. A new stage of development arises when a new or transformed system becomes dominant and functionally subordinates or incorporates previously existing systems. In this way, personal continuity is maintained as discontinuous stages evolve.

The thesis is that evolution is a synthetic process that interweaves two antithetical organismic tendencies: to maintain continuity in order to conserve one's integrity (survival and organizational coherence) and to elaborate discontinuity in order to develop. This dialectical conception was formulated by Werner and Kaplan (1963):

> There is, on one hand, the tendency of organisms to *conserve* their integrity, whether biological or psychological: in the face of variable and often adverse, external or internal conditions, the organism tends to maintain its

existence as an integrated entity. There is, on the other hand, the tendency of organisms to *develop* towards a relatively mature state: under the widest range of conditions, organisms undergo transformation from the status of relatively little differentiated entities to relatively differentiated and integrated adult forms. (p. 5)

The understanding of genetic emergence and of developmental transformation is the major focus of organic lamp theory. The theory recognizes that the human begins life in the intrauterine and early postuterine period as an organism composed of biological action systems, such as the systems for breathing and for ingesting food. But he evolves psychological action systems, such as that for thinking, as he develops into an adult, mature form. Organic lamp theorists propose that much of man's psychological functioning grows out of and is the highest expression of his biological functioning. Psychological organization is the end product toward which biological evolution is directed. The problem is to determine how psychological action systems such as thinking and perceiving develop out of, and become integrated with, biological foundations to create the total organismic unity that characterizes the mature person. This is seen as a twofold, complementary task of working out (*a*) the taxonomy of stages from the biological to the psychological (and within the psychological), and (*b*) the genetic and developmental processes of change.

THE TAXONOMIC TASK

The taxonomic task of working out the stages serves as a concrete example of the more abstract question of evolutionary processes. The working assumption is that both the child's biological and his psychological organizations are, in Gesell's terms, composed of "action systems." Consequently, the task is to determine the transitional stages during which the child's acts are most clearly biological and psychological at the same time. Organic lamp theorists tend to agree that such acts are to be found primarily at the first great stage of postuterine development, namely, the sensorimotor (s-m) stage of infancy.

Human characteristics are not superadded as a late installment upon a lower primitive stage. They were in the beginning of fetal and post-natal behavior. (Gesell, 1946, p. 296)

Verbal or cognitive intelligence is based on practical or sensorimotor intelligence which in turn depends on acquired and recombined habits and associations; these presuppose, furthermore, the system of reflexes whose connection with the organism's anatomical and morphological structure is apparent. A certain continuity exists, thus, between intelligence and the purely biological process of morphogenesis and adaptation to the environment. (Piaget, 1952, p. 1)

That is, psychological action is immanent in the propensity for action of the biological structures with which the child is born. The biological organization of infancy constitutes the foundation or ground plan for future growth:

> Infancy was evolved to subserve the need of individual growth. It lengthens as the organism becomes more complex. (Gesell, 1946, p. 297)

The importance of human infancy for the scope of later psychological development lies in its range, depth, duration, and plasticity of functioning. Werner (1948) has suggested a more general formulation:

> The difference in plasticity of development comes clearly into view in a comparison of various ontogeneses in the animal and the human sphere. That is, the epoch of plasticity in any form of life appears . . . of longer duration and richer in content, the higher the species. (pp. 29–30)

For example, Gruber (personal communication) compared the ontogenesis of object permanence in kittens with that of children. It took kittens only three months to begin to search for disappearing objects in a fashion that is comparable to the conduct that takes eight to ten months to develop in children (see "Objects," p. 124). However, the comparative precocity of kittens is inversely related to the scope of their cognitive development. Object cognition in cats does not progress beyond the level developed at three months. Children progress more slowly through infancy, but as we shall see in the section on cognitive development, they eventually develop to much more advanced stages of cognition (for example, see "Objects," p. 143.

The child's earliest psychological means of constructing experience are sensorimotor acts, such as sucking, grasping, or looking at things. Neither perceptual nor intellectual acts can arise unless the child has passed through a stage of s-m activity that is functionally analogous or precursory (as a mode of adaptation to and interpretation of the world) to the perceptual and contemplative or operational activity that will evolve out of it (see pp. 96–98 for a fuller explanation of functional analogy). At the s-m stage, the child creates cognitive forms that are precursors of the perceptual and operational forms of knowledge that develop out of them at later stages. In this sense, functional and structural continuity between psychological stages of development is assumed:

> The sensorimotor sub-structure is necessary to the conceptual for the formation of the operational schemes which are destined to function finally

in a formal manner and thus to make language consistent with thought. (Piaget, 1952, p. xi)

Because of their bodily nature, the child's sensorimotor acts are little differentiated from their biological base; that is, they are adaptive means of functioning. At the same time, they already constitute representational and exploratory means because of their concomitant graphic and manipulatory character. They therefore constitute the essentials for the child's psychological interpretation of events, in which his functioning is no longer directed toward purely biological adaptation. In this sense the child's s-m acts are both biological and psychological.

The general picture of human development that emerges is the following. Three major stages of evolution in the person's organization and consequent interactions with the psychological environment develop (Werner & Kaplan, 1963, p. 9) (see Table 4.1). The changes from stage to stage exhibit the directiveness of evolutionary progress, namely, progressive construction and interpretation of, and dominance over, the environment. In this sense, development is marked by a shift in man's psychological functioning from (*a*) passive motions or relatively conforming reactions to external stimulation to (*b*) interpretative actions or relatively spontaneous constructions of himself, his experience, and his environment.

THE PROCESS TASK

The fundamental theoretical problem in the study of change in the composition of the child's mental organization from biological to s-m to contemplative systems is to determine what self-generative processes are innate. Two complementary processes of autogenesis have been posited, the orthogenetic and the equilibration processes. Whereas the orthogenetic process is characterized in topographical terms, equilibration is described in more probabilistic terms. The reader who is not already well acquainted with developmental theory is advised to skim the next two parts, on orthogenesis and equilibration, and to come back to them after reading the section on cognitive development.

Orthogenesis

Werner (1948) adapted the biological principle of orthogenesis as the process governing long-term psychological development. The thesis is that the inherent direction of development is toward

Table 4.1 *Diagram of Developmental Transformations* [a]

Organism-Umwelt Relationships		Means-Ends Relationships
I. Tropistic-reflex reactions *to*	Stimuli	Biophysical and biochemical transmission culminating in stereotyped reaction patterns of parts of, or whole, organisms
II. Goal-directed sensorimotor action *upon*	Signaled things	Species-specific behaviors and individually learned patterns of response ("habits"); formation of signals (mammals); "natural" tool usage (apes) —all predominantly in the service of biological ends
III. Contemplative knowledge *about*	Objects	Construction of tools and formation of symbols in the service of knowing about and manipulating the environment

[a]From Werner and Kaplan (1963). Reproduced with the permisson of John Wiley & Sons, New York.

a. increasing differentiation and specification of primitive action systems that are initially fused with each other in one global organization, causing

b. the emergence of novel and increasingly discrete action systems that are also increasingly integrated within themselves, such that

c. the most advanced (differentiated, specialized, and internally integrated) systems hierarchically integrate (functionally subordinate and regulate) less developed systems.

Progressive *differentiation* and specification of the global organization of action systems, their functions and structures, is one side of development. Functions are either fused with each other (syncretic), or they have no operative relationship to each other (are segregated) and operate in a rigidly fixed and unstably fluctuating (labile) fashion at the onset of development. They progressively differentiate into increasingly discrete yet internally integrated means of action and intended ends that operate in a flexible and stable fashion. Structures are indefinite in boundaries and diffuse in character and relationship to each other early in development. In the course of development they become differentiated into increasingly definite and well-articulated parts that are internally integrated.

Progressive *hierarchic integration* and centralization of differentiated and internally integrated parts (individual action systems) into the total mental organization is the other side of development. The evolving relationship between action systems is directed toward a structural hierarchization and functional integration of parts to each other and to the whole mental organization. The result is the progressive formation of a holistic mental organization such that the most central and developed action systems increasingly subordinate and regulate the less developed systems.

Thus, in the course of development, the human's systems for action unfold into a complex of varied forms (von Bertalanffy, 1933; Werner, 1948). Consequently, the human progressively, and sometimes regressively, changes. His development is not linear, however, but multilinear. Many "selves," individuated systems of action, arise side by side. The mark of normal development is that these differentiated "selves" are progressively related into a functionally and structurally hierarchized organizational whole in which the constituent parts are not lost but integrated. Regression, by contrast, is characterized by increasing dedifferentiation and disintegration of the higher organization of action systems (Goldstein, 1939; Angyal, 1941).

Developmentally lower action systems need not be lost with the elaboration of new, higher forms. Typically, they are transformed into the higher systems or are integrated as subordinates of the new systems that comprise the more complex organization of later personal development. Behaviorally, this means that the normal individual does not ordinarily operate at one and the same level even during a given stage of life. Developmentally, it means three things, according to Werner (1948, 1957). First, earlier modes of acting are continually present as the basis of all mental life. Faced with a novel situation, problem, or task, the person approaches it through a developmental sequence of actions that ranges from his lowest to his highest systems. In the adult the sequence may extend all the way from sensorimotor to contemplative operations. Werner calls this developmental process *microgenesis;* others have called it *actualgenesis,* to indicate that it is a part of a developmental unfolding process that may occur at any stage of ontogenesis (the life cycle of an individual). Microgenesis is such a rapid process that it must be slowed down, in effect stretched out over time, by special research methods so that it can be empirically observed (for a review of research methods for the study of microgenesis, see Flavell and Draguns, 1957). The second and third developmental implications follow from the first one. Since earlier modes of acting are continually present as the basis of all mental life, they may appear as normal supports of higher modes of acting. Under special conditions earlier modes may serve as substitute (vicarious) means for the more advanced modes. For example, the fingers may be used to count sensorimotorically when more conceptual means of calculation are not available.

Equilibration

An equilibration process postulated as the prime mover of long-term self-development is the theoretical complement of orthogenesis. Gesell (1946) provided an early formulation of equilibration in order to understand the process of maturation, particularly physiological maturation. Gesell hypothesized that a principle of self-regulatory fluctuation governed the direction of maturation. The principle asserts that the organism restricts the "oscillations" that characterize its growth.

> The growing organism is of necessity in a stage of unstable and shifting equilibrium. Also, of necessity, it must restrict the modes and degrees of instability. (p. 298)

Development, then, is a process of "formative instability combined with a progressive movement toward stability." Its course is spiral: it consists of "progressive involutions by which structure and function are jointly matured."

Piaget (1967) provides a general and a particular interpretation of the equilibration process of psychological development in which the core force is interaction rather than maturation. The general interpretation is that the functional relations within the child's action systems are always in disequilibrium, but more so early in life and progressively less so as the child develops. That is, the child is endowed with self-regulating biological systems that are directed toward establishing increasing equilibrium. Development is the progressive approximation to an ideal equilibrial state that is never fully achieved.

The child's self-regulating systems themselves evolve as a consequence of the new levels of equilibration that his prior systems create, and intelligence is his most advanced self-regulatory system for establishing equilibration. Intelligence evolves (materializes) out of prior self-regulatory systems, which are more purely biological and less psychological. At base, then, intelligence is still a biological system. Even within intelligence itself there is progress from pragmatic, sensorimotor to logical, operational self-regulatory systems. But all self-regulatory systems are mechanisms for the progressive development of coordination and compensation (reversibility) among his structures, which they both conserve and transform.

The particular interpretation is that the equilibrial level achieved by the child at a given moment of his life may be disrupted by an environmental perturbation whenever he (*a*) biologically or psychologically recognizes that something is disturbing him and (*b*) lacks the means (adequate physiological regulations, s-m acts, or mental operations) necessary to deal with the perturbation. When this is the case, the child's physiological, s-m, or mental self-regulatory systems begin to act so as to establish greater equilibrium. This state can only be achieved when the child performs actions that actively compensate for the perturbation and then feed back the information obtained from the compensatory activity to the acting system. Usually the system of action in question is then transformed. This means that new ways of acting are created that may more functionally anticipate and efficiently deal with future perturbations of the same order. For an example of how the equilibration process of cognitive development is beginning to be studied experimentally, see pp. 138–139.

A complementary, or possibly alternative, hypothesis is that the child's equilibrium may be disrupted by a perturbation that is internal, that is, a perturbation between structural parts of his action systems (Langer, 1969). Disequilibrium may occur whenever the child's means of action outstrip the desired ends, or vice versa. That is to say, whenever the child develops a novel structure of action that has functional capacities (means of action) that outstrip his present adaptive needs (ends), then the operative system is in disequilibrium. The child's tendency will be to develop novel ends for action (functions) to be served by these means and thereby to establish greater equilibrium. In complementary fashion, whenever the child develops a function that has ends for action (adaptive needs) that outstrip the means of action available to him (structural capacities of the system), his tendency will be to develop novel means (structures) to serve these ends. This is consistent with Werner and Kaplan's (1963) assertion that

> wherever functional shifts occur during development, the novel function is first executed through old, available forms; sooner or later, of course, there is a pressure towards the development of new forms which are of a more function-specific character, i.e., that will serve the new function better than the older forms. (p. 60)

Now, in establishing greater equilibrium the child tends to overcompensate for the perturbation (the lack). This means that the novel means constructed to serve an unsatisfied end will tend to have functional potentials that outstrip the purpose for which it was originally created. Likewise, novel ends will also tend to have need potentials that outstrip the capacities of the present means. Consequently, the system never remains in a stable equilibrium but rather shifts from one state of disequilibrium to the next. The mutually regulating and impelling effects of the structure and functions directed toward establishing greater equilibrium cause development to follow a spiral course (see Figure 4.1) in which structures and functions continuously outstrip each other. In this sense, the child's present operations are directed toward the construction of future nonformalized organs and intuitions in order to transform them into formal operational systems and cognitions.

Accordingly, the loops of the spiral in Figure 4.1 may be said to represent stages that are transformed into each other. Thus, the loops overlap and grow out of each other, indicating developmental continuity between stages of an action system. They also progressively form quantitatively and qualitatively separate and higher-level configurations, indicating developmental discontinuity between stages. The figure also shows that in order to go forward it is first necessary to go backward: the first step toward progress is regress. Progress is based upon hindsight (backward action), upon past functioning (means and ends), achievement of some stable but not completely satisfying resolution between present action and past operations, then foresight (anticipatory action) of future ends (needs) and means (instruments) of operation. The clearest example of dedifferentiation as the first step toward progress is the spiral process from egocentrism to perspectivism that is manifested throughout

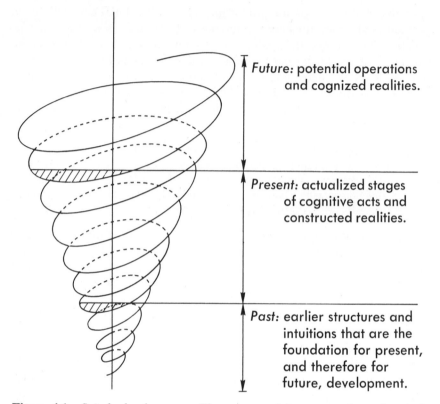

Future: potential operations and cognized realities.

Present: actualized stages of cognitive acts and constructed realities.

Past: earlier structures and intuitions that are the foundation for present, and therefore for future, development.

Figure 4.1 *Spiral development: The constructivist assumption of spiral development*

development; it is described in detail on pp. 105–107. Another example, described below, is the spiral construction of object knowledge, in which the recurrent first step is dedifferentiation of the perception or conception of objects.

THE EVOLUTION OF MENTAL ACTIVITY

Many stages and systems of action develop as a consequence of the process of autoregulative equilibration from biological to psychobiological stages and systems. The developmentally most advanced and sophisticated self-regulatory system that evolves is intelligence, and the invariant functions of human intelligence are the mental representations of the two most general functions of the autoregulative equilibration process, namely, to organize oneself and to adapt to the world. Biological and psychological stages and systems are, then, functionally analogous with respect to the process of autoregulative equilibration.

Functional analogy between stages and systems of action may imply anything from the notion that they are recursively isomorphic to the idea that earlier stages and systems are the material cause of (precedents or precursors necessary to) the development of later higher-order stages (Werner, 1957). For example, Piaget's work points to the functional analogy between the following stages of object cognition:

   a. sensorimotor construction of object permanence from
     1. action, in the first few months of life, indicating that when an object moves out of the child's perceptual field it has disappeared for him, to
     2. transformed action, toward the end of the first year, indicating that objects maintain their permanence for the child even when they have disappeared from his perceptual field
   b. the development of perceptual constancy such that an object eventually is seen as maintaining its size even when it is receding into the distance, as maintaining its shape even when only part of the object is visible, and so forth
   c. the construction of object identity from
     1. preconceptual notions of object metamorphosis until the age of four or five years—for example, the child asserts that a plant he has observed growing from one time to another is not the same plant—to
     2. intuitive concepts of object identity—for example, he understands that it is the same plant even though it has changed
   d. the development of the concept of conservation of objects in thought from
     1. the intuitive stage, at which the child intuits that, for example, the amount of liquid changes when it is poured from one beaker into another of different shape, even though the entire operation is performed in front of him, simply because he perceives that the water level has changed, to
     2. the concrete stage, at which the child knows that the amount of liquid is conserved and he can use the principle of conservation, although he does not yet understand it, to
     3. the formal stage, at which the child both understands the principle of conservation and can use it as a means of regulating his operations; that is, he has developed a "theory" of objects, their transformations, and actions
   e. the development of the concept of conservation in the history of physics (In an insightful account, Kuhn (1962) analyzes the process of paradigm change (stages) in the history of physical thought that culminated in the quantum revolution.)

Piaget (1967) and Werner (1948) hypothesize that analogous functioning is one of the most general laws of development. The knowledge that the child constructs at the initial, sensorimotor stage he *re*constructs into new, richer and more comprehensive configurations at each subsequent stage. These configurations are composed of *schemes*, which have functional and structural aspects. Functionally, they are forms of action that have structure, that structure experience into percepts and concepts, and that have self-constructive capacities from the outset, as contrasted with habits, which are the result of conditioned associations between unrelated elements. As such, the child's schemes of action are his instruments for (*a*) cognitive generalization, (*b*) the satisfaction of needs, and (*c*) the organization of interests and attitudes. Structurally, the child's schemes are the forms of his knowledge (for example, permanence, identity, and conservation), needs, and attitudes, which are constructed by their own active operations. They constitute the "stuff" out of which the child's knowledge is made at each stage of his development. Thus, the structural and the functional aspects of schemes are reciprocal because their organizational and adaptational aspects are two sides of the autoregulative process of equilibration.

A scheme of action or schematizing activity is therefore any class of cognitive acts that is coherently interrelated and discernible at different stages of life as belonging to a class. Later schemes are presumed to unfold out of earlier ones. For example, the child's sensorimotor construction of permanent objects is precursory and prerequisite to the various manifestations in later life of the conceptual construction of conservation. Both types of schematization have a system of action and an end in common—namely, intelligence—and both construct forms or schemes of object knowledge, that is, permanence and conservation of objects. Of course, the child's specific actions and ends and the content of the knowledge he constructs are different since one of his schemes establishes the permanence of objects while the other establishes their conservation properties.

The child's schemes have two complementary functional forms of action: assimilation and accommodation (Piaget, 1950). The function of *assimilation* is to modify (integrate) the aliment (experiential "food for thought") incorporated through interaction with the environment and thereby to conserve the structure of the operative schemes. To assimilate the child restructures the relevant environmental data so that it becomes coherent with his existing schemes, that is, so that the data fit in with what he already knows. Thus, assimilation is the function that ensures that experience will have significance.

The function of *accommodation* is to modify (differentiate) and elaborate the child's schemes so that they will be consistent with the character of the external environment. Accommodation thus integrates new information from the environment into the child's existing schemes so that they are modified but not destroyed.

Short-term local development is a process by which assimilation and accommodation are equilibrated. Local disequilibrium occurs whenever assimilation or accommodation is the dominant feature of the child's action. When this is the case, the other function is likely to be brought into play, and increasing equilibration is the probable result.

One of the earliest ontogenetic schemes of action described by Piaget (1952)—prehension—may be used to illustrate these two functions, how they naturally come to be in disequilibrium, and how disequilibrium leads to local development. In the first months of life the infant already grasps at anything with which his hands happen to come in contact. At first he tends to grasp in a stereotyped fashion regardless of what kind of object is involved (even when from an adult point of view it is not an object, such as the nostrils of the person holding the baby, for which grasping is an appropriate reaction), what shape it has, and what distance it is from himself. Two major characteristics of this activity indicate the assimilatory function. First, the infant makes the object he is interacting with into a "grasping" object, whatever its characteristics. "Grasping" is the significance he attributes to it. Second, he grasps at all objects in the same characteristic fashion no matter what they are like. In short, he constructs the thing through his actions into an object of knowledge that fits the prehensile scheme with which he has come to the situation and which determines the way in which he may interact with things.

Dominance of the assimilatory function, with its attendant lack of discrimination on the part of the child's grasping activity and consequent perturbations, puts the prehensile scheme of action in disequilibrium. In normal development the most probable outcome is the eventual accommodation of prehensile activity and the establishment of greater balance. Thus, beginning at the second or third month of life, the infant begins to modify (accommodate) the way in which he grasps at different things. The result is increased equilibration between assimilation and accommodation and, thus, local development of the child's scheme of prehension and cognition of objects.

In sum, two characteristics of humans are organization and development. Therefore, the child must have inherent functions that permit him to take in outside material so that he will develop. Accordingly, there is the root organismic hypothesis of *interaction:* the person actively takes in and digests "food" that is present outside of himself. The fact that he takes in and digests food or experience means that he grows physiologically or develops psychologically. Of course, he can digest food only in accordance with the digestive structures available to him. In the same way he can digest experience (information) only in accordance with his cognitive structures. Thus, the structures determine the meaning of experience by their assimilatory and accommodatory functioning.

Moreover, if the person stops ingesting food he will die or at least be harmed. For this reason all living organic systems are said to be developing (Werner, 1957). The same is true of the organism as a psychological rather than a physiological being. Normal psychological existence implies development, and abnormal existence is characterized by a lack of development—arrest, retardation, or regression.

A key reason why studying the form of each stage and the sequence in which the stages evolve is important to the understanding of development lies in the root hypothesis that development is a process of interaction. The structure of each stage delimits the range of actions the individual can make at that stage. Consequently, it determines the kinds of interactions he can have with the environment and the experiences he will encounter. His experiences feed back upon the present structure, and eventually, in ways that are still little understood, the present structure is qualitatively altered to become the structure of the next stage. It is in this sense that we may understand the organic lamp view of the material causation of development described in Chapter 1. The organization of preceding stages implies but does not contain the organization of subsequent stages.

GENETIC EPISTEMOLOGY AND DEVELOPMENT

Around the turn of the century, James Mark Baldwin established a discipline he called "genetic epistemology." This is the study of how "thought or experience makes to render reality." According to Baldwin, this study involves comparing the progressive "stages of thought" in cultural evolution and in ontogenesis, thereby establishing "a natural history of interpretation itself." This idea is at the core of the organic lamp study of development. Piaget (1964) has summarized it succinctly:

> The psychology of development (or genetics) studies the subject as gradually constructing and continually correcting his own knowledge, in part under the influence of the environment but in part spontaneously. By studying the formation and transformation of knowledge, from birth to adolescence and to maturity, we thereby raise all the problems of knowledge proper to the subject in general . . . and we grasp them in the perspective of an "embryogenesis" or an ontogenesis of knowledge that can

perform the same services for epistemology that organic embryology has performed for comparative anatomy and biology in general. (p. 31)

Baldwin (1915) marked out three progressive stages in the subject's interpretation of reality. The first is the *prelogical* stage, at which his mode of action is "intuitive" and "quasi-discursive" or quasi-linguistic. The child makes no distinction between the subjective and objective factors in his experience. He accepts "the reality of the datum" of experience. Thus, knowledge in the prelogical period "is a meaning of immediate presence and intuition." The mode of action at the next, the *logical*, stage is "discursive" or linguistic. Imaginative, aesthetic schemes are used to unite thought (mediated interpretation of reality) with "the singular and the immediate."

> The imagination takes the lead, . . . projecting its schematic and tentative readings forward with various shadings and semblance and probability. . . . It has the character of assumption, proposal, hypothesis. . . . Reality is embodied in all sorts of "as-if" constructions. . . . All its interpretations have the force of possibility and probability. (pp. 26–27)

At the highest, *hyperlogical* stage, contemplation is the interpretive mode of action. This mode

> erects into postulates its ends, values, and goods. . . . Conditional and relative ends become absolute values seeming to be imposed by the very nature of things, and to disclose the essence of the real as a system of practical goods. (p. 29)

Baldwin hypothesized that this evolution of subjective (individual) interpretation is paralleled by the evolution of objective (societal) embodiments of interpretation "in laws, rites, customs, sanctions." He therefore proposed three stages of cultural evolution that formally parallel the stages of individual interpretation. At the prelogical stage, the group's mode of action is mystical, and it takes mythical and religious forms. At the logical stage, the group's mode is speculative, and it takes scientific and critical forms. The mode of action is transformed into "aesthetic contemplation" at the hyperlogical stage, and it takes the form of advanced philosophical theory.

Thus, there is parallel "movement in the internal organization of thoughts and values" between the individual and society, but it is "the individuals who . . . give to the group its vital impulse and its progressive 'uplift' " (Baldwin, 1915). The core of the study of genetic epistemology is therefore ontogenesis, although Werner (1948) and Cassirer (1953, 1955, 1957) have argued that a comprehensive view must include more general comparative laws that relate individual development (onto-genesis) to societal development (ethnogenesis) to species evolution (phylogenesis) to the development of pathology (pathogenesis), as well as to microgenesis:

> It is necessary to consider the problem of a comparison of mental develop-ments in different fields as a question of essential importance for a com-parative developmental psychology. (Werner, 1948, p. 24)

Indeed,

> the mental development of the individual is . . . but one theme in genetic psychology. Related to the developmental psychology of the individual is the development of larger societal units. . . . The question of the develop-ment of the human mentality . . . must lead further to an investigation of the relation of man to animal and, in consequence, to an *animal psychology* oriented according to developmental theory. (Werner, 1948, p. 3)

The aim is therefore to bring together and compare primitive and advanced forms of cognition. This means establishing the formal similari-ties and differences in the progressive or regressive development of cognition, regardless of the particular content and where it is found, whether, for example, in ontogenesis or in pathogenesis. For example, Werner (1948) hypothesized that all primitive cognitions of time are egocentrically bound to the concrete actions, feelings, and social life of the subjects. With respect to ethnogenesis, Werner provides many illus-trations, among which is the following.

> Uganda tribesmen who raise cattle have a complicated system of dividing up the day but it is by no means a generally applicable, abstract schema. The temporal divisions are implicit in the series of events constituting the day's work; e.g., six o'clock is "milking-time"; three o'clock in the afternoon is "watering-time"; five o'clock, "home-coming time for the cattle," and so on. (p. 182)

As to primitive forms of temporal cognition in ontogenesis, he finds that

> The temporal values of the child are primarily expressed in terms of affec-tive and motor activities which contain an implicit temporal reference. A two-year-old child says, for instance, "Bath, bath!" and by these words expresses a desire in which the time element of the near future is involved by implication. (1948, p. 185)

Other examples from ontogenesis will be cited in the section on cognitive development. Werner's hypotheses on the primitivization of cognition in pathogenesis are particularly intriguing because of their formal compara-bility with hypotheses of primitive forms in ontogenesis and ethno-genesis. Since we will not again consider pathogenesis, it is worth looking in some detail at Werner's (1948) exposition of the pathology of temporal cognition because it illustrates his comparative analysis. The key hypothesis is that

> however different in clinical cause and appearance the pathologically degenerated ideas of temporality may be, all the regressive changes exhibited have certain formal characteristics in common. The basic factor behind these structural changes is a de-differentiation of the acting subject and the objective world against him. Through this shrinking of the gap between object and subject, the individual is plunged into a swift stream of events; he more or less loses the ability to enmesh this flux of activity within a temporal schema, and thus fix and order it. (p. 188)

As a consequence,

> in various psychoses—as in schizophrenia—when the fundamental polarity of ego and external world is disturbed, the ego time with its affective content becomes independent and dominant with respect to world time. The objective temporal order may collapse completely. Time, says one schizophrenic, falls together like a pack of cards. Another schizophrenic's experience of time during his quiet phase differed from his temporal experience during the phase of terrible anxiety. In the calm phase time moved on with great rapidity; ten months were as one. In the anxious phase, on the contrary, events hung motionless in a temporal vacuum. (pp. 189–190)

Werner also considers cases of brain damage among adults:

> Head describes aphasiacs who, following a loss of the abstract schema, employed a concrete time-of-action. Although such a patient could not tell time by the clock, he was nevertheless able to order his day punctually. He had a concrete-qualitative time scale made up of dominant moments in the succession of daily events: "Then, when you eat." "Then, when we arrive there," etc. . . . For these aphasiacs the temporal is fused with the concrete flow and thrust of events. (p. 190)

Comparison with phylogenesis is not as easy because little animal work has been done on the difficult but important problem of the phylogeny of temporal behavior since the promising beginning made by von Uexküll (1934). Von Uexküll's comparative inquiry was directed toward studying the psychological "world as it appears to the animals themselves, not as it appears to us." He called this psychological world of the animal its *Umwelt*. For example, he analyzed the world of the tick. Picking up his analysis at the point where the female tick has become a hunter for warm blood, we find her climbing to the tip of a twig on a bush at a height from which she can drop onto small mammals that run under her and at which she can be brushed off by larger animals. The tick is eyeless, but she is directed to this watchtower by a general photosensitivity of the skin. She finds her prey through her olfactory sensitivity to butyric acid, which is secreted by the skin glands of all mammals. Butyric acid acts as the releasing signal for her to throw herself downward. If she falls upon something warm she finds a hairless spot, burrows deep into the skin, and slowly pumps herself full of blood. Then she drops to the earth, lays her eggs, and dies. If she falls on something cold she has missed her prey and must start all over again. As to the temporal aspect of the tick's *Umwelt*, von Uexküll points out that the tick can wait eighteen years for her prey without starving. Whereas, in the human, duration ceases only during the hours of sleep, in the tick it can stop for years. Von Uexküll concludes:

> Time, which frames all happenings, seems to us to be the only objective stable thing in contrast to the colorful changes of its contents, and now we see that the subject sways the time of his own world. Instead of saying, as heretofore, that without time, there can be no living subject, we shall now have to say that without a living subject, there can be no time. (p. 13)

> Without a living subject, there can be neither space nor time. With this, biology has ultimately established its connection with the doctrine of Kant, which it intends to exploit in the *Umwelt* theory by stressing the decisive role of the subject. (1957, p. 13)

Notwithstanding the apparent differences in the content of the examples taken from ethnogenesis, ontogenesis, and pathogenesis, important features of the reasoning processes that underlie primitive conceptions of time are formally similar. Consequently, Werner (1948) argues that

> For all practical purposes one may speak of a principle of parallelism: development in mental life follows certain general and formal rules whether it concerns the individual or the species. Such a principle implies that, apart from general and formal similarities, there do exist specific material differences in the comparable phenomena. (p. 26)

Even though his developmental psychology focused upon the formal similarities, Werner did not neglect the differences:

> These parallels must be taken as such, as merely indicating a similar mental structure in a general and purely *formal* sense. In a particular and *material* sense, there will be irreconcilable differences. (p. 28)

Thus, for example, Werner (1948, p. 26) points to three major factors that make cognition different in ontogenesis and ethnogenesis. First, the child is growing and his cognitions will change. The adult in a primitive society is already developed and "fixed in tradition." Second, the child develops "out of his child's world into an alien world of adults." His cognition "is the result of an interaction between these two worlds." The world of an adult in a primitive society is fairly permanent. Third, the "social pattern" of the child is not well organized and established, as the world of the adult in a primitive society is.

So far some of the parallels between formal aspects of different evolutionary lines, such as ethnogenesis and ontogenesis, have been sketched. It is now necessary to indicate the formal parallels *within* ontogenesis between the individual's personal-social, cognitive, and perceptual development before characterizing each of these lines of development in detail.

The basic dimension used to conceptualize the formal parallels between personal-social, cognitive, and perceptual development is the egocentrism-perspectivism dimension, which derives from the orthogenetic principle. The argument for formal parallels between affective and intellectual development, as Inhelder and Piaget (1958) put it, is that emotional transformations

> are parallel to intellectual transformations, since affectivity can be considered as the energetic force of behavior whereas its structure defines cognitive functions. (This does not mean either that affectivity is determined by intellect or the contrary, but that both are indissociably united in the functioning of the personality.) (pp. 347–348)

Even though it is possible to point to some of the affective aspects of development, it is the intellectual features that have actually been worked out in some detail.

The social, as well as cognitive, process of differentiating from, yet integrating into, the physical and cultural environment takes place throughout development, albeit in different ways. Early in life the child's interactions are characterized by a radical egocentrism or lack of differentiation between himself and his actions and the characteristics of the situation he is in.

> The childlike world . . . is *ego-centered* and concrete; it is a world of *nearness at hand*. The younger the child the "nearer" it is, and the distance separating subject and object increases with age. (Werner, 1948, p. 383)

Toward the end of infancy the child develops some distance and perspectivism. He

> differentiates his own ego and situates his body in a spatially and causally organized field composed of permanent objects and other persons similar to himself. This is the first decentering process; its result is the gradual coordination of sensori-motor behavior. (Inhelder & Piaget, 1958, p. 343)

The second form of egocentrism appears with the development of symbolic processes and linguistic communication with others:

It still takes the form of an initial relative lack of differentiation both between ego's and alter's point of view, between subjective and objective,
but this time the lack of differentiation is representational rather than
sensori-motor. (Inhelder & Piaget, 1958, p. 343)

Events are not seen from the standpoint of things or from that of other
persons, but are interpreted according to their meaning for the child's own
life. (Werner, 1948, p. 384)

Thus, for example, the child's graphic representation of a mountain
changes as he views it from different sides even though the s-m permanence of objects is well established. During the same period, however,
the symbolic processes of representing objects and actions lead the child
to consciousness of (a) the differential status of objects—himself and other
things—and (b) the differential consequences of actions—his own and
those of others. By the time he develops concrete mental operations, at
about seven years,

the decentering process has gone far enough for him to be able to structure
relationships between classes, relations, and numbers objectively. At the
same stage, he acquires skill in interindividual relations in a cooperative
framework. (Inhelder & Piaget, 1958, p. 343)

The third major form of egocentrism appears at adolescence with the
development of formal mental operations. Formal operations have two
major characteristics. First is what Goldstein (1939) called the "attitude
towards the possible," or the ability to deal with possibilities as well as
with actualities. The second is the ability to think about one's own
thoughts. These new-found intellectual powers lead the adolescent to
construct "theories" of operations, his own, society's, and those of his
future role as an adult participant in and transformer of society. The
adolescent

feels he has to work out a conception of life which gives him an oppor-
tunity to assert himself and create something new. . . . Secondly, he wants
a guarantee that he will be more successful than his predecessors (thus
the need for change in which altruistic concern and youthful ambitions
are inseparably blended). (Inhelder & Piaget, 1958, p. 342)

The adolescent goes through a phase in which he attributes an unlimited
power to his own thoughts so that the dream of a glorious future or of
transforming the world through Ideas (even if this idealism takes a mate-
rialistic form) seems to be not only fantasy but also an effective action
which in itself modifies the empirical world. (Inhelder & Piaget, 1958,
pp. 345–346)

When this sense of a personal freedom of choice exists, the individual acquires a new sense of responsibility, however limited, in relation to the society in which he lives and carries on his personal struggle. This expanding consciousness of personal responsibility signaling release from the egocentric structure of the child is the primary cause for the external conflict of generations within our culture. (Werner, 1948, p. 456)

These intellectual powers eventually result in the breakdown of adolescent egocentrism and the further elaboration of perspectivism. When the adolescent thinks about his thoughts as well as about things, so that he becomes capable of seeing his own acts from a relatively detached perspective, almost as if they belonged to some other object, he becomes capable of seeing others' as well as his own point of view. This decentering is supported by two social factors. First, the adolescent becomes conscious of the weakness of his own "theory" when he begins to discuss it with friends and "has to test it against the theories of others." Second, and most important, is the effect of taking on an occupation:

It is then that he is transformed from an idealistic reformer into an achiever. In other words, the job leads thinking away from the dangers of formalism back into reality. (Inhelder & Piaget, 1958, p. 346)

These, then, are the conditions that cause disequilibrium, which the adolescent becomes increasingly conscious of, and that lead to his self regulative transformation into adulthood. Their efficacy is dependent upon a reciprocally perspectivistic social context:

The personality grows and becomes differentiated in reciprocity with respect to the differentiation of the social organism to which it belongs. It develops as it participates in the formation of objective values and as it bends itself to achieve ends established by the group. (Werner, 1948, p. 458)

Personality normally grows and becomes differentiated against the growth and differentiation of the social world. (Werner, 1948, p. 467)

PERSONAL-SOCIAL DEVELOPMENT

The organic lamp view is that personal-social development reveals correlative progress in the interactions (1) between the child and the social milieu and (2) within the child himself between personal intuitions and socio-objective assessments. As we have just begun to see, intraorganismic or personal development proceeds from an initial egocentric or nondifferentiated state of organization in infancy, when the precursors of inner subjective and external objective actions, feelings, and judgments are totally fused. The process of development is directed toward the evolution of an operating subject who (*a*) assigns a different status to his personal feelings and subjective reasons than to his logical understanding and objective assessments, such that (*b*) they are integrated into a unified whole in which one or the other usually dominates.

Organic lamp theory specifies only the general coordinates of orthogenesis according to which such personal-social development can be conceptualized. These coordinates are syncresis (fusion) versus discreteness, rigidity versus flexibility, lability versus stability, and diffuseness versus articulation (Werner, 1948). This generality reveals the broad outlines of the theory's treatment of major lines of human development.

Syncresis (fusion) of subjective and objective personality aspects early in development is reflected by the young child's inability to differentiate "between the 'outer' and 'inner' aspects, between the behavioral and motivational dynamics of personality" as *discrete* entities (Werner, 1948). The child views inner phenomena as if they were concretely tangible entities like outer phenomena. Piaget (1929) cites many examples of the belief, in children, that thoughts and dreams are material events of the same kind as the external events they perceive. When a four-year-old girl described a dream, a man asked the child if he too could have seen the dream. The little girl responded that he could not have because men were not allowed in her bedroom. When he asked if her mother could have seen the dream, she responded that of course she could have because her mother was allowed in her room.

Progressive differentiation between subjective and objective factors is exemplified by Piaget's (1932) early findings on ethical development. The young child does not make a distinction between the subjective reason for a person's action and the phenomenal characteristics of that action. Asked to judge which of two children is naughtier, the one who purposefully makes a small mess or the one who accidentally makes a large mess, the young child characteristically affirms that the latter is naughtier because he made the largest mess. Intention and consequence are undifferentiated. Only at about eight or nine years of age does the child distinguish between the subjective intentional and the objective phenomenal character of events so that he makes an ethical judgment in terms of subjective intention.

Concomitantly, according to Werner (1948), the child's operations shift from *rigidity* to *flexibility*. Early in development functioning is rigidly bound to subjective or objective attitudes. Progressively, the child integrates these attitudes so that he may (1) flexibly attribute differential status, that is, subjectivity or objectivity, to his actions and (2) flexibly shift from one to the other attitude depending upon such factors as his needs and the demands of the situation.

Lability of personality early in development is reflected by fluctuation in the self (Werner, 1948). For example, the child may think that he and others radically change by wearing different clothes or by saying that they are different animals. Often the child's lability is expressed in his play, for example, in the creation of imaginary friends, and in the "split" character of his personality, for example, in his idea that he is two selves, a good one and a bad one. Sometimes the "good" child scolds the "bad" child for doing something naughty, or the "bad" child transforms himself into the "good" child or vice versa. Development is directed toward the progressive formation of a *stable* personality that no longer permits the individual to act as if he is radically changing or is "split" in character; rather, different aspects may become differentiated but integrated parts of the total personality.

The basic hypothesis about the evolution of the child's interaction with his milieu is that it is directed toward the progressive elaboration of perspectivism. His development is directed toward (*a*) integrating himself as a participant in and member of his social world, that is, acquiring the same type of objective status as other social beings, yet at the same time (*b*) differentiating himself as a subjective entity that is distinct from other social objects so that he feels and acts as an individual of a particular nature. This progression evolves out of the neonatal radical egocentrism in which the child does not differentiate himself from other physical objects and their actions, let alone from social objects and their actions.

Individuation is in part a process of identifying oneself as a discrete entity. At first, however, identification is of a syncretic nature; that is, the child hardly differentiates himself from those around him. "The earliest symptom of identification appears on some such empathic response as crying or smiling with the tears or smiles of another person" (Werner, 1948, p. 441). Piaget (1951) reports that the first sounds that wake the neonate are the cries of other infants. Then the awakened infant himself begins to cry. The assumption that this empathic crying is true imitation would mean that the newborn child already discretely differentiates himself from other infants and then imitates the models. Therefore, it must be assumed that the initial, syncretic process of identification is co-action. Co-action is the neonate's response to the contagious excitatory qualities of things around him. A good example of excitatory contagion and consequent co-action is Zazzo's (1953, p. 72) report that when a twenty- to thirty-day-old infant sticks out his tongue and is imitated by an adult, then the infant will co-act in turn by sticking out his tongue.

An important instrument of identification is symbolic play, in which the child fuses his own actions with those of other things (Werner, 1948). The child may ascribe some of his own childlike characteristics to other things. Werner reports, for example, that his four-year-old niece attributed her own misbehavior to her doll and forbade it to do all the things she herself was not allowed to do. Or the child may syncretically fuse himself with other things so that he takes on some of their characteristics. An example of this is the fairly typical play pattern in which the child strikes his legs with a whip while running in a galloping fashion; in this way the child is both horse and rider.

The *diffuse* way in which the young child perceives himself and the boundary between himself and his milieu is illustrated by some recent ontogenetic studies on the perception of one's own body size (Wapner & Werner, 1965). When the five-year-old child is asked to indicate the width of his head while his eyes are closed, he greatly overestimates. With ontogenetic *articulation* of the boundary between himself and the milieu, the estimate greatly diminishes. The natural articulation that takes place between the child and the environment in the course of ontogenesis may be artificially induced temporarily. For example, if one side of the child's head, but not the other, is touched, his estimate of the size of the touched side is much smaller than his estimate of the other side.

In complementary fashion, Wapner (1964) hypothesizes that (a) the development of body articulation is slower in retarded children, so that they more greatly overestimate head size than normal children of the same age, and (b) regression leads to greater diffuseness of the body, which is evidenced by increased overestimation of head size. The findings support the hypotheses: retarded children overestimate their head size more than normal children; schizophrenics overestimate their head size more than normal individuals of the same age; increased overestimation accompanies old age; and adults given LSD-25, a drug that is assumed to induce regression, overestimate more than normal adults.

These hypotheses about personal-social evolution are derived from the orthogenetic principle. In applying the principle to psychological development, Werner (1948) specified the major dimensional coordinates for assessing whether and to what extent orthogenesis has taken place. These are, then, coordinates for the formal description of development. It should be recognized, however, that as they now stand these coordinates only indicate the general nature of the most primitive initial stage and the most advanced mature stage; they do not detail the intermediate stages.

As to the understanding of development from stage to stage, the data generated in terms of these coordinates fit the general thesis that the evolution of advanced stages out of primitive stages is an orthogenetic process of increasing differentiation and hierarchic integration. They do not, however, characterize the specific features of personal-social functioning in the detail necessary for the full explanation of its development. The theoretical and empirical details necessary to the understanding of the developmental process have begun to be worked out only for cognitive development.

COGNITIVE DEVELOPMENT

Following the lead of James Mark Baldwin, contemporary organic lamp theorists attempt to delineate stages in cognitive evolution, particularly as they unfold in ontogenesis. They have been more interested in the study of cognitive than other lines of ontogenesis because they assume that cognitive development is intimately associated with, and the most important influence upon, all other lines of psychological development. This assumption, which dates back at least to Coleridge, has been described by I. A. Richards as "knowledge is growledge." The neologism "growledge" succinctly expresses the organic lamp view that, in humans, knowledge is a more important reason for psychological change than any other single factor (Cassirer, 1957). Intelligence is considered to be the most advanced instrument for autoregulative equilibration.

In more contemporary evolutionary terminology, organisms find themselves in a variety of ecologies or environments that make different demands upon their adaptive or survival functions. Mutant forms whose action systems are most successful in adapting to their ecology, by either modifying their own behavior to fit the environment or changing the environment to suit their needs, are most likely to survive and reproduce. What is desirable then is the evolution of organisms whose organization is most plastic and most successful in interpreting the ecology and reformulating it into a manipulable environment.

Consequently, local (short-term) acquisition of particular bits of knowledge, for example, how in a particular instance the child comes to identify, classify, name, and so forth, an object like a "dog," is only of secondary concern to organic lamp theory. Its primary interest is in paradigmatic cases of long-term development from the concrete to abstract reasoning processes that underlie the acquisition of knowledge (Goldstein & Scheerer, 1941). The focal strategy has been to study the evolution of the actions by which children come to know and communicate about the most important characteristics of themselves and the world around them. For this reason the major effort has been to determine the progressive s-m and mental stages of acting whereby fundamental physical concepts (for example, objects and space) and logical concepts (for example, coherence and classification) are constructed and expressed. This taxonomic work has led to the delineation of ten substages of progressively constructive cognitive activity that develop in a necessary order. The first six substages comprise the s-m gestural stage of the child's cognitive development, and the last four make up his symbolic operational stage.

In the course of development from substage to substage, the child's interactions increasingly shift from (*a*) motions made in response to environmental stimulation to (*b*) actions upon and thoughts about the environment and himself as an object in the environment to (*c*) thoughts about his own thoughts and about possibilities as well as actualities. Insofar, then, as organic lamp theory considers significant the reflex, conditioning, and imitational mechanisms that mechanical mirror theory assumes to determine all development, it restricts that significance to the first few substages and months of life. However, even during this early period the process of cognitive development is much more complex, according to organic lamp theory. The baby's schemes of action are already directed toward both assimilating and accommodating to the environment.

In sum, the theory maintains that the emergent genetic function that determines and gives significance to human development is the intention *to know*. This intentionality is reflected by the child's progressive tendency to construct knowledge, rather than to mirror or react to a preformed reality, as he develops. The emergent activity subserving this end is representation, or symbolic operations (Cassirer, 1953).

The description presented here of the stages and substages of cognitive development up to adolescence is my own construction based upon the best available information, mainly upon the work of Piaget, Werner, and their respective co-workers. The presentation necessarily ends at adolescence because organic lamp theorists have no clear conception of adult cognition that is qualitatively different from adolescent cognition, although they would hesitate to equate the two. One may well ponder this lacuna in organic lamp theory (see Langer, 1964, for a more detailed discussion of this theoretical problem).

Sensorimotor: Gestural Stage

As noted earlier, organic lamp theory considers the s-m stage as the transitional stage between biological and psychological organization. It is the foundation period of psychological life. During this stage (from birth to almost two years of age) the child begins to cognize the world through s-m explorations and experimentation. His means of constructing knowledge are exterior assimilatory and accommodatory actions upon the environment. The forms of knowledge he therefore creates are things-of-action, that is, pragmatic and objective forms of knowledge about the spatial, temporal, and causal characteristics of the world (Werner, 1948). It should be noted that the term *knowledge* or *cognition* is used without prejudice as to whether the child is conscious of knowing or not at this stage; nor is it meant to imply that the child is trying to understand his world in the adult sense of understanding for the sake of understanding. What is proposed is that there are many means of cognizing: both bodily and mental operations may serve this end. The concepts constructed through these two classes of means are of course different: s-m acting leads to practical concepts, while mental operations lead to contemplative concepts.

It is possible to distinguish six substages of sensorimotor activity that are the progressive means by which the young child constructs the four fundamental forms of knowledge—namely, objects, space, time, and causality (Piaget, 1954). The unfolding of substages is hypothesized to occur in a fixed sequence; each is necessary to the emergence of all subsequent substages. Although approximate ages for each substage are provided, there are individual differences in rate of development. Age is merely an indicator of the average; the true theoretical concern is with the sequence of stages.

The underlying genetic hypothesis with respect to the relationship between the construction of practical concepts of objects, space, time, and causality is that their developments are correlated. For example, the child's formation of object concepts is correlated with his organization of the spatial field. During the earliest months of life, things do not exist for the child apart from the actions he performs upon them; these actions gradually give objects their permanence. So, too, at first there are as many practical spaces for the child as there are different activities. Since his cognition of space is of a property (the result) of his action, space becomes organized and unified only to the extent that his different actions upon and knowledge of objects become coordinated. Consequently, the child first apprehends space not as a container but as the objects it contains. Space becomes cognized as a container only to the extent that he perceives these objects as interconnected into a coherent whole.

During this stage, the child stays outside of his cognition of space to the extent that he does not act upon himself as an object and thus does not know himself. Obversely, to the extent that he begins to act upon himself he comes to know himself as an object, but as an object that is at first undifferentiated from all other objects. In general, his cognition is characterized by an egocentric syncresis between subjective feelings and objective states, his actions and external events, and his body and external objects.

Egocentricity or lack of subject-object differentiation means that primitive concrete action will be characterized by "immediacy, limited motivation, and lack of planning" (Werner, 1948, p. 191). The immediate character of primitive action is most evident in the global, helpless, and noninstrumental movements of the neonate. Chimpanzees and young children have been tested in many problem situations that require circuitous behavior, such as extending a rake through bars beyond a desired object in order to haul it in. All these tests demonstrate the difficulty of problems that require circuitous behavior when the organism's action capacities are limited to manipulations of direct, concrete contact.

Perhaps the most striking mark of the evolution of circuitous behavior and "the release of the subject from the domination of the concrete field is the extension of the action beyond the visibly given field" (Werner, 1948, p. 194). Chickens and sea gulls do not seek food that they have seen hidden, but crows and jackdaws, like higher vertebrates, do. The human infant only begins to search for an object hidden before him at about nine months of age, and he shows some freedom to retrieve hidden objects at thirteen months.

Personal motives do not play a role in primitive action, which is "set in motion by vital drives on the one hand, and the concrete signals of the milieu on the other" (Werner, 1948, p. 194). Much animal and infant behavior is primitive, in this sense. For example, animals learn mazes more rapidly when they are hungry and infants learn to find an object more easily if it is rewarding.

During the early phase of the sensorimotor period, children's activity lacks the specificity and direction that is the mark of intentional planning. Bühler (1928) has demonstrated, for example, that infants are even unable to brush away a cloth laid on their faces. At 1½ months, only about 25 percent of infants show purposeful movements directed toward getting rid of the cloth; even at 4½ months, only about 50 percent of movements are purposeful; and the majority of purposeful manipulations become successful only at seven months.

In the first two years of life, then, the cognized world is ordered to the child's bodily activity. There is a direct egocentric link between each of his schemes of action and the objects which they assimilate. Only when the child's schemes become numerous and internal structural links are established between them does it become possible for him to begin to differentiate and integrate himself and other objects, to comprehend the independent status of the external world, and to deduce the spatio-temporal and causal relationships between objects. In this sense, the assimilating subject (the child) enters into a reciprocal (accommodatory) relationship with the world he is assimilating; the child is no longer limited to activity in which he is unaware of himself and his role in constructing his own world.

During this same stage the infant begins to use natural, gestural means of external representation (Piaget, 1951; Werner & Kaplan, 1963). In this way he constructs two kinds of symbols: expressive imitations of, and playful pretenses of, things-of-action. The forms of representation constructed are therefore signals-of-action.

The child's bodily and vocal gestural signals are precursory to his later use of verbal symbols (Werner & Kaplan, 1963). Insofar as his signaling is a means of eliciting overt action, it is functionally discontinuous with his later symbolizing, which is also a means of contemplating things and relations. Insofar as the medium of signaling he uses is gestural, its structure is also discontinuous with that of later symbolic media, which range from the verbal to the mathematical. On the other hand, there is functional and structural continuity between these two extreme types of representation. The child's pragmatic, gestural means are gradually transformed into contemplative, symbolic means. Moreover, it is only through internalization and transformation of the natural forms of depicting and referring to things that the child eventually changes these signals into symbols. Therefore, the earliest verbal expressions which develop after the s-m stage are not purely arbitrary and conventional symbols; they have many of the imitative and playful metaphorical qualities characteristic of gestural signals.

Substage 1 (to 1½ months): Radical Egocentrism. The first substage of the child's cognitive development is marked by extreme nondifferentiation (global fusion) among himself, his acts, external objects, and their actions. There are, however, actual correspondences and differences between the neonate's acts, such as his posture and motion of sucking, and the objects of his action, such as the nipple he sucks.

Radical egocentricity, then, means that the actual correspondences between the neonate's acts and their objects are not at first psychologically real for the neonate himself. They only begin to become psychologically real for him as a consequence of the assimilatory and accommodatory functions of his own acts. The neonate's assimilatory function "modifies" the objects of his acts into things that will psychologically fit his inborn schemes, thereby making these objects into food for cognitive digestion. For example, at first the neonate sucks at anything that touches his mouth; that is, he treats all objects that he acts upon with his mouth as things-to-suck.

Even this early in life, the neonate assimilates cognitive nourishment in three ways that he will use throughout life (Piaget, 1950). First, he practices his capacities for action (functional reproductive assimilation) even when appropriate objects are not present; for example, he sucks in the absence of any object. Second, he extends the application of his schemes of action (generalized or transpositive assimilation) to the treatment and understanding of new objects; for example, he sucks on any object that touches his mouth. In this way the infant incorporates new objects of knowledge into his body of cognition. Third, his actions come to recognize (recognitory assimilation) familiar objects so that he immediately understands them and treats them appropriately.

The differentiation between the neonate's acts and their objects begins to become psychologically real to the neonate himself through the accommodatory function of his acts. One of the earliest manifestations of accommodation, which will develop throughout life, is discrimination between objects or situational complexes. For example, toward the end of the first month the neonate begins not to suck upon previously unsatisfying objects that touch his mouth. Another early manifestation of accommodation is co-action; for example, contagious crying in the first few days of life. Co-action will eventually develop into truly imitative accommodation.

In sum, the psychological reality of mutuality and of differentiation between the neonate's acts and their objects of reference (situational complexes) is constructed by the innate assimilatory and accommodatory functions of the child's schematizing action. The construction of correspondence and distinction between his own acts and their objects of reference is the necessary basis for the neonate's production of action signs. For example, sucking action becomes a postural gestural sign of desire to suck that has communicative value, at least to the mother.

On the basis of his acts, the neonate constructs and expresses his first cognition of the fundamental categories of experience—objects, space, time, and causality—as follows:

OBJECTS. The neonate's objects of cognition, constructed by his s-m action, do not yet have a permanent and "substantial" form; for example, when the child is no longer in immediate contact with an object he acts as if it has disappeared, not only perceptually but cognitively. Piaget hypothesizes that the functional prerequisite to the cognitive construction of permanent objects is present because if the object resists the activity of the sensorimotor schema sufficiently to create a momentary maladjustment while giving rise soon after to a successful readjustment, then assimilation is accompanied by recognition. (1954, p. 6)

The equilibration process of development, then, is assumed to operate from the first substage of the child's life.

SPACE.   The infant's cognition of space is of a constantly shifting panorama. Moreover, what he learns about space through the actions of one of his sensorimotor modalities, such as his mouth, holds nothing in common with what he apprehends through other modalities, like eyes and hands. Within individual modalities, however, the child is introduced to the most primitive form of organized spatial experience: coordination between displacement from one point to another, $A \rightarrow B$, and subsequent return to the point of origin, $B \rightarrow A$. This experience is first provided by neuromuscular coordination between extension and flexion. It is the precursory activity and experience upon which the child's subsequent forms of cognitive *reversibility* are built, for example, retracing his path to get to his point of origin.

TIME.   In the same way that spatial cognition "begins as the simple practical co-ordination of body movements . . . so also time begins as simple duration immanent in the practical series" of the child's own acts. The infant coordinates his movements so that he performs certain acts in order, one before the other; for example, he opens his mouth and seeks contact before sucking. At first, then, the infant's cognition of duration

is mingled with impressions of expectation and effort, with the very development of the act, experienced internally. As such it certainly fills the child's whole universe, since no distinction is yet given between an internal world and the external universe. (Piaget, 1954, p. 326)

CAUSALITY.   At the beginning, the child's cognition of causality is nothing more than "a sort of feeling of efficiency or of efficacy linked with acts as such," which he experiences as being neither internal nor external (Piaget, 1954, p. 227). Preceding his action there may be feelings of desire, effort, and expectation. Therefore the result of his act is experienced as only an extension of these feelings/action; for example, food is experienced as an extension of the act of sucking, and visual images as an extension of the act of seeing. This primitive form of cognition contains the seeds of two causal types of reasoning which are gradually differentiated from each other in the course of ontogenesis. The first is the child's feeling of personal efficacy, which is a necessary condition for his subjective awareness. It becomes his intentional mode of causality, that is, the child's subjective, internal reasons and feelings for things. The second is his feeling of phenomenal connection between things he percieves contiguously in space and time. It becomes his physical mode of causality, that is, the objective relationships he attributes to aspects of an external event.

Substage 2 (1 to 4 months): Anticipating and Generalizing. During the second substage the child begins to construct anticipatory signs. For example, he cries because he anticipates that crying may result in the return of an absent person. To call an absent person not only serves to communicate an appeal but also suggests his initial differentiation between his sign activity and its object of reference, since the referent is not present. Insofar as true representation is only manifest when the signifier is differentiated from the signified, anticipatory signs may be transitional representational forms between the signs of the first substage and the signals constructed in the third. Thus, they are a further step in the breakdown of the child's initial egocentricity.

The earliest means the child uses to construct anticipatory signs are co-active (contagious) forms of accommodatory action and reproductive forms of assimilatory action, which he already possessed, at least rudimentarily, during the previous substage (see p. 116). The infant still co-acts with bodily movements or vocalizations analogous to actions previously made. The consequence is his continuous performance of acts he has seen others make that are analogous to his own actions. For example, Piaget (1951) describes the vocal contagion between, or mutual stimulation of, a baby (one month, four days) and his older brother. The baby started and stopped crying three times in succession when his older brother started to cry, as if the baby anticipated that his own crying would reevoke the sound of his brother's crying.

The reproductive aspect of the child's anticipation is that, at this substage, he performs repetitive activity for the functional pleasure he obtains from it. Piaget (1951, p. 91) cites the example of a baby of three months who "played with his voice, not only through interest in the sound, but for 'functional pleasure,' laughing at his own power."

It is clear from the above examples of the infant's co-active and reproductive anticipation that his schemes of action are beginning to generalize genuinely. Generalization may take place in two ways. The first is a relatively passive extension of the child's schemes of action to new things by conditioning mechanisms such as those described in the previous chapter. The second is the infant's "spontaneous" extension of his action schemes to new things. Piaget (1950, p. 100) asserts that this "extension of the reflex schemata, through the incorporation of a new element, involves by this very fact the formation of a schema of a higher order (a genuine habit) which then integrates the lower schema with itself."

Progress in cognition at this substage may be summarized as follows:

OBJECTS.   Whereas in the previous substage the infant was hardly able visually to follow a moving object through its trajectory, he now begins to be able to do so. His following activity gradually extends from movements of his eyes to movements of his head and torso. However, he does not yet begin to search for things that have left his visual field. Thus, the child begins to know objects as things-of-action/posture-in-progress. In addition, he shows increasing signs of recognition, as exemplified by his smiling at familiar people.

SPACE, TIME, AND CAUSALITY.   Advance in the child's spatial, temporal, and causal cognition is limited to consolidating and extending the progress begun in the previous substage. For example, the child begins to look in the direction of a heard sound in order to find it. He begins to be able to coordinate different percepts in space and time when one is a signal for the other.

Substage 3 (5 to 8 months): Static Coordinating.   Functional coordination between different schemes of action progresses rapidly during this substage of development. The baby of about four and a half months begins to integrate his vision with his prehension (grasping) so that, for example, he begins to be able to grasp intentionally a string that he sees hanging in front of him.

This development heralds the further consolidation of two other aspects of intelligence, the abilities to analyze and to generalize, which are illustrated by the following example (Piaget, 1954). If a string is attached to some rattles so that when the baby grasps the string he shakes the rattles, he will, for the first time, actively try to reproduce the result by again reaching for the string. This indicates his initial and rudimentary capacity to disarticulate and internally recompose parts of an event. His rudimentary analysis is suggested by the fact that after he has observed the order of events, the sight of a new object suspended from the same place will cause him to reach again for the string. It is almost as if the child has reconstructed, after the event, that grasping the string is the means to the end of achieving an interesting spectacle. That his causal analysis is not yet adequate is demonstrated by the further fact that if the baby observes something interesting across the room that is obviously not attached to the string, he will still grasp the string. Overextending his scheme of action indicates the continuing development of another aspect of intelligence, namely, external generalization or transposition of action schemes to new objects.

The baby's imitative activity is still limited to reproduction of simple acts he has performed previously. He still cannot imitate actions suggested to him by models but not yet in his repertoire. The baby's primary interest is in the result of his action and not yet in the movements he has to make to achieve that result. His imitation is still limited to attempts to reproduce an event previously achieved by chance (circular reaction). In addition, however, the baby begins more systematically to reproduce more complicated, coordinated acts. Indeed, he begins to be able to imitate almost all sounds and bodily movements that he can make spontaneously. He will at times make a sound he has made before in an attempt to influence others to make that sound. This, then, constitutes a rudimentary communicative and anticipatory signal-to-action.

Cognitive development makes great progress during this substage:

OBJECTS   The baby's schematic knowledge is no longer simply of things-of-action in the present or in progress but also of immediately past things-of-action. This new knowledge finds its expression in the beginnings of a practical permanence; for example, the baby begins to look for a thing which has disappeared from his perceptual field. However, this permanence is still very primitive, for it is bound to current activity. The baby only searches for an object whose trajectory he has just been following. He never initiates an active search for an object perceived at another time. Thus, this permanence is based upon the sensorimotor expectation and anticipatory assimilation begun in the previous substage.

SPACE.   The baby achieves his first cognitive systemization by integrating different schemes of action with each other, particularly those of hand and eye. This makes it possible for him to form a tactile-kinesthetic sense of space (an aggregate of visual, buccal, prehensile, and bodily space) to which his other forms of spatial accommodation will be gradually added. The marked advances in the child's prehension at this substage result in two essential changes in spatial cognition. First, he begins to make spatial relationships between things, and not only between things and the action of his appendages, as in the previous substage. Second, he begins to watch himself because of his intervention in the detail of displacements and spatial connection.

At this substage it becomes possible for the child to "transcend the level of the simple practical group and to form what we shall call the subjective group" (Piaget, 1954, p. 113). The subjective group is transitional between the practical and the objective groups: "it involves an incipient objectification but within the limits of momentary activity" (Piaget, 1954, p. 114). When the child perceives movements with manipulated objects that can be repeated and perceives the movements as governed by his own action, then it is sufficient that he recognize the permanent aspects and kinematic regularities in such events for him to

> perceive in objects at least a trace of the structure characteristic of groups. The group is therefore in process of being objectified and of being transferred from the action itself to the displacements perceived in objects as such. (Piaget, 1954, 132–133)

This, of course, does not imply that the infant has understood anything about how these connections are established. Moreover, spatial interrelations between things or between the various displacements of the body itself are still not taken into account in their totality. When a moving object leaves his perceptual field, the infant seeks it where he first perceived it, as if the group were self-enclosed in terms of the subject (his own activity) and not the object (the physical relations of the thing in space).

In psychology, the concept of groups (of transformations) is used to characterize the forms of cognitive invariance that the organism's acts construct at each stage of its development (see Cassirer, 1944, for a detailed analysis of the concept of groups in psychology and mathematics). For our purposes it is sufficient to realize that groups refer to the universe of transformative mental operations used by the organism to create conceptual invariance out of the flux of its experience. Since the child develops new mental means at each developmental stage, his group of transformations progresses and so does his construction of invariant forms. For example, during the sensorimotor stage the child's acts are limited to pragmatic groups of transformation. Consequently, their most advanced conceptual product is limited to an invariant here-and-now container made up of permanent objects and retraceable trajectories. During the symbolic operational stage the child's acts extend to logical groups of transformation. Consequently, their conceptual product includes invariant, theoretically possible, as well as actual, space in which object properties are conserved and trajectories are reversible.

TIME.   The example of the string and rattle indicates the child's nascent capacity to relate *before* and *after* in connection with his own action. Thus, his actions begin to bear upon two objects at once, and not only upon one. This is the primary condition necessary for his formation of a sense of temporality. However, he still cannot temporally arrange aspects of an event into an ordered series when they succeed each other independently of his own action. Moreover, the child's first signs of locating memories in a temporal series are restricted to phenomena involving his own action. In the midst of doing something, the child may turn to look at his mother, who is sitting motionless nearby. If the mother leaves the room, the child may look at the place where she was sitting. However, he would not look for her if he had not previously been actively engaged in looking at her. Localization in time is then purely a subjective series (that is, dependent upon the child's own activity) and not an independent, objective temporal series.

CAUSALITY. The baby's egocentricity with respect to causality still reveals itself in the fact that he treats the relations between the movements of objects and those of the body itself as no different in principle from those between parts of the body. For example, one hand will manipulate the other as it would any other object. However, because he has begun to control his own movements and other objects, the baby becomes more capable of distinguishing within an event between desire, action, and result. He exhibits the first signs of differentiating efficacy from phenomenalism. Phenomenalism is indicated by the child's imitation of head shaking by an adult who has stopped shaking his head until the adult recommences. However, efficacy is still immanent in the conception of the connection among objects. That is, efficacy is still apparent from the repetition of the original gesture in exact form, as in the string-rattle illustration, with no allowance for the objective character of the spatial relations. For this reason, Piaget (1954, p. 321) calls the causality of this stage magico-phenomenalistic causality. It constitutes the child's first awareness of the purposefulness of his own movements: "cause reveals a tendency to be internalized and effect to be externalized."

Substage 4 (8 to 10 months): Mobile Coordinating and Signaling. In the fourth substage, the child develops signal activity that is fully precursory to the first forms of symbolic activity, which will arise in the sixth substage of development. The baby's signal activity now clearly includes the depictive characteristics of representation and the denotative characteristics of reference that are the hallmarks of symbolization (Werner & Kaplan, 1963).

Signal depiction by the very young child takes the form of bodily and vocal (onomatopoetic) gestures that mimic some selected aspect of the event represented. An example of the child's use of his body as a gestural signal is given by Piaget (1951), who describes an infant who ordinarily sucked her thumb before going to sleep at night. While playing with her pillow she began to suck on its fringe. This sucking activity seemed to remind her of going to sleep because she lay down in her sleeping position while holding the fringe of the pillow and sucking her thumb. She did this for half a minute and then got up and went back to playing with the pillow. This depictive signal-of-action is precursory to true symbolic play, but the child is not yet aware of using gesture as a make-believe means of representing something. Vocal gestural signaling is illustrated by the productions of a baby who at nine months made sounds like *dididi* to represent scolding or comforting, at ten months *nenene* to represent disapproval, and at twelve months *mjamjam* to represent food or tastes (Werner & Kaplan, 1963).

The above examples of signal depiction indicate the baby's beginning capacity to represent referents intentionally and in a flexible fashion. He begins experimentally to imitate new events, that is, configurations of objects and actions that are new to him but that are analogous to those he knows. The child tries out different actions of which he is already capable until he feels that he has achieved a proper fit. Thus, the stage marks the first major shift from co-action, based upon identity between the child's reproduction and the object of reference, to real imitation, based upon similarity between the child's gesture and its referent.

Signal denotation by the very young child also takes bodily and vocal forms. The former is exhibited by the child's initial use of bodily movements of reaching-for-touching, touching, and, a little later, turning-for-looking as gestural means of signaling that he is referring to things (Werner & Kaplan, 1963). An example of turning-for-looking that comes from Stern & Stern (1928) is that of a ten-month-old girl who turned toward the clock in her room when asked, "Where is the tick-tock?" even if the clock was making no sound. Such signal reference

> typically arises in an interpersonal context and indicates for oneself and for others a "something" articulated at a distance from the self and the other. (Werner & Kaplan, 1963, p. 79)

At the same time, the child begins to use vocal gestural means of reference. Often he uses vocal gestures in unison with bodily gestures because

> The first sounds uttered in the context of object-directedness are manifested as ingredients of the straining movements of the child towards objects in the environment which are beyond his immediate reach. (Werner & Kaplan, 1963, p. 81)

For this reason Werner and Kaplan (1963) call these early vocal gestural forms of signal reference "call-sounds." Toward the end of this substage and the beginning of the next, according to Werner and Kaplan, the child produces specific forms of vocal demonstration, such as *da*. At first these sounds may be accompanied by bodily gestures of reference, but in the next substage, vocal reference is often used with a new symbolic means of referring, namely, pointing.

The baby's beginning capacity for mental representation in the form of signals is the necessary basis for the flexible or mobile coordination between his schemes of action that develops at this substage. Piaget (1954) provides the following example to indicate the type of mobile coordination between schemes that are, in some cases, previously acquired means and others that may, for example, set the goal for an action. If a thing is concealed behind a screen, the child for the first time is able to use his "schemata of grasping or striking" in order to remove the screen and grasp at the objective. Thus, the end is represented before the means because it is the intention to get the thing which leads the child to the action needed to achieve the end. The child's interaction with the environment, then, is no longer limited to direct contact. Rather, varied and indirect interaction between the child and the environment becomes possible through his emerging capacity to apply old means to new ends. The advance is limited, however, insofar as the child does not construct new means but is restricted to already available ones.

The development in the child's fundamental conceptions may be summarized as follows:

OBJECTS. For the first time, objects take on some of the substantive character of permanent, past as well as present, things-of-action. This is indicated, for example, by the child's attempt to find a hidden thing. Even so, the progress is small and still dependent upon the child's activity. He will seek and find a thing hidden behind a screen on his right. But if the thing is then hidden behind a screen on his left while he is watching, he does a curious thing: he first looks for the thing on his right, the place of his original activity and success.

SPACE. This is still a transitional period between the child's construction of subjective and objective spatial groups and his discovery of reversible relations. The group is subjective because it is still based upon the coordination of the child's own activity and not upon the movement of objects in space. He does not yet take into account the displacements in the objects themselves. But the group is becoming objective insofar as the child now sees things as existing in space outside of his immediate perception; "outside," however, is still limited to the first displacement of the object. The child begins to distinguish between changes of position and state as evidenced by the facts that (*a*) objects acquire some permanence of state and (*b*) he shows some searching behavior when presented with a rotating object, indicating that "he considers moving objects capable of following autonomous trajectories independently of his own action" (Piaget, 1954, p. 169).

TIME. Temporal series are also beginning to be objectified. This is indicated by coordination of the child's means with his ends in such a way that his goal is constituted before his action; that is, he reverses the time order of activity. It is also indicated by the child's ability to look for hidden things, which means that he remembers a series in which his own activity plays only a partial role. His confusion, however, when the objective is moved from one hiding spot to another reflects the fact that this stage is still transitional between the construction of subjective and objective temporal series.

CAUSALITY.   According to Piaget (1954), this is also a transitional phase in the child's causal cognition insofar as "causality becomes detached from the child's action without, however, being attributed once and for all to objects independent of the self." Again, a good example is the child's application of old means to new ends and his inability to construct new means. That is, causality is tending toward being spatialized without being differentiated from the efficacy of gestures. The child no longer considers his own action to be the sole source of causality, and he attributes particular powers to other bodies. This partial detachment of causality from his own action is indicated by his recognition that others may play an intermediary role in the causal sequence. But causality is still partially seen as dependent upon his own activity; for example, he may appeal for help in getting something.

Substage 5 (12 to 15 months): Experimenting.   In the fifth substage, the baby's intended ends for the first time lead him to experiment actively with new means of achieving them. For example, the child who has discovered and watched the path of a falling object will drop the object in different ways or from different positions to see what happens. On the one hand, this involves reproductive (assimilatory) dropping of the object to see what happens to the path of falling. On the other hand, it involves trial and error activity (differentiated and intentional accommodation) to induce new information and possibilities.

Experimenting is no longer limited to direct bodily action. Indirect bodily activity, that is, gestural representation, begins to be used as a major means of determining the possibilities within a situation. Piaget (1951) describes a child at one year and twenty days who watched him remove and then put back the top of his tobacco jar. The child could have done the same because the jar was well within her reach, but instead she gesturally imitated the type of movement his hand made by raising and lowering her own hand without touching the jar.

During this period, the child also becomes capable of reproducing new movements by nonvisible parts of his body. For example, at one year, one month, and nineteen days this same child imitated Piaget when he put out his tongue against the left corner of his mouth. As a consequence of such reproductive experimentation, the child often and by chance combines unrelated gestures. Subsequently, he "repeats these gestures as a ritual and makes a motor game of them" (Piaget, 1951, p. 94). For example, at one year and five days the child held her hair with her right hand while taking a bath. Her hand slipped and hit the water. She immediately reproduced the event, putting her hand on her hair and then quickly dropping it on the water. For days after, this action became a ritualistic part of her bath.

Pointing as a bodily gestural means of reference becomes well established during this substage. Indeed, Werner & Kaplan hypothesize that

> all these preliminaries to motor reference, occurring within reaching-for, touching, and turning-to activities, culminate in *pointing*. (1963, p. 79)

Thus, when asked where the clock was at the age of fourteen months, the child observed by the Sterns pointed to it. Pointing is often accompanied by the vocal demonstrative *da*; another child observed by the Sterns pointed at things they named and said "da" at the age of 12½ months.

The child's conceptual progress may be described as follows:

OBJECTS.   Things maintain their permanent individual substance as long as changes in their position occur within the child's field of perception. In the hidden object experiment, the child will no longer look for the object at the first place he found it if he sees its position being changed. If, however, the change in position is not visible, the child looks for it in the first place. This suggests that objects have still acquired only the permanence of a here-and-now thing-of-action.

SPACE.   The child's spatial group begins to be objective. As just noted, his search for vanished objects takes into account their sequence of displacements as long as he has perceived the sequence. Here, then, there is an objective elaboration of the relation of movements within space or of contents within a container. However, imaginal and representational spatial groups have not yet been elaborated. The child is not able to take into account displacements outside of his immediate perception: he perceives space but cannot imagine it. In addition he cannot locate himself as a moving object because this requires imagining himself as a trajectory and not merely perceiving his own movements.

TIME.   The child begins to have exact memory of spatial displacements he has perceived, for example, he is capable of reaching for something behind him after being involved with something else. However, this is true only for short time intervals. If the interval is long, the child is not capable of remembering what happened.

CAUSALITY. The child progressively notices and uses the intermediaries between his own movement and the culminating effect. Henceforth, he conceives of his own body as inserted in the external causal sequence. He conceives of himself as subject to the actions of things, and not only as the source of actions that operate upon things. For example, if the child's sweater is caught on a nail at his back, he tries to detach himself by moving toward the nail rather than by simply pulling to overcome the resistance, as he would have done in the fourth substage. Thus appears the beginning of the end of the child's placing his own activity in the center of events: he begins to conceive of dependence between his acts and those of objects in space that are separate from him. His increasing objectification and spatialization of causality is marked by his apparent subscription to the principle that every desired effect has a cause for which it is necessary to determine (to search and experiment for) effective means.

Substage 6 (15 to 21 months): Symbolizing. The final s-m substage is marked by the development of mental operations or interiorized schemes of action. In some situations the child behaves as if he is thinking rather than immediately acting. The coordination between his internal mental operations occurs at such a rapid pace, as compared with the coordination between his external s-m acts, that thought sometimes gives the appearance of immediate insight.

The major instrument for the performance of mental operations is symbolic representation (Werner & Kaplan, 1963). At this substage, the media of representation are still primarily nonverbal, although symbolization is already moving in the verbal direction.

Nonverbal symbolic representation has two major characteristics—delayed imitation and symbolic play (Piaget, 1951). Delayed imitation is the capacity to produce gestural or imaginal copies of events no longer present. Piaget gives an example of a child, J., at one year, sixteen months and three days who was visited by a little boy. The guest, who was in a playpen, threw a tantrum—screaming, stamping, pushing the playpen and trying to get out of it—in the course of the visit.

> J. stood watching him in amazement, never having witnessed such a scene before. The next day, she herself screamed in her play-pen and tried to move it, stamping her foot lightly several times in succession. The imitation of the whole scene was most striking. (1951, p. 63)

In this way the child imitatively symbolized an event that was no longer spatio-temporally present and that she did not imitate at the time of its occurrence.

Symbolic play is the use of gestural or imaginal means to pretend that nonexistent events are present. Piaget (1951) describes a child (one year, three months, and two days) who was aware of the make-believe ("as if") character of her playful symbol. She pretended to be going to sleep, performing all the gestures she makes when she is really going to sleep, and laughed at her activity.

At this substage the child develops not only motor gestural but also vocal gestural means of symbolization, according to Werner and Kaplan (1963). Unlike vocal *signalization*, vocal *symbolization* is not limited to the representation of heard sounds by vocalizations. Rather, sounds may be used as analogues (physiognomic depictions) that represent properties of events, other than those heard, that is, properties that are not physically present in the event. For example, a long vowel sound may be used to symbolize a large object or something that is liked, and a short vowel may be used to represent a small object or something that is not highly valued. The child continues to use pointing and vocal demonstratives as means of reference. Pointing is, of course, a means of reference that is sustained throughout life. Vocal demonstratives, on the other hand, eventually change so that they progressively approximate the verbal symbolic forms of reference, for example, *this* or *that*.

The most advanced s-m concepts develop as follows:

OBJECTS. There is a rapid decrease in the child's external, pragmatic activity on and with objects, culminating between the ages of fifteen and eighteen months, and a reciprocally rapid increase in his visually regarding and beginning to contemplate objects. As his s-m activity

> becomes subordinated to visual regard or contemplation, it is possible that sensory-motor activity undergoes a partial *shift of function:* freed from involvement in the satisfaction of preemptory demands, sensory-motor activity can now accompany visual regard in the form of a deictic gesture (pointing). (Werner & Kaplan, 1963, p. 70)

Object permanence is no longer limited to immediately perceived objects. Representation permits the child to conceive of objects that are not spatio-temporally present and leads to his internal expectation that when an object disappears it does not dissolve; for example, the child will search for objects he has seen a while ago.

SPACE. The child is now able to locate a hidden object even when he has not perceived its displacement because he can now represent the displacement to himself. A practical, objective system of relations between objects in space is constructed, for example, the relations "placed upon," "behind," and "inside."

The child's internal representation of space is now of an objective group structure because three necessary conditions are met, namely, permanence of objects, differentiation of his own movements from those of other things, and representation of his own displacements. The importance of the fact that the child's cognition of space is of a group is its implication that the child is cognizant of which changes of state or displacements are reversible and which are not. Reversibility is dependent upon the conception of a permanent object. Permanence in turn is dependent upon differentiation between subjective action and objective movement. Cognition of a group structure thus implies cognition of the reciprocity between objects and space, permanence and reversibility, subject and object. Of course, the child is not conscious of the group nature of his cognitive structure, yet he puts the group into practice. This is at least one major reason why his cognition is still limited to the implications of a pragmatic group and cannot extend to a theoretical one.

TIME.   The child's cognition of temporal series is now extended beyond the limits of the present. It is particularly influenced by his reproductive assimilation, which mentally reconstructs an increasingly extensive past, permitting the child to remember things that have happened beyond the immediate past.

CAUSALITY.   The child now becomes capable of reconstructing causes in the presence of their effects alone, without having perceived the action of those causes. Conversely, he also becomes capable of foreseeing and representing to himself the effects of a cause, given a perceived object as the source of potential action. Piaget (1951) provides an example: A child was taken away from her game and placed in a playpen. First she cried; then she indicated that she wanted to go "pottie." As soon as she was taken out of the playpen she returned to her game, indicating that she anticipated the effect of her action.

Symbolic Operational Stage

The child's mental operations are structurally discontinuous from his s-m acts in four major ways. First, s-m acts are performed in slow motion and are tied to the sequence of events to which they are relevant (Piaget, 1950). Consequently, successive experiences of acts/events are not schematically integrated into an all-encompassing representation. They are schematically linked only by brief s-m anticipations and reconstructions. Mental operations, on the other hand, are performed in fast motion, and in the course of the child's development, they become increasingly liberated from the sequence in which he experiences events. This permits simultaneous mental consideration of events that actually occur separately and, schematically, integration of the events into a comprehensive representation. Consequently, true experimental reversibility has become possible, that is, the child begins symbolically to consider experiences (acts and events) in different orders than that of the temporal sequence in which they happened. Memory of past events and anticipation of future possibilities are added to his consideration of present involvements.

The second difference between the child's s-m acts and his symbolic operations, which is related to the first, is that the former only lead to practical satisfaction whereas the latter are directed toward reflective satisfaction (Piaget, 1950; Werner & Kaplan, 1963). This interpretation is consistent with the general organic lamp concept of man as essentially contemplative in nature and of his development as directed toward the progressive actualization of his essential nature.

The third difference, which is related to both of the preceding ones, is that the scope of the child's s-m acts, but not of his symbolic operations, is limited to dealing with real material entities (Piaget, 1950; Werner, 1948). At best, s-m acts construct only very short psychological distance between the subject (the child) and his objects of experience (the environment). This egocentricity means that the baby cannot view the world from perspectives other than his own. On the other hand, the scope of his mental operations includes the construction of conceptual knowledge. Consequently, the psychological distance constructed by the child between himself and his objects of experiential consideration progressively increases. Theoretical possibilities become potentially imaginable: multiple perspectives and the flexibility to shift between them become the mark of intelligent activity itself.

Subject-object orthogenesis (differentiation and hierarchic integration) and developing perspectivism lead to mental mediation, internal or personal motivation, and intentional planning (Werner, 1948). The child's acts become progressively circuitous—no longer limited to the immediate—and means (instruments and devices) for mediation are developed. Lewin's famous film of the three-year-old who cannot sit down directly on a stone but must climb on to it and then turn around demonstrates that even such a simple circuitous act is not accomplished until well after the end of the sensorimotor stage proper. Internal or personal motivation implies willful intentionality which only begins to appear at about the age of four to six years, when the child begins to make choices that are not totally determined by the signal value of external objects. At this age the child begins to plan intentionally and to organize willfully or to rearrange situations in terms of his mediating devices. He begins to anticipate the end effect of his actions; for example, he can name what he is going to draw before he has drawn it rather than being limited to naming what he has drawn after the drawing is done.

The fourth difference is the result of the first three. The child's sensorimotor activity is individualized and lacks the social focus of his mental operations, which are the source of his representational, particularly conventional linguistic, social interaction.

On the basis of these four differences, Piaget (1950) derives the following four necessary conditions for the transformation of the child's s-m acts into mental operations. The first is that the speed with which he coordinates discrete experiences into "one simultaneous whole" must increase radically. The second is that the child must become conscious of the nature of his cognitive activity, rather than merely of the results he desires. Third, he must develop the symbolic function of representation, which is necessary for both progressive subject-object differentiation and cognition that transcends the spatio-temporal bounds of immediate experience of acts and events. Finally, the child must use representation as a means of conventional social communication so that his thinking becomes integrated with the way of life and thinking of his community.

The derivation of these conditions for the emergence of mental operations is based upon the assumption that the child's mental and social development are interdependent and genetically parallel processes (as described in the section on genetic epistemology). The child's mental development proceeds from (*a*) practical structures that rigidly relate external actions/events to each other and the knowledge obtained from relating them to (*b*) contemplative structures that flexibly relate reversible mental operations to each other and to external actions and the knowledge thereby obtained. As we have seen in the previous section, the child's personal-social development proceeds from (*a*) egocentric fixations to (*b*) "inter-individual coordination" of respective actions and perspectives, thereby "ensuring both general reciprocity of points of view, and correspondence between the detail of the operations and their results" (Piaget, 1951, p. 239).

The child's cognitive development during the symbolic operational stage progresses through four sequentially ordered substages attributed to age ranges that are again only approximate.

Substage 7 (1½ to 4 years). Preconceptual: Gestural-Verbal Acts. The seventh substage is the major transitional stage between the child's usage of naturalistic, gestural forms and conventional, linguistic forms of representation. Werner & Kaplan (1963, pp. 58–59) hypothesize that young children "perceive and conceive their expanding universe in terms of certain formula-like schemata or connotative models." They suggest that the major model used "for connoting states of affairs and articulating them linguistically is the human action model." That is, the child uses human action as a kind of metaphorical model for making sense out of many types of events and understanding them. Werner & Kaplan cite the example of a three-year-old girl who was watching her mother turn on the hot water. The water spurted out of the faucet in jets, and the child exclaimed, "O, mamma, the water is choked; see how it coughs!" The human action model may also be the basis for the child's animistic thinking. For example, young children attribute life to all sorts of inanimate things, such as stones, if they perceive them in motion (Piaget, 1929).

Besides continuing to use imaginal and playful gestural symbols, the child actively imitates (accommodates to) the language he hears around him. However, he can only meaningfully use speech in a fashion that is significant for him by transforming (assimilating) it, often playfully, to what he already knows. That means that, for the most part, its expressive form and meaning are not yet primarily conventional but rather individual. For this reason communication between the child and his community is still partial; others have a great deal of difficulty understanding him.

Individualized verbal forms of representation begin with the use of words to designate "global, rather undifferentiated" referents (Werner & Kaplan, 1963, p. 114). Linguistic ontogenesis is dependent upon the development of mental operations that permit the child to "differentiate among and to specify events in his environment, so that the referents of his vocables progressively approximate the referents of adult names." Consequently, he begins to use different words for different referents. As an example, Werner & Kaplan cite the development of the use of the word *mammam* by a little girl. At twelve months of age, the child used *mammam* as a name for her sister, for bread, and for cooked dishes. At seventeen months she began to use it also to designate milk. Only between nineteen and twenty-one months did she stop using *mammam* for all of these things and begin to use separate names for each. At the same time she began to use the word *mama* as a specific form of reference to her mother.

Even when the child begins to use specific words to represent discrete things, actions, and properties, the symbols still refer to ideas that stand midway between the particularity of referents constructed by s-m activity and the generality of referents constructed by later mental operations. Piaget (1951) hypothesizes that these symbols are "fluctuating incessantly between the two extremes" and that they thereby exhibit a lack of understanding and a confounding "of individual identity and . . . general class." His observation of a child at the age of three years, two months, and twenty-three days who could not comprehend that the city Lausanne, where her grandmother lived, was all the houses in that city together provides the following type of evidence for his hypothesis:

> for her it was her grandmother's house "Le Cret" that was *"the Lausanne house."* . . . The next day I wanted to see if my explanation had been understood. "What is Lausanne?" *"It's all these houses"* (pointing to all the houses around). *"All these houses are Le Cret."* "What's Le Cret?" *"It's granny's house; it's Lausanne."* (1951, p. 225)

This conceptual fluctuation is reflected in the child's inability to classify, that is, to relate general classes to particular instances or the whole to its parts. As a consequence of this cognitive syncresis, the child may use terms such as *all* and *some* as if they were interchangeable. This is because he does not yet clearly comprehend that elements in a spatial continuum are discrete units. Without such differentiation there are no elements for classification according to, for example, a class (whole) or subclass (part).

The major developments in the child's conceptualization of object, space, time, and causality may be summarized as follows:

OBJECTS. The child still tends to conceive of objects in terms of their immediately experienced phenomenal configurations from moment to moment; he does not yet relate the changes leading from one situation to another into an integrated concept. As a consequence, for example, he believes that the shape of a mountain changes in the course of his journey past it. This indicates that the child maintains a concept of object *permanence* similar to that found late in the s-m stage. At the same time it demonstrates that he does not yet conceive that objects maintain their identity regardless of spatial position.

SPACE. It is clear from the above example that the child's conception of spatial relations is not yet that of a stable and unified (Euclidian) container in which things occupy specific positions and have particular, fixed relations to each other, thereby sustaining changes in position without being intrinsically modified. That is, he does not conceive of space in terms of an abstract framework (group) independent of the objects he is ordering in space, that is, their particular topographical characteristics, which shift with changes in the perspective from which they are viewed. Rather, the child's spatial schemes are dependent upon the degree to which (a) his locomotory powers permit him to explore his environment and (b) his still limited memory capacities permit him to remember familiar places. In this sense, the child's cognition of space is a "personal space-of-action" (Werner, 1948). Consequently, for example, three-year-olds are very likely to be disoriented if they enter a familiar place through a doorway they usually use as an exit.

TIME. The child, as we have seen, begins to distinguish between the symbolic forms he uses to represent and the things that are the referents of his expressions. As a consequence, he begins to be able to use symbols as means of evoking and reconstructing absent events. This is, of course, the major condition necessary to mentally remember experiences, concepts, and so forth. It is, then, the basis of a psychological memory system. As an example we may cite a report by Piaget (1951) of a seventeen-month-old child who named aloud the food she had previously eaten while she was in bed during her nap time and thought she was alone. Thus, the symbol is no longer simply an accompaniment to the child's action, but it becomes his means of reconstructing the action in memory.

According to Werner (1948), the child's temporal schemes have a "concrete and affective character-of-action." They are

> primarily expressed in terms of affective and motor activities which contain an implicit temporal reference. A two-year-old child says, for instance, "Bath, bath!" and by these words expresses a desire in which the time element of the near future is involved by implication. (p. 185)

Thus we see that the child's nascent symbolic powers support the ever-widening extension of his mental life not only into the remembered past but into the anticipated future. This is the basis for the child's developing a future time perspective.

CAUSALITY. The child's reasoning becomes increasingly independent of his phenomenal experience and subordinates it. An early example, reported by Piaget (1951, p. 231), is of J., who at two years, ten months, and eight days wanted an orange and was told that it was not possible to get oranges yet because they were still green, so that it was too soon to eat them. J. seemed to accept this, but while drinking camomile tea a moment later, she said, "*Camomile isn't green, it's yellow already. . . . Give me some oranges!*" Piaget interprets this as meaning that "if the camomile is already yellow, the oranges can also be yellow." Reasoning here is then independent of experience, but by analogy to it, the condition of one is made to participate in the other. It is this reasoning by participation that is now at the root of the child's conception of causal relations. Objects that are clearly different, and spatio-temporally removed from each other when viewed from the adult perspective, are taken to participate in each other by the child. For example, a shadow thrown on a table by a screen in a closed room is explained as if it were the result of shadows found under trees in a garden, at night time, and so forth. Necessity is purely subjective because the child does not differentiate physical causality from social obligation and desire. That is, the child thinks in a magico-phenomenalistic fashion such that desires for physical proximity influence objects, which are obedient.

Substage 8 (4 to 7 years). Intuitive: Quasi-Verbal Acts. The child's mental operations are still relatively tied to phenomenal experience: thought is still intuitive. The child thinks and communicates in representational symbols that are relatively imitative, imaginal, and playful. This means that his mental operations and linguistic expressions are still (*a*) egocentric, because they are still determined by his own present action, and (*b*) phenomenalistic, because they are still tied to perceptual experience without transforming it. Werner & Kaplan (1963, p. 188) observe that the child's

> verbal concepts are rooted in specific, concrete, action-contexts, and that their meaning cannot be formulated in symbols remote from such contexts.

As evidence they cite studies of children's definitions of verbal concepts such as *bottle*. Typical definitions given by five- and six-year-old children were: "there's lemonade in it"; "where you put water"; "when a little boy drinks milk out of it"; "where you pour something out of".

The child classifies objects in terms of his phenomenal experience. He begins to distinguish between *all* and *some* and to differentiate a continuous configuration into classes (wholes) and subclasses (parts). Nevertheless, these meanings still fluctuate for him because the relationships between the general concept and the particular exemplar, the class and the subclass, the whole and its parts, are only understood in an intuitive way. Inhelder and Piaget (1964) offer the following type of demonstration. The child is presented with a bunch of flowers, some of which are roses, and is asked whether there are more flowers or more roses. The response is that there are more roses.

Thus, the child's symbolic activity is still quasi-verbal at this substage because he continues to construct the significance of words primarily by assimilating them to his cognitive schemes rather than by accommodating to conventional usage (Werner & Kaplan, 1952). His assimilatory constructions have two major aspects. First, the child's spontaneous *production* of speech is particular to this substage. When dealing with conservation problems, for example (Inhelder *et al.*, 1966, p. 162), the child at the intuitive substage (*a*) does not use relational, *more* and *less*, terms, but rather absolute, *big* and *small*, terms; (*b*) does not simultaneously use differentiated, *long/short* or *fat/thin*, terms to describe an object but rather uses "one term to refer successively to two different dimensions" (that is, *big* and *small,* and then, *large* and *small*); and (*c*) does not use coordinated descriptives such as *more but smaller* when the problem involves more than one dimensional difference, but rather refers to only one of the dimensional differences, that is, to *more* or to *smaller* but not to both. It is only at the next, concrete substage that the child spontaneously produces relational, differentiated, and coordinated descriptive terminology. The natural progression of cognitive development, then, is marked by parallel changes in mental operations and verbal production.

As always, cognitive comprehension outstrips cognitive production of that understanding. The second characteristic, then, is that the child's *comprehension* of speech is quasi-idiosyncratic. On the one hand, he seems to understand the meaning of relational terms, descriptive terms, and coordinated descriptives when used by adults: he performs adequately when given verbal commands in which such words are used. Moreover, he can be trained to produce and to use the more advanced terminology. On the other hand, his understanding of these terms does not affect his cognitive conceptions, such as conservation, even when he is trained to use the advanced terminology in a conservation problem situation: "Our evidence offers little, if any, support for the contention that language learning per se contributes to . . . the achievement of the conservation concepts" (Inhelder *et al.,* 1966, p. 163). This suggests that the child's mental operations do not progress through linguistic communication. Rather, such findings support the hypothesis that the meaning of language is not passively acquired from environmental sources, but rather is mentally constructed (assimilated) by the child to accord with his internal schemes.

Findings of this kind lend credence to Piaget's (1967) general hypothesis that intelligence is the only truly autonomous self-generative system of action. Other systems such as language, but also mental imagery, memory, and perception are not. They are subordinate to intelligence and dependent upon maturation, experience, and social communication. It has already been indicated to some extent how language is subordinate to intelligence, and Piaget's views on the relationship between perception and intelligence will be described in the section on perceptual development. This section will therefore be restricted to his views on the subordinate role of mental imagery and memory. The exposition will necessarily be brief and will refer only to the major aspects of his complex and lengthy views, which encompass two books (Piaget and Inhelder, 1966; Piaget and Inhelder, 1968) and numerous articles.

The child's mental imagery grows out of his s-m activity. It is made up of deferred imitations of "gestures, attitudes and movements" that he has interiorized (Inhelder, 1965). Consequently, it is "limited to copying, or, more precisely, to imitating in a schematic way" the object of his knowledge. Since it copies the figure of the object it is said to constitute part of the figurative aspect of thought. By contrast, the function of intelligence is to operate upon objects of knowledge by transforming them. (For a fuller exposition of Piaget's distinction between figurative and operative processes, see the section on perceptual development.)

The child's formation of mental images is particularly influenced by the operative level of his intelligence. For example, in one of numerous experiments, children were presented with a piece of wire shaped in an arc and asked (a) to draw or cut out another piece of wire that would show how long the piece of curved wire would be if straightened out and (b) "to draw successive intermediate stages of the transformation." Children at the intuitive stage had great difficulty imagining what the transformations would look like. In addition, they tended to imagine that the length of the straightened out wire would be the straight-line distance between the ends of the curved wire. Only during the next stage of cognition were they able to imagine the transformations appropriately. Inhelder concludes, "The data available . . . show that the formation of operations directs the progress of figurative symbolism, which serves as a support for operative thought" (1965, p. 17).

Of course, if we take a more critical view, we must question the inevitability of this conclusion. Although they are important in their own right, the results of experiments of this kind lend themselves equally well to the alternative interpretation that mental imagery and intelligence have parallel developments and that each supports (and sometimes possibly directs) the functioning of the other.

The development of memory is dealt with in a similar fashion. Again, the hypothesis is that the child's memory is figurative (imitative) and that much of his mnemonic activity is dependent upon operativity. In one experiment, for example, children were presented with ten sticks ranging in length from 9 to 15 cm, in a series from shortest to longest. The findings show that after one week, memory of the presentation corresponded to the operative level, that is, to the child's own arrangement of the sticks when he was instructed to arrange them from shortest to longest. Four- to five-year-old children remember the sticks as (a) paired, a long with a short, or (b) in groups of three or four, with short, long, and intermediate ones, or (c) divided into two groups, one long and the other short. The most important finding for our purposes is that when asked to recall the presentation after six to eight months, the majority of the children's memories improved in accordance with the progress in operativity that children would ordinarily make during that period of time. From findings of these and other studies, Inhelder & Sinclair (1967, p. 22) draw the general conclusion that

> operative structures . . . control not only strictly logical behavior but become manifest as determining factors in many different fields; this has been shown in experiments on perception, on the mental image, in learning, and now also in memory.

Operatively, the child develops the symbolic capacity to coordinate simple representations of kinetic events, that is, actions upon objects, at this stage, but he still tends to understand the relations between static events in terms of their phenomenal configurations rather than of the transformations that must have transpired between them. For example, the child believes that the quantity of liquid changes when it is poured from one container into another of different shape. To the extent that he recognizes that transformations have taken place, "he assimilates them to his own actions and not as yet to reversible operations" (Inhelder & Piaget, 1958). This means that his cognitive schemes consist of "incomplete or approximate compensations" (regulative operations) between his percepts or representations. Completely compensatory mental operations of transforming percepts or representations of events begin to appear only at the next substage.

Although the child's regulative operations do not permit complete mental transformations at the intuitive substage, they

> do thrust a small wedge of potential transformations (i.e., elementary processes based on "possibilities" as distinct from "reality") into a type of cognition which is still almost completely bound to reality (either in the sense of external perceptual reality or in the sense of imagined actions). (Inhelder & Piaget, 1958, p. 248)

Regulative operations are the basis for an imbalance between the child's cognitive schemes that appears toward the end of this substage. Together with external perturbations, internal imbalance causes the disequilibrium that, according to the principle of autoregulative equilibration, is the necessary and sufficient condition for development toward the next substage of cognitive functioning (Langer, 1969).

The clearest reported example of the progressive influence of external perturbation upon cognitive development occurs in a study on the conservation of continuous quantity (Inhelder & Sinclair, 1967). The child is presented with six transparent glasses stacked in two parallel columns of three glasses each. Five of the glasses are identical, but the middle one in one column is taller and thinner than the others. In the bottoms of the top two glasses in each column are taps that can be opened to let the water flow to the glasses beneath. An equal amount of water is poured into the top glass of each column, and the child is allowed to familiarize himself with the workings of the apparatus. He is asked to predict what the water level will be at each glass, then to observe the actual levels, and finally to compare his prediction with the outcome. In this way the child is confronted with a discrepancy between his anticipations and his observations. The apparent contradiction of equality of quantity from glass to glass, and the child's actual observation of the successive trans-formations, facilitate partial progress in children confronted with this experiment at a transitional conceptual phase between this substage (the eighth) and the next.

> Only 25% made no progress at all, whereas the others (75%) benefitted from the learning procedures in varying degrees. (Inhelder & Sinclair, 1967, p. 7)

Children who entered the experiment at the truly intuitive substage, rather than at a transitional phase between intuitive and concrete think-ing, did not progress:

> Not one child . . . succeeded in learning the logical operations that underlie the elementary notions of conservation of physical quantities. The great majority (87.5%) did not make any real progress, while a minority (12.5%) attained an intermediary level, characterized by frequent oscillations be-tween judgments of conservation and judgments of non-conservation. (Inhelder & Sinclair, 1967, p. 6)

The child begins to construct the concept of number at this substage. The evolution of this concept and of the other fundamental concepts may be summarized as follows:

OBJECTS.   Although the child begins to conceive of objects as relatively permanent in the last substages of the s-m period, only now does he act upon things as if they maintained their *identity* in spite of change in position; for example, the child no longer maintains that the shape of a mountain changes when he views it from different perspectives. Now, when an object is transformed by an action, the child recognizes the identity of the object. Yet, as we have seen, he still does not comprehend conservation of objects.

NUMBER.   The child's conception of number begins as an intuition of whether there is more or less in one configuration than another. His understanding is based upon phenomenal experience rather than upon a notational system (group) for representing different numbers; that is, the child fixates upon the qualitative arrangement rather than upon the quantitative amount of the things considered. For example, Piaget

(1941) has demonstrated that the child does not conserve number when the phenomenal display is transformed. When presented with two rows containing an equal number of buttons such that they are lined up with each other, the child judges the rows to be equal. But if one row is then spread apart in front of the child, he will assert that it has more buttons than the other.

Toward the middle of this substage the child begins to use parts of his body, such as his fingers, to represent the quantity of things. He concretely analogizes parts of his body to things or to numbers in a fixed order, in such a way that if the series is broken up he becomes totally confused. Nevertheless, these gestural representations provide the initial basis for his performing additive and subtractive operations.

The child develops a truly quantitative conception of number toward the end of this substage. The association between parts of the body and the number of things is gradually given up. Moreover, the idea of quantity begins to be separated from the concrete phenomenal quality of the configuration.

SPACE.   The child is still not able to compensate completely for difference in perspective due to change in position. This is seen, for example, in his inability to (*a*) rotate the plan of his school 180° and indicate the placement of things and (*b*) reconstruct a route he has traversed in the reverse direction from his own movement. Although the child is developing an understanding of distance, he lacks the idea of an empty space which has invariant geometric properties that are conserved and that are partially independent of the objects in the space. Thus, he claims that the distance between two objects is altered when a third one is placed between them.

TIME.   The child does not yet regard time as the relation between distance and speed, nor does he differentiate between duration and succession. Rather, his intuition of time is bound to the phenomenal quality of the objects he is observing and the type of movement they are engaged in. Consequently, he will maintain that something that traverses a longer distance takes a longer time, even if it started and stopped at the same time as the thing with which he is comparing it. Two sources of water flowing into differently shaped beakers such that they achieve different levels are judged to have taken different durations even when the child sees them start and stop at the same time.

Werner (1948) hypothesizes that the child "masters time as he masters space." During this stage, space and time are not well-differentiated cognitive schemes:

The embedding of the temporal in the actual current event . . . may result in the phenomenon of temporal ideas possessing spatial characteristics. The duration of year and day is understood by many children to be an entity materially extended in space, a dynamic entity. The Scupins' six-year, eight-month-old son "looked up at the sky and said, pointing with his finger: 'That's where the day comes out, and there, farther along, is the night, and right up at the top is Christmas day.'" (1948, pp. 185–186)

The child's temporal sense is highly personalized and egocentric. At four years almost all children (86 percent) assert that time in a neighboring town is different; by seven years only half (54 percent) maintain that the time is the same (Oakden & Sturt, 1922).

CAUSALITY. The child begins to have the first inklings of genuinely physical explanations of phenomena. That is, he begins to see the need for continuity and contact between objects, rather than motives and intentions, as the basis of causal relations. That his causal understanding is still highly intuitive and rudimentary is revealed, for example, by his belief that clouds set themselves in motion by an act of internal force and desire. His nascent concern with physical explanation, on the other hand, is attested to by his addition, for the first time, that once the clouds are started they are driven along by the wind which the clouds produced by their flight. Nevertheless, even the child six to eight years old still accepts his immediate perceptions as true. Thus, he thinks that the sun and moon move because they follow him, never questioning whether they also follow other people and whether they then can follow him (Piaget, 1927).

Substage 9 (7 to 10 years). Concrete: Verbal Acts. Concrete operations are "formed by a kind of thawing out of intuitive structures, by the sudden mobility which animates and coordinates the configurations that were hitherto more or less rigid despite their progressive articulation" (Piaget, 1950, p. 139). The child's newly acquired flexibility of mental operations has three major consequences:

1. His thought is no longer bound to the particular phenomenal state of events, but begins to take into account successive transformations ("detours and reversals").
2. His thought can and does change from egocentrism to perspectivism, and it becomes possible for him to perform multiplicative operations. He begins to coordinate different points of view (his own and others) into a system or logical group of objective reciprocities. He begins to realize that the nature of things is not absolute but relative to the viewpoint from which it is considered. For example, when the child views liquid being poured from one container into another, he no longer sees

only the change in height or in width, but both. Simultaneous recognition that from one viewpoint the amount has increased while from another viewpoint it has decreased is necessary for the multiplicative coordination of these two variables.

3. He begins to be capable of mentally performing transformational operations upon phenomental configurations. He can mentally isolate the relevant variables of a display and can apply first approximations of reversible operations upon these variables. This ability is the mental source of the ability to form such concepts as conservation.

Thus, the logic of the cognitive activity that develops at this substage is the product of the child's differentiation of two reversible operations, inversion and reciprocity, that he will not coordinate, however, until the formal (tenth) substage (Inhelder & Piaget, 1958). Mental *reversibility* is the "permanent possibility of returning to the starting point of the operation in question." Mental *inversion* is the operation of negation whereby an operation that has already been performed is canceled. For example, the child may arrive at the concept of conservation of quantity by mentally inverting the act of pouring liquid from a beaker of one shape into a differently shaped one. The product, then, is a null operation or class structure. Mental *reciprocity* is compensation for a difference such that the product is an equivalence operation or relational structure. For example, in order to hit an object by bouncing a ball off a wall, the child makes the angles of incidence and reflection equivalent, that is, reciprocal.

The child's lack of integration between the mental operations of inversion and reciprocity means that his mind cannot yet function like a combinatorial system that relates mental operations to each other. It is presumably for this reason that the child cannot, for example, explain why a ball he bounces off a *crooked* wall does not hit the objective when he has kept the angles of incidence and reflection equivalent. His mental operations are not sufficiently integrated to enable him to assert a general principle which holds when all other things are equal. According to Inhelder and Piaget (1958), this ability is dependent upon the mental organization that develops at the next substage as a result of integration (coordination) of inversion and reciprocity. It allows the child to understand both (*a*) the principle of equivalence that governs hitting an objective by bouncing a ball off a wall and (*b*) the fact that failure to hit the objective must be due to another factor, such as the irregularity of the wall.

In sum, this substage is marked by the true beginnings of mental differentiation, as is seen by examining the child's classificatory conceptualization. He begins to take account of and to differentiate between the quality (intension) and quantity (extension) of the elements in a spatial configuration when he classifies them into wholes and parts. However, he still does not adequately integrate the intensive and extensive characteristics of class membership. Consequently, he still vacillates in his usage of *all* and *some*. Here is an example from an interview with a boy of nine years, eleven months (Inhelder & Piaget, 1964, p. 115):

> Are there more animals that fly in the world or more birds?
> *I don't know.*
> If you make a collection of animals that fly, and I make one of birds, who will have more?
> *The collection of animals, because there are more animals than birds.*
> Could one put the birds in the collection of animals?
> *No.*
> But are they animals or not?
> *Oh, yes.*

Surprising as it seems at first blush, it appears that important features of the child's acquisition of language meaning are still idiosyncratic at this substage. Werner and Kaplan (1952) cite the example of a seven-year-old girl who thought that vanity meant "a person looking in a mirror." These authors conducted an investigation into the acquisition of word meaning. They presented children with series of six sentences, each of which contained the same artificial word. For example, the artificial word in one series was *hudray,* and its adequate translation was "grow," "increase," or "expand." One of the sentences in that series was "If you eat well and sleep well you will *hudray*." After each sentence was presented, the child was asked what *hudray* meant, how it fit the context, whether or not the meaning he gave fit the preceding sentence, and why. The authors analyze many features of the child's preponderantly idiosyncratic assignment of meaning to these artificial words. To give just one illustration, the child does not differentiate between the meaning of a word and its context. Thus, one ten-year-old child defined *hudray* as "feel good" when she first encountered it in the sentence given above. She then proceeded to ascribe this context-determined meaning to *hudray* in the other five sentences even though it did not fit. "Mrs. Smith wanted to *hudray* her family" became "Mrs. Smith wanted her family to *feel good*."

In the ninth substage, the development of physical, but not logical, conceptions of objects, number, space, time, and causality are finally consolidated.

OBJECTS. The child begins to be able to relate successive appearances as reversible transformations. Objects that have changed not only maintain their permanence and identity but are *conserved*. At about six years, the child achieves conservation of discontinuous quantity, for example, when a quantity of marbles is poured into a glass that is shaped differently from the one they were in. Typically, children do not achieve conservation of a continuous quantity, such as water, for another year. Conservation of weight is not achieved until about nine years and volume until about eleven years. Piaget (1950) explains these age differences as due to the progressive difficulty in isolating the variables involved in the transformations that have to be compensated for in order to make a judgment of conservation.

NUMBER. The child differentiates the number of objects being counted (quantity) from the actions he performs upon the objects and the configuration in which the objects are perceived (quality). As a consequence, a few numbers suffice to deal with an extensive range of potential arithmetic problems. The developing distinction between quantity and quality is most clearly seen in the fact that the child no longer believes that there are more points in one configuration because the points are spread farther apart than in another configuration (Piaget, 1941). It is also seen in the fact that his enumerative activity becomes further freed from the gestural use of his body parts as a means of quantification.

SPACE. The child develops a limited, objective group coordination of parts in a total space. Thus, for example, he is able to indicate the location of some but not all things in the plan of his school when he rotates it 180°. He begins to understand that space (the container) has invariant properties that are independent of the objects in it (the contained); for example, he now asserts that the distance between two objects remains the same (is conserved) even when other objects are introduced between them. He also begins to use measuring objects, for example, a yardstick, as intermediaries for measuring and comparing the relative size of two objects. This development expresses his growing understanding of transitivity; if $A = B$ and $B = C$, then $A = C$, or if $A > B$ and $B > C$, then $A > C$. The child begins to be able to use any ruler, whether it is larger or smaller than the distances measured, as a means of determining their relative length, indicating that he is now able to coordinate two reference systems—the one that applies to the ruler with the one that applies to external space.

TIME. The child coordinates succession (the temporal relation between *before* and *after, first* and *second,* and so on) with duration. Consequently, he groups events into a coherent system such that velocity is taken into account. He asserts, for the first time, that two objects must have moved for an identical duration if they started and stopped at the same time, even if the distance they traversed is not equal. Likewise, for the first time he understands that the shape and height of flowing water does not affect the duration of the flow. Yet it is not until the end of this stage, at nine or ten years, that almost all children understand that time is the same in a neighboring town as where they are (Oakden & Sturt, 1922). According to Werner (1948), this understanding marks the development from an egocentric "personal" time to an abstract and objective "universal" time scheme.

CAUSALITY. The child of nine to ten years discovers the idea that if objects like the sun and moon move because of the desires or action of people, then they must follow other people besides himself. Since he now also recognizes that the sun and the moon cannot follow everyone at the same time, he deduces that they follow no one; everybody sees them as just above and following himself. Thus

> the child, after having regarded his own point of view as absolute, comes to discover the possibility of other points of view and to conceive of reality as constituted, no longer by what is immediately given but by what is common to all points of view taken together. (Piaget, 1951, p. 247)

Consequently, the child gives priority to the spatio-temporal or the mechanical properties of events to account for the behavior of objects. For example, clouds are said to move because the winds push them. This is causal explanation by spatio-temporal contact and transference of movement or force, but it is still based upon concrete, perceived facts. It is not understanding based upon deductive reasoning that imposes logical necessity upon causal relations.

Substage 10 (10 to 15 years). Formal Operations. When the child has well established the concrete, physical properties, that is, object, number, space, time, and causal properties, of events, he is ready to construct a formal "logical theory" of events that (a) stands independent of any particular event or instance and (b) considers possible events in addition to actual ones.

> Formal thinking is both thinking about thought (propositional logic is a second-order operational system which operates on propositions whose truth, in turn, depends on class, relational, and numerical operations) and a reversal of relations between what is real and what is possible (the emirically given comes to be inserted as a particular sector of the total set of possible combinations). (Inhelder & Piaget, 1958, pp. 341–342)

The transition in the child's mode of thinking from concrete to formal operations is dependent upon two necessary conditions, virtuosity and conscious discovery of perturbations. In order for his reasoning processes to progress, his concrete mental operations must have developed to the extent that his system of mental operations is in equilibrium and is efficient. This is what is meant by virtuosity. According to Inhelder and Piaget (1958, p. 282), the more the child's concrete operations attain virtuosity, the more likely he is to discover and be perturbed by the fact that events contain a "mixture of partial regularities and exceptions . . . which he cannot explain with any degree of certainty."

Virtuosity and perturbation result in the emergence of a new attitude which characterizes the child's transitional phase between concrete and formal operations. This attitude consists of (1) certain observational and experimental procedures of verification, and (2) isolation of variables by negation, which allows him to understand that an event observed to occur in some instances does not occur in others. The ability to perform the operation of negation is limited to situations in which a factor can be eliminated physically; the child is not yet capable of isolating variables by purely logical elimination. Thus conservation of weight and volume is more difficult to comprehend than conservation of objects. Moreover, the child is still limited to consideration of one variable at a time. He cannot simultaneously consider that variable in relation to another.

Children at the concrete substage attempt to understand puzzling events by "multiplication or association of empirical correspondences."

> They simply multiply correspondences and make new attempts to find relationships, hoping that something meaningful will automatically emerge from the abundance of data. (Inhelder & Piaget, 1958, p. 286)

Their new attitude at the transitional phase of the formal substage develops because

> sooner or later they have to retrace their steps, for if too complicated linkages are built up, the variables left unanalyzed at one moment will later reappear as disturbing influences. (p. 286)

This new attitude

> consists of setting aside y in order to analyze x free from disturbing interference and vice versa. Thus, the need to exclude one factor so as to vary another results from a reversal of direction in structuring correspondences; it involves an attitude toward abstraction or separating out variables instead of toward multiplication or assocation of empirical correspondences. Furthermore, it appears when the subject is faced with excessive complexity and too many contradictions in the raw empirical situation. (p. 286)

The culminating mental operation of the final phase of the formal substage is the integration and simultaneous usage of the two reversible operations, reciprocity and inversion, such that they become functionally equivalent. This development leads to the "structuring of a combinatorial system" that permits consideration of possibilities that "exist in the subject's mind as expectations" and that "can be formulated by means of implications, equivalences, disjunctions, conjunctions, exclusions, incompatibilities, etc., depending upon the particular case" (Inhelder & Piaget, 1958, p. 288).

The combinatorial system consists of the grouping of four cognitive operations or mental means of transformation: direct, inverse, reciprocal, and the inverse of the reciprocal transformations. These operations transform a variable into its direct identity (I), negate or inverse it (N), transform it into its reciprocal (R), or transform it into the inverse of its reciprocal, or its correlative (C). The combinatorial group is, thus, INRC, such that

$C = NR$, the correlative implies the inverse of the reciprocal
$R = CN$, the reciprocal implies the corrrelative of the inverse
$N = CR$, the inverse implies the correlative of the reciprocal
$I = NRC$, identity implies the inverse of the inverse or the negative of the reciprocal of the correlative.

According to Inhelder and Piaget (1958) this is the most integrated and equilibrated group structure of mental operations achieved; it is assumed to constitute the logic of the most advanced cognitive activity, even though the child is hardly aware of it.

It is this integrated structure of mental operations that henceforth underlies the invariant theoretical cognition of the physical concepts of object, number, space, time, and causality. For example (Inhelder & Piaget, 1958, p. 16), when faced with the problem of hitting a target by bouncing a ball off a wall, the adolescent no longer reasons as he did at the concrete substage by proceeding "from one partial link to the next in step-by-step fashion, without relating each partial link to all the others." Rather, he hypothesizes a law that governs the incidence and reflection of bouncing objects. It is a law precisely because it asserts that, in general, bouncing objects must necessarily behave in a certain way; yet it allows for qualifications that will accommodate the behavior of a particular ball. This law is that reciprocal implication between angles of movement produces equivalent trajectories.

> Thought proceeds from a combination of *possibility, hypothesis,* and *deductive reasoning,* instead of being limited to deductions from the actual immediate situation. (Inhelder & Piaget, 1958, p. 16)

Mental differentiation and integration of intension and extension underlie the adolescent's capacity to conceptualize a hierarchical classificatory system. The first step is differentiation between intension and extension. Intension is the quality of the class, that is, the properties that are common to the members of a class. Extension is the quantity of members in a class; it is based upon the precise symbolic numeration of the extent of elements belonging to a class. Mental differentiation between these concepts is not, however, sufficient to hierarchic classification.

> An accurate use of the quantifiers "all" and "some", which is what the co-ordination implies, . . ., means simply that the ascending process $(A + A' = B)$, and the descending process $(B - A' = A)$, which is its inverse, have become fused to form a single operational whole. (Inhelder & Piaget, 1964, p. 288)

> Such a state [of group transformations that construct theoretical invariance] exists if and only if a subject, when confronted with a set of elements which he has to classify, can anticipate the several stages involved in the complete classification and can also at the same time anticipate these stages in reverse order. In other words he must anticipate both the unions and the subdivisions. Thus there is equilibrium when the ascending method and the descending method together form a unique system of transformations, as they are bound to do when the subject anticipates the transformations as such instead of their static results. Both the anticipations and the hindsights enter into such a system, but because they are so integrated, they have the additional character of direct and inverse operations. (Inhelder & Piaget, 1964, pp. 288–9)

PERCEPTUAL DEVELOPMENT

Both Piaget (1961) and Werner (1948) assert that the child's perceptual acts, like his symbolic operations, evolve out of s-m activity. The apparent differences between these two major organic lamp theorists of perceptual development are more definitional differences about what belongs to perception and what to conception than theoretical differences.

Werner maintains that perception is one of the child's autoregulative systems of cognitive action. In the construction of the human world, many means or action systems are available to cognition. Perceptual judgments are only one major class of means by which it is possible to cognize; the other two classes are s-m acts and contemplative operations.

The developmental relationship of these three means to each other is governed by the orthogenetic principle that with progress the less differentiated mental means—sensorimotor and perceptual ones—do not drop out but become increasingly subordinate to the higher mental functions of contemplation. Consequently, it is highly unlikely that an operation of pristine perception independent of contemplative judgment can be found in normal adult behavior.

Moreover, Werner takes a holistic view of the relationship of different parts or modalities within perception. His idea that early in development the child's perceptual modalities, such as vision and audition, are relatively little differentiated from each other is the basis for the hypothesized greater frequency of synesthesia in childhood. A synesthetic phenomenon occurs whenever a sense-specific stimulus results not only in the corresponding perception but also in one or more others; for example, a color may be perceived as warm or cold. Synesthesia, then, is an intersensory relationship reflecting fusion (syncresis) of perceptual modalities.

Werner also characterizes the relationship of the child's perception to his objects of experience as initially undifferentiated. Objects are perceived only in terms of the child's perceptual reactions to them. This psychological undifferentiatedness of subject and object is termed "egocentric perception." Thus, the child who considers a few wisps of straw as a doll is not aware that he is imaginatively supplying the objective qualities of a doll. Rather, his perception of a doll is the result of a lack of differentiation in the total psychological organization between his subjective (motor-affective-perceptual) activity and the objective, factual attributes.

Egocentric perception often involves cognition of phenomena as animate or as having some "inner form of life." Werner calls this mode of perception *physiognomic* and contrasts it with the *geometric-technical* mode, which recognizes phenomena in terms of their everyday matter-of-fact qualities, such as shape and color. Physiognomic perception is different from and developmentally earlier than anthropomorphism and personification. It involves a lack of differentiation between subjective and objective factors. In anthropomorphism, the child is aware of the distinction between animate and nonanimate, but he intentionally projects an animate perspective upon a nonanimate event. In the same fashion, in personification the child has already distinguished between persons and nonpersons, but he finds it useful in realizing his desires to treat things as if they were people.

In sum, Werner thinks of perceptual activity as a cognitive system because it is *judging about* (reconstructing) the selected field of attention. He therefore places it within the general constructivist position; it is one of the child's general active means of cognizing things, acts, and events.

Although Piaget has never directly addressed himself to a consideration of Werner's position on perception, we may surmise from his view of perception and intelligence that he would not deny Werner's concepts. He would probably, however, incorporate them into his overall scheme of cognitive development, specifically in the preconceptual and intuitive substages, and would thus reserve the term *perception* for nonconstructive activity.

Piaget reasons in the following way. He admits that there are some partial similarities (partial isomorphisms) between perceptual and operational activity. He draws attention to the analogous results obtained in some experiments dealing with corresponding percepts and concepts. For example, when perceptual judgment is tested by presenting two lines of equal length as follows

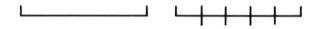

the young child judges the second to be longer, whereas when they are presented like this

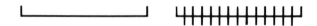

he judges the first to be longer. In an analogous, but operational, situation, when a lump of clay is broken into four parts in front of the child, he judges the four parts to have more quantity than the whole out of which they were broken. When, however, the whole is broken into twelve parts, he judges the whole to have more quantity.

One possibility, then, according to Piaget, is that there are formal ontogenetic parallels between perception and operativity. His reasoning is based upon the general principle that immediate knowledge due to perception and mediated knowledge due to operations are really only ideal poles of the continuum of cognition. In reality the child's perception is never truly immediate but always involves comparison of presently with previously regarded objects. On the other hand, the child's mental operations, particularly in their early manifestations from the intuitive until the concrete substage, are often very much dominated by the immediate nature of the spatio-temporal configurations to which he is attending. Moreover, like his operativity, the child's perception is never centered (as a unitary fixation), in the ideal egocentric sense, but is rather progressively decentered ("perspectivistic").

Consequently, Piaget rejects the possibility that perception and operativity are totally unrelated functions. He attaches little importance or plausibility to this hypothesis partially because his idea of the organismic organization of the child's functions has a generally holistic orientation and partially because perception and operativity share a common material source, namely, s-m activity.

A third possibility is that the child's perceptual development is often more precocious than his development of mental operations and may therefore be precursory to (prefigure) his operativity, as Michotte (1963) maintains, but that his perception will not progress as far as his contemplation. An example of the precocity of perception is the development of perceptual constancy of size and shape, which begins at least as early as five or six months of age, and possibly as early as two or three months (Bower, 1966). This kind of perceptual constancy clearly precedes the s-m construction of object permanence and the operational construction of object identity and conservation.

The "systems of compensation" that lead to perceptual constancy are strikingly analogous to those that lead to operational conservation. Both derive from and are influenced by sensorimotor activity, but Piaget's view is that they develop along divergent lines and even functionally are only analogous: both their functions and their invarient final achievements are different. Perceptual constancy is the result of inductive sampling (focusing upon and comparing different points of the configuration) that leads the child at each instance to a probabilistic approximation, if no objective change has been wrought in the perceived configuration. Consequently perceptual judgment—even the perceptual judgment of adulthood—is never absolute, nor is it completely accurate. Rather, perception of constancy may vary in the course of ontogenesis from under- to overestimation. By contrast, conservation is the result of a strictly deductive, symbolic readjustment of a configuration whose phenomenal properties have actually changed. Consequently, the judgment becomes absolute when the child is capable of mentally reversing the transformation he has perceived. Thus, before the child is capable of making reversible mental transformations his judgments are invariably of nonconservation, but when he becomes capable of reversible transformations, his judgments are of conservation.

The fourth possibility is Piaget's central thesis. The child's perceptual and mental operations are different in terms of (*a*) the relations they establish between himself and the environment with which he interacts, (*b*) their respective functions, and (*c*) their ontogenesis.

The divergent development of perception and cognition is clearest in the ontogenesis of some corresponding notions and percepts. Piaget presents the following type of experiment as evidence that perception and operativity may develop in completely opposite directions. In a perceptual experiment the child is presented with two lines of equal length:

Five-year-old children judge the lines to be equal. From five to eight, there is a progressive increase in overestimation of the top line. When the same material is used in an experiment on operativity, the results are the opposite. The two lines are first superimposed upon each other so that subjects of all ages judge them to be equal. Then, in full view of the child, the lines are separated until they appear as above. Now five-year-olds judge the top line to be longer because it juts out to the right, and they do not compensate for the jutting to the left of the lower line. Eight-year-olds, on the other hand, judge the lines to be equal because they operationally conserve the length of objects that change position.

Werner asserts not only that perception is a stage in cognitive development but that the development of perceptual activity continues, at least until adulthood, as a parallel system of action that is a hierarchically integrated part of the person's cognitive organization. Sensorimotor development is part of the same pattern, so that Werner's picture of cognitive ontogenesis is something like the branching tree shown in Figure 4.2.

Development is not only an ontogenetic but also a microgenetic process, whereby a psychological act unfolds over a brief period of time. The assumption is that

> activity patterns, percepts, thoughts, are not merely products but processes that, whether they take seconds, or hours or days, unfold in terms of developmental sequence. (Werner, 1957, p. 143)

The most frequently used experimental technique for investigating perceptual microgenesis is to present scenes in such a way that "the time of exposure is increased from trial to trial" (Werner, 1957, p. 128). Thus, Werner reports findings of parallel development in the maturity of percepts of Rorschach inkblots for ontogenesis (inkblots were exposed to three- through ten-year-old and adult subjects) and microgenesis (inkblots were exposed to adults for 0.01, 0.10, 1, and 10 seconds). From findings of this kind he concludes:

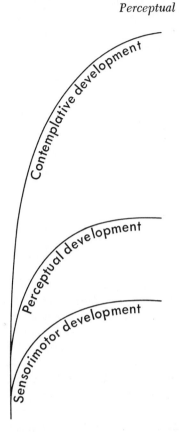

Figure 4.2 *Werner's conception*
of cognitive development

In both microgenesis and ontogenesis the formation of percepts seems, in general, to go through an orderly sequence of stages. Perception is first global; whole qualities are dominant. The next stage might be called analytic; perception is selectively directed towards parts. The final stage might be called synthetic; parts become integrated with respect to the whole. (1957, pp. 128–129)

The first two stages have been studied with respect to perceptual ontogenesis in subject-object differentiation (Wapner & Werner, 1965). Subjects are required to indicate where a luminescent rod must be placed in order to indicate their own body position (subject) and the true vertical (object) when they themselves have been placed in a tilted position in a dark room. The change in apparent body (AB) and apparent vertical (AV) judgments from childhood (six years) to

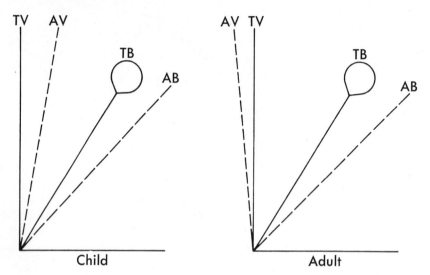

Figure 4.3   *Ontogenetic changes in apparent body (AB) and apparent vertical (AV) perceptions of the true body (TB) and true vertical (TV) positions*

adulthood (eighteen years) is shown in Figure 4.3. The shift from seeing body and vertical positions as relatively next to each other to seeing them as separate is interpreted as reflecting development from subject-object syncresis (global perception) to discrete perception of self and objects (analytic perception).

Underlying the achievement of a perceptual end product is an equilibration process defined as the resolution of sensoritonic forces (issuing from environmental and cognitive factors) within the organism-environment field. This sensoritonic theory of perception (Wapner & Werner, 1957) assumes that although sensory and tonic (postural-muscular) factors appear to be different sources of perception, they "must be essentially of the same nature" since they have parallel effects, and they interact and influence each other. A stable psychological field is therefore one in which stimuli impinging upon the person result in sensory states that are in equilibrium with his tonic state. An unstable field is one in which stimulation results in sensory forces that disrupt the tonic state, or vice versa. For example, when an adult is tilted to one side, sensoritonic forces alerted to the direction of the tilt cause him to try to reestablish equilibrium in the field by tonic forces (implicit muscular strain or movement) exerted in the opposite direction. When he is tilted, he therefore perceives a rod as vertical when it is actually tilted in the opposite direction from his own tilt.

With normal ontogenesis there is a tendency to overcompensate for perturbations in the field, such as those due to body tilt. Since the primary aim is to reestablish equilibrium by compensatory forces, perception is not directed toward progressive approximations to veridicality. Rather, it pursues the same adaptive aim as all other cognitive activity, namely, to construct the known world in such a fashion that the field of action is in increasingly stable equilibrium. For this reason the developmental shift in the child's perception of the positions of his body and the vertical need not be and is not toward his true body and the true vertical position (see Figure 4.3). In sum, Werner's position is that the perceptual end product is a judgment in which configurational, sensoritonic, and conceptual aspects are intertwined.

Piaget's thesis, on the other hand, is that perception is not a stage in cognitive development because perception is *attending to* (fixating or centering upon) the figural characteristics of the field of presentation. Perception is somewhat outside the general constructivist position: it is a *mechanism* (not an intellectual means) that is passively bound to stimulus configurations, as compared with cognitive means, which actively construct the field of concern.

The mechanism governing perception is probabilistic equilibration, which is defined as the statistical result of the child's sampling of a stimulus configuration through successive centrations or fixations. Now, a single centration is always biased (essentially because looking at anything from a single perspective must necessarily distort what is seen). The bias is in the direction of overestimating the part attended to as compared to that which is only given peripheral attention. The child's successive centrations can therefore only reach a perfect balance when:

1. His sampling includes the total population of parts or the entire configuration. This, of course, would be a highly inefficient means of sampling. It would save no work, and the child can therefore hardly ever be expected to use it.
2. He centers upon all parts with equal frequency. This is also highly unlikely because certain parts tend to be more compelling than others.
3. The child's memory system for short-term storage of the information obtained by each of his centrations is completely efficient, that is, he forgets none of the information gathered. This, too, seems highly unlikely.

Since it is highly improbable, in most instances, that any of these three conditions will be perfectly met, most if not all percepts are only partial isomorphs, or distortions, of the stimulus configuration. This is particularly true when the child perceives irregular figures. The larger parts will draw his attention more than the smaller parts, so that his overestimations in successive fixations will not cancel each other out; rather, he will overestimate the difference in size. This hypothesis has been confirmed by Piaget and his associates in a number of experiments on illusions and constant errors in perception. For example, children overestimate the difference between the longer and shorter sides of a rectangle in proportion to the actual difference. They are less likely to distort a regular form, such as a square. Their overestimations in successive fixations will balance each other out so that finally no leg of the square will be overestimated: the square will be perceived as a square.

Piaget maintains that with development the three conditions for perfect perception are increasingly approximated. Drawing an analogy to the ontogenetic decrease in operative egocentricity, he hypothesizes that the child develops an increasing tendency to focus upon configurations from many perspectives (to decenter). This tendency to increase the number of fixations on a given configuration as the child grows older leads to progressive compensation of each distortion by another. Consequently, Piaget expects that primary overestimation of larger parts of a configuration will decrease with age, even though the biasing tendency will never completely disappear because perception remains an inductive process (probabilistic sampling). This is precisely what Piaget and his associates have found for most illusions (primary illusions); for example, the relative overestimation of the longer sides of a rectangle decreases as the child grows older. Some illusory effects (secondary illusions), however, increase with age, for example, the overestimation of the vertical in the configuration

Piaget tries to attribute these increases to other intruding variables that are semiperceptual and semioperational, such as anticipatory sets, but he has not yet found empirical confirmation of this idea.

In sum, Piaget's hypothesis is that the child's perceptual end product is a partial isomorph of the stimulus configuration to which he attends. His percept approximates the configuration to the extent to which his sampling fixation procedure covers the stimulus. For this reason percepts are said to be figurations, that is, the perceptible partial isomorphs of the stimulus configurations. As the child grows older figurations usually, but not always, become more isomorphic, and less distortive, of the perceived stimulus configurations.

SUMMARY AND CRITIQUE

Organic lamp theory assumes that development is a process of interaction between organismic and environmental factors, but it focuses upon the individual's self-generative rather than upon the environment's socializing part in the developmental process. It assumes that the person is affected by social (and for that matter, physical) stimulation only to the extent that he first actively assimilates the stimulation to his schemes; assimilation is logically, if not temporally, prior to accommodation.

Thus, the child does not even clearly distinguish between the physical and the social milieu until the fifth s-m substage. For example, the baby will smile at a circular piece of cardboard with two holes in it just as he smiles at a person's face; or he will make the same gesture at objects as at people to signify that they should continue their interesting spectacle. It is true that during the symbolic operational stage the child increasingly discovers that there is a world external to himself which has physical and social properties that affect him. However, we have seen that he still transforms (interprets) these physical and social properties in accordance with his own schemes; he uses language idiosyncratically at least until the concrete substage; and he constructs personally meaningful "theories" of society even at the formal substage. It is only during the final phase of the formal substage that accommodation fully balances assimilation and development achieves an optimal state of equilibrium. Formal operativity is thus the theoretical end (most mature) stage toward which development is directed.

The environment, then, in organic lamp theory is merely the occasion for or scene of, and not the cause or agent of, development. It provides the nourishment or content for the child's emotional and cognitive digestion, which is necessary for autogenesis. It provides the occasions for communicative experience (from the "primordial sharing situation" of the infant in his mother's arms to the conventional linguistic intercourse) about values, norms, attitudes, and rules that are necessary for the child's integration into his cultural community (Werner & Kaplan, 1963).

It is to be expected, then, that the chronological onset of cognitive substages varies with the child's experiences and that cross-cultural differences obtain in average rate (see, for example, Price-Williams, 1961; Goodnow, 1962). It is also a theoretically plausible hypothesis that advanced substages may not develop in individuals in societies that do not provide the minimal experiential nourishment necessary to them. For example, Greenfield (1966) reports that some unschooled rural Wolof children in Senegal do not develop the concept of quantity conservation, whereas all schooled rural children acquire it. Findings of this kind, if they are replicated, are a first step toward determining the specific minimum experience necessary for the development of each substage. The general research strategy is to compare the cognitive development of children with different patterns of experience in order to assess what is required for continued progress and what is likely to result in slow, average, and fast progress.

The developmental sequence of cognitive progress posited by organic lamp theory would be tested in a crucial way if additional or substitute substages that do not logically fit into the posited sequence, or a theoretically plausible alternate sequence of substages, were hypothesized and empirically verified. To date such crucial tests have not been performed. If anything, the bulk of the empirical findings, including the cross-cultural data, lend strong support to the described sequence.

The major theoretical criticisms that may be leveled at the organic lamp portrayal of the sequence of cognitive substages are threefold. First, even though the sequence makes good intuitive sense, it is not theoretically clear why each substage posited is the sole possible, and logically necessary, successor to the immediately preceding one. Thus, the second problem is the lack of clarity about the process by which substages are generated. There are the theoretical assertions that each substage is a more differentiated and hierarchically integrated or equilibrated transformation of the previous one. However, precise and detailed empirical descriptions and theoretical explanations of the orthogenetic or equilibration process are not provided. Moreover, it is not at all obvious in organic lamp theory which substages are the result of transformation or alteration of the action systems of previous substages and which are the result of genetic emergence or coming-to-be of completely novel action systems. In the third place, then, the formulations of both the orthogenetic and the equilibration principles seem most applicable to alteration, that is, to developmental change that is both a continuous and a discontinuous transformation. Even the orthogenetic principle does not appear appropriate to the concept of coming-to-be (or passing-away), that is, to the genetic or maturational emergence of a novel function or system of action that may hierarchically integrate previous systems of action. The principle asserts that new developments are more differentiated and integrated transformations of previous, more global manifestations.

Chapter 5

Conclusion

A T ROOT, ALL THEORETICAL APPROACHES to developmental psychology make basic assumptions about the psychological nature of man, his actions, his change in the course of a lifetime, and the ways to explain all this. Among the three major theories, there are some important similarities and differences in these basic assumptions. As a consequence, there are both similarities and differences as to what constitute the central theoretical issues, what are psychological phenomena, and what is devolopment. In turn, there are similarities and differences as to what are the psychological units of analysis and the most appropriate research methods. In order to begin to make clear the basic similarities and differences it is necessary to compare the three theories briefly on some important common dimensions.

MAN AND HIS DEVELOPMENT

The mechanical mirror view of man and his development denies the possibility of any but quantitative changes. The child is born with certain reflex mechanisms that ensure that he will acquire and reflect the content inherent in the environmental agents that stimulate and shape his behavior. Change occurs only in the quantity of behavioral content (impressions, associations, and responses) that the person acquires in the course of life and the strength with which he maintains these impressions, associations, and responses once he has acquired them. Progress is the increase in behavioral content with time, whereas regress is the decrease in behavioral content with time.

The basic assumption, then, is that man's psychological nature is his behavior. Growth is a continuous process of learning (acquiring, remembering, and performing) behavior: "like a sculptor who shapes a lump of clay," the environment gradually shapes the behavior of the child (Skin-

159

ner, 1953). Consequently, the theoretical focus is upon the child's behavioral achievements, particularly those that bring him into increasing conformity with his physical and social milieu. And the empirical focus is upon the efficient cause of short-term or local change: the general aim is to determine how a given impression, association, or response is acquired over a short period at any given time of life. The idea is that gradual and continuous acquisition of these elements adds up to the growth observed at any age. The aim is to demonstrate (a) long-term memory of acquired elements and (b) the effect of these elements upon related impressions, associations, and responses acquired at a later period of life.

The organic lamp theory's view of man is much more complex. Its assumption is that psychological phenomena are acts and the experience, knowledge, and feelings constructed by these acts. Man develops many ways of acting in the course of his lifetime, however. The most primitive ways are the child's sensorimotor acts, which range from purely pragmatic movements to symbolic gestures and images. But these acts already include more than the unconditioned and conditioned behaviors that mechanical mirror theory usually assumes to constitute the totality of psychological acts. The most advanced means of psychological acting are mental operations, which range from egocentric intuitions to self-conscious thinking about one's own actions, thoughts, feelings, attitudes, and so forth, in relationship to those of others.

Organic lamp theory distinguishes between the form and the content of man's personal and social experience, knowledge, and feelings. The forms are progressively constructed by his own actions: since man's actions develop, the forms he constructs also develop. The content, however, is influenced by the particular interactions the person has with his environment. In sum, the forms constructed are determined by the stage of action to which the person has developed, while the content varies with the physical and social environment in which he lives. For example, a person's awareness of his own social status cannot take the form of a personal "theory" until he reaches the stage at which formal operations develop. Then, the specific content of the personal "theory" he constructs will vary according to the environment he has been interacting with.

The organic lamp view of development is also much more complex. It does not deny that development is continuous. As a matter of fact, it stresses continuity in its definition of alteration. It asserts that a system of action must be conserved in order for a transformation in its state (A_1 to A_2 and not A to B) to be legitimately observed. Moreover, not all changes are developmental; there are, for example, cyclical changes such as those of the menstrual cycle.

Organic lamp theory centers its attention, however, upon the qualitative discontinuity that marks development, although it by no means denies that many changes may be quantitative. Discontinuity implies that development is composed of a sequence of progressive stages that build upon each other. It also implies gaps or breaks between stages. This raises the central and most difficult question of how the transitions from stage to stage take place. The form of the solution proposed depends upon whether the development of a new stage is taken to be the result of a process of coming-to-be of new systems of action or one of alteration of existing systems.

Alteration means that a new functional stage is the transformational result of an earlier stage, which is the prime source of the transformation. An appropriate environmental setting is merely a necessary occasion, but not the source of development. The functional organization of the initial stage has within it the dual tendency and capacity to conserve and to transform itself under appropriate environmental conditions. The direction of the child's development is, then, immanent in his functional structures; the environment merely provides the appropriate and necessary scene.

The assumption that most of development is both a continuous and a discontinuous process has led organic lamp theory to focus upon alteration. The theory maintains that the developmental process is an autogenetic internal process of self-differentiation and hierarchic integration. The person is a self-regulatory organization of functional structures that continuously renew and transform themselves by their own actions upon (interactions with) the environment. These actions lead to the developmental reorganization (equilibration) of the person's structures, which subserve these actions, at a new functional level or more stable stage of adaptation.

In sum, the working relationships among acts constitute the functional structures of the self-regulatory system to which these acts belong. A system of action may be considered as the "logic" by which actions operate in terms of each other. The differentiation and hierarchic integration that characterizes the working relationships that develop among self-regulatory systems of action may therefore be considered to constitute the functional organization or the "logic" of the total mental organization.

Psychoanalytic theory, like organic lamp theory, assumes that the organization with which the child is born constitutes the initial functional and structural basis of his development. Biologically rooted functions are the organizing forces that differentiate and relate inborn structures into increasingly complex organizations, subject to the nature of the individual's particular history of interactions with his environment.

Unlike organic lamp theory, psychoanalytic theory focuses upon the energy it assumes to fuel the functioning of the individual's structures. It further assumes that this energy is instinctual sexual and aggressive energy. These instincts are invested in different bodily zones in accordance with a predetermined maturational code or epigenetic principle of order and tempo of unfolding. The instinctual activation of a bodily zone causes it to function. When the functioning of one zone is predominant, a stage of development is said to be constituted.

The clearest example of this formulation is seen in the psychoanalytic conception of psychosexual development. For example, oral functioning precedes anal functioning. The child must necessarily engage in the first before he can normally progress to the second. In and of itself, oral functioning does not lead to anal functioning, however. The maturation of the anal zone, that is, its predominant investment with instinctual energy, is the sufficient condition for anal functioning.

The assumption, then, is that psychosexual development is a process of coming-to-be. In such a process, each stage of functioning is not a transformation of an earlier stage, but rather a new stage that emerges at a given point of life and that takes precedence over the previous form of functioning. This conception is based upon the model of physiological maturation, which assumes a critical period for the emergence of a new functional structure. The implication is that the new function is potentially encoded in the child's maturational sequence. At the proper time, under appropriate environmental conditions, it emerges or becomes actualized. The previous stage of functioning is therefore only a necessary condition for the emergence of the new stage.

This view of the developmental process may be appropriate for psychosexual phenomena, at least for their physiological components. But psychoanalytic, like organic lamp, theory maintains that man develops many other psychological processes of a less instinctual and more rational, intellectual, and social nature. These are far removed from purely physiological functioning and from its biological roots. When we turn to these processes, however, we can no longer discern a clear and consistent psychoanalytic view of development.

Freud assumed that rational ego functioning is a transformed part of arational id functioning and that it is subject to environmental forces. Superego functioning, which includes at least some aspects of social functioning, is a transformed part of rational ego functioning that is the direct result of environmental influences. By contrast, ego psychologists assume that the child is born with the initial structures necessary for ego functioning. Loevinger goes so far as to accept the transformational processes described by organic lamp theory to explain all ego functioning and its development. Since ego functioning includes at least intellectual and moral functioning, according to Loevinger, it is not clear whether she would separate ego from superego functioning. Erikson attempts to make a greater theoretical distinction than Loevinger between the development of intellectual and social functioning and between the development of ego and superego functioning. He is not clear, however, as to which aspects of social functioning are part of ego functioning and which are part of superego functioning. Nevertheless, he assumes that to some extent the process of psychosocial development is governed by epigenesis. He has little to say about the nature of intellectual functioning and its development.

ORGANISM-ENVIRONMENT INTERACTION

As must be apparent, a core concept of all three theories is interaction: all maintain that psychological phenomena and their change are the result of interaction between the organism and the environment. The difference between theories lies in which action is emphasized in the interaction.

Mechanical mirror theory most clearly emphasizes the action of the environment. Environmental action is the cause of psychological phenomena, which mechanical mirror theory alone takes to be nothing more than behavioral reactions to environmental stimulation. Environmental action is therefore also the cause of the growth (accumulation) of acquired behavior.

Organic lamp theory is clearest in the assertion that the action of the organism is the primary source of interaction. The action of the child himself is the primary cause of both his own psychological phenomena (behaviors, feelings, experiences, and so forth) and the behavior of the environment. The child's own action is therefore also the primary cause of his psychological development.

Psychoanalytic theory sometimes emphasizes the organism and sometimes the environment, depending upon which part of the personality structure is being considered. The original source of id-environment interaction is assumed to be the individual's innate instincts. The prime source of superego functioning is the action of the environment upon the individual. Depending upon the theorist, the emphasis is more upon the environment (Freud) or upon the individual (ego psychologists) as the original source of ego operation. Erikson's position is somewhere between these two and somewhat unclear. Psychoanalytic theory is clear in its concern with psychological phenomena that are conscious, preconscious, or unconscious mental experiences, feelings, thoughts, and so on, although it by no means excludes behavior. It does not, however, provide a clear or consistent picture of the interactive sources of these phenomena. A reason for this is the lack of clarity as to their relationship to id, ego, and superego functioning and development.

CRUCIAL EMPIRICAL PHENOMENA

The performance of crucial experiments is often thought to be a basic means of assessing the comparative adequacy of two or more theories. The idea is to deduce contradictory hypotheses from the different theories about an empirical phenomenon that all consider important. An experiment is then constructed in which the different expectations are pitted against each other.

The difficulties in performing such crucial tests at this point in developmental psychology, and probably in the rest of psychology as well, are manifold. First, it is practically impossible to determine what, if any, are the common crucial psychological phenomena for two or more theories. In fact, as we have just seen, the theories disagree more than they agree about what psychological phenomena are—for example, whether they are physical movements only or also mental operations.

The second obstacle is the difficulty of designing adequate research techniques for pitting opposing hypotheses against each other. Aside from the purely technical problems of design, the difficulty is that there is little agreement about what constitute sound empirical methods. Chapter 1 points out that the choice of research method is intrinsically related to the theoretical approach to psychological phenomena and development. The mechanical mirror perspective is wedded to the experimental and correlational approach; the psychoanalytic perspective to the psychotherapeutic method; and, although it is methodologically eclectic, the organic lamp perspective places most faith in the clinical method.

A third obstacle is the difficulty of deducing theoretical hypotheses that explicitly contradict each other. A major source of this difficulty is the lack of clear and explicit definition of central theoretical concepts and terms. Thus, any experimental result could probably be interpreted to fit mechanical mirror propositions. The stimulus and response terms used to describe all psychological phenomena can be, and most often are, used in such a general and ill-defined fashion that they are nothing more than verbal substitutes for some vaguely conceived experiential antecedent and behavioral consequent. In addition, the mechanisms assumed to govern the acquisition (conditioning, imitation, mediation) and organization or connection (association) of behavior are also used in such a broad and usually vague manner as to make them convenient but uninformative, and perhaps misleading, labels whenever a change in behavior takes place.

One might also accuse organic lamp theory of not precisely defining its central concepts, such as orthogenesis, equilibration, schemes, assimilation, and egocentricity. However, this theory has at least the actual and potential advantage of precision because its taxonomic strategy is directed toward establishing and delimiting the meaning of such terms as egocentricity and schemes at different substages of development.

The central psychoanalytic concepts, such as id, primary process, instincts, consciousness, ego, and secondary processes, are poorly defined. They can be extended to almost any psychological datum. These terms would be less ambiguous if the taxonomic strategy implicit in developmental hypotheses about psychosexual, psychosocial, and competence activity were made explicit and the concepts were formally delineated and empirically justified.

Another important source of difficulty in deducing and testing opposing hypotheses is that the theories have different focal concerns. This is most clearly true for mechanical mirror and organic lamp theories. Mechanical mirror theory is concerned with how the environment modifies behavior. Basically, it assumes that the environment works through the mechanisms of conditioning and imitation. Organic lamp theory is concerned with how the individual transforms his mental structures and functions. Basically, it assumes that the individual transforms himself by his own actions.

This difference in approach has led proponents of mechanical mirror theory to try to demonstrate that at least some of the developments that organic lamp theory claims to be mental alterations are really modifications of behavior due to conditioning and imitation. The paradigm of the mechanical mirror argument can be seen in the following type of experiment. Take a conceptual problem such as whether the quantity of plasticine is conserved when its shape is changed. According to organic lamp theory, the child uses different mental operations, which lead to different judgments, at successive stages of development. Test children on this problem in order to determine what organic lamp theory would consider their initial conceptual level of performance. Then expose the children to an adult model who consistently gives judgments that are different from their own. Expose some of the children to models who respond at theoretically higher levels and others to models whose responses are theoretically lower. Reinforce (reward) the children for subsequent responses to similar problems if they change their performance to accord with the model's responses. The mechanical mirror claim is that if the children's responses change to accord with the model's, then these phenomena, which organic lamp theory considers to represent mental development, are really nothing but the shaping of behavior by imitation and conditioning.

The greatest success with this mode of argument has been reported by Bandura and McDonald (1963). Children made moral judgments of acts in terms of either consequence (theoretically low) or intention (theoretically high). An attempt to replicate this study (reported by Langer, in press) revealed many empirical and criterial difficulties that shed doubt on the findings. One is that about half the children keep their original judgments and about half change to the model's responses. This suggests that the children are confused because of the apparent differences between their own judgments and the model's responses. This does not mean that their underlying reasoning processes or conceptual competence has been modified. It does suggest, as studies of conformity behavior have long indicated, that situations like this one may lead to some short-term acquiescent behavior. That is, the child tries to say what he thinks the model is saying and what the experimenter wants. This would hardly reflect profound or lasting modification in the child's cognitive competence.

There is, however, a more important and general logical difficulty with this type of mechanical mirror argument. Perhaps it can be best illustrated by analyzing the following phenomenon. Revesz (1924) reports a study in which domestic chickens were trained to choose the smaller of two figures. Then they were presented with Jastrow's illusion (see Figure 5.1), in which the lower of two equal figures is perceived as smaller by humans. The chickens also chose the lower figure as smaller. Similar results on the Mueller-Lyer illusion in ring doves have been reported by Warden and Baar (1929).

Now, consider the hypothetical but plausible idea that the strength of the Jastrow illusion may be modified in both humans and chickens. It is equally likely, however, that modification can be achieved by genetic

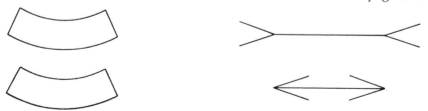

Figure 5.1 *Left, the Jastrow illusion; right, the Mueller-Lyer illusion*

selection (breeding) as by conditioning. Therefore, any behavior modification attributed to conditioning could also be obtained by nonconditioning processes. Consequently, experimental demonstrations of modification by conditioning are not determining evidence that conditioning is, in fact, the natural cause of the development of the phenomenon.

Moreover, the same illusion is found in two different species of animals with radically different physiologies and experiential histories. This means that the *genesis* (*origin* in organic lamp terms or *acquisition* in mechanical mirror terms) could hardly be the same even though the achievement appears to be (but is not necessarily) the same. If the mechanisms of acquisition are different, the same behavioral achievement may have different causes. In that case, even if it could be demonstrated that conditioning may cause the acquisition of a behavior, other causes are not ruled out, nor is conditioning demonstrated to be the natural cause of the phenomenon.

Organic lamp attacks upon mechanical mirror theory have been more subtle, but they also are the result of the theory's focus. In general, the attempt is to demonstrate that mechanical mirror theory underestimates the complexity and variety of psychological phenomena and of the mechanisms by which they develop. Organic lamp theory attempts to demonstrate that all the conditioned and unconditioned mechanisms can be subsumed under the developments it finds during only the first few substages of life. Conditioning mechanisms do not account for all the phenomena found during even those periods. And mechanical mirror theory says nothing at all about later mental developments. Organic lamp theory also attempts to show that imitation is a complex process that takes different forms during successive stages of development, rather than a unitary mechanism that does not change. And as the analysis of pigeons playing ping-pong in Chapter 3 indicates, organic lamp theory attempts to show (*a*) that even the behavior of animals is more complex than mechanical mirror theory suggests and (*b*) that it is incorrect to generalize from animal behavior to human behavior.

HEURISTIC POWER

Another important criterion for comparing theories is their relative heuristic power. Psychoanalytic theory has great potential for studying both normal and pathological personality development. To date, however, its long-standing promise has not really been fulfilled. As compared to its great productivity in the realm of theory, psychoanalysis has produced little systematic research on normal or abnormal development.

Mechanical mirror theory has generated very little research based on a developmental rationale. It is most concerned with explicating the nuances of general learning mechanisms regardless of ontogenetic status. The theory typically has not proposed ontogenetic differences in the operation of transmitting mechanisms because it assumes a blanket continuity of behavior. A notable and fruitful exception is some of the research on mediational processes. In the best of this work, however, the concepts come close to the organic lamp perspective.

Organic lamp theory, by contrast, has been fruitful in developmental research. Most of its research has yielded rich descriptive-interpretative data on the taxonomy of mental development, particularly its cognitive aspects. To some extent, the theory is also beginning to generate research on the processes of development from stage to stage.

NOTES TOWARD A COMPREHENSIVE THEORY

Two major tasks face developmental psychology if it is to create a theory that is descriptively comprehensive and has explanatory power. The first task has some resemblance to what Aristotle called final determination or how the end determines the process leading to it. The theoretical method is to specify the formal determinants of the end (most advanced and mature) stage that will be achieved in life and the direction that development must take in order to reach that final stage. When this is done, it should become possible to postulate tentatively the functional structures that must make up the organization of the initial (most primitive) stage if development is to take the course specified. That is, the procedure is to determine with what biopsychological capacities the child must be genetically endowed in order to develop to the final stage. Once initial and final stages have been well defined, it should begin to become possible to derive logically and investigate empirically what the intermediate stages must be.

The second theoretical task is the complement of the first. It is to specify the generative rules that must be built into the organization of functional structures of the initial stage if this stage is to determine the direction of development. The issue is: With what generative rules for the emergence or transformation of functional structures must the child be genetically endowed if his original organization is to evolve toward the end stage of development?

The resolution of both tasks requires specification of the logical structure of each functional stage of action in such a way that the first stage logically implies but does not actually contain the structure of the second, the second logically implies the third, and so on until the end stage. At present, the most appropriate mode of explaining how new stages of functional structures and systems of action are generated seems to be logical implication. In general, one suspects that logical implication is a more appropriate explanation than efficient causation, which at best has been useful for conceptualizing a limited set of mechanical aspects of physical phenomena.

We must formulate two sets of self-regulatory rules and their method of interaction. The first set of formal rules applies to the self-regulatory mechanism of coherence. These are conservative rules that, so to speak, tell the child not to accommodate to novel experiential nourishment, to ignore new facts or to treat them as familiar, already well-digested experiences (information) so that they can be easily assimilated to prior schemes. The second set of rules applies to the self-regulatory mechanism of progressive directionality. These are transformational rules that, so to speak, tell the child not to assimilate novel experiences (information) to prior schemes, but to discover new and anomalous facts and construct new schemes to accommodate them. When the conservative mechanism of coherence is dominant, the child is in a relatively stable state and there will be no change. When the balance tips in favor of the progressive mechanism, then the disequilibrating conditions for change are present. The child will develop new functional structures that can accommodate novel experiences so that the self-regulatory mechanism of coherence is once more dominant and the child is in a state of greater equilibrium.

The Cross-Sectional Theoretical Method

Prerequisite to the undertaking of these central theoretical tasks, then, is the clarification of what is involved in the kind of phenomena dealt with in developmental psychology. A comprehensive cross-sectional look at any given moment or stage of development would reveal a picture somewhat like that outlined in Figure 5.2. The observable local phenomena for theoretical consideration are interactions between the overt outputs of the individual and the environment. These outputs are quite different from each other; for example, the child's sucking behavior is different from the mother's nurturent activity. Each is directed toward eliciting reciprocal, but not identical, behavior. Moreover, the course of development is such that the ontogenetic changes in the individual's observable output are immense; consider, for example, the change in his patterns of behavior toward his mother from infancy to adulthood. The individual perceives the world as changing radically in the course of his own growth; yet in actuality, the output of the environment that is directed toward him remains relatively stable. Of course the environmental output changes somewhat; in particular, the person is treated differently. But the change in the output of the physical and social environment is not equal to the change in the individual's output over the course of development. Consequently, it seems illogical to assert that the environmental output is a primary cause of the individual's output, even in the sense that individual output is composed of learned inputs of environmental output. Man's output and its development could hardly be a mechanical and mimetic reflection of the environmental output.

The external outputs—acts and achievements—of the person must be regulated by nonobservable internal structures and functions. A necessary corollary of this axiom is that his initial organization of functional structures must be innately given in phylogenesis. Lorenz (1965, p. 44) has formulated the thesis precisely:

> Phylogenetically adapted structures and their functions are what effects all adaptive modification. In regard to behavior, the innate is not only what is not learned, but what must be in existence before all individual learning in order to make learning possible.

This innate organization constitutes the constructive equipment for ontogenetic action and growth with which the person is born. Here Lorenz (1965, p. 42) provides us with a happy analogy:

> What rules ontogeny . . . is obviously the hereditary blueprint contained in the genome and not the environmental circumstances indispensable to its realization. It is not the bricks and the mortar which rules the building of a cathedral but a plan which has been conceived by an architect and which, of course, also depends on the solid causality of bricks and mortar for its realization. This plan must allow for a certain amount of adaptation that may become necessary during building; the soil may be looser on one side, necessitating compensatory strengthening of the fundaments.

The constructive process is mediated by schemes of action, which must be part of both the internal organization and the external output of the person. That is to say, innate endowment with functional structures is the condition for the development of schematizing (assimilatory and accommodatory) activity upon the external world. External activity produces behavioral achievements, and these products feed back (consciously or nonconsciously) to the internal organization through development and modification of schemes (internal and external mental representation) of information. The result is further development of the internal functional structures and consequent changes in schematizing activity.

As used here, a scheme is a theoretical bridge between internal structures and external achievements, while schematizing is a bridge

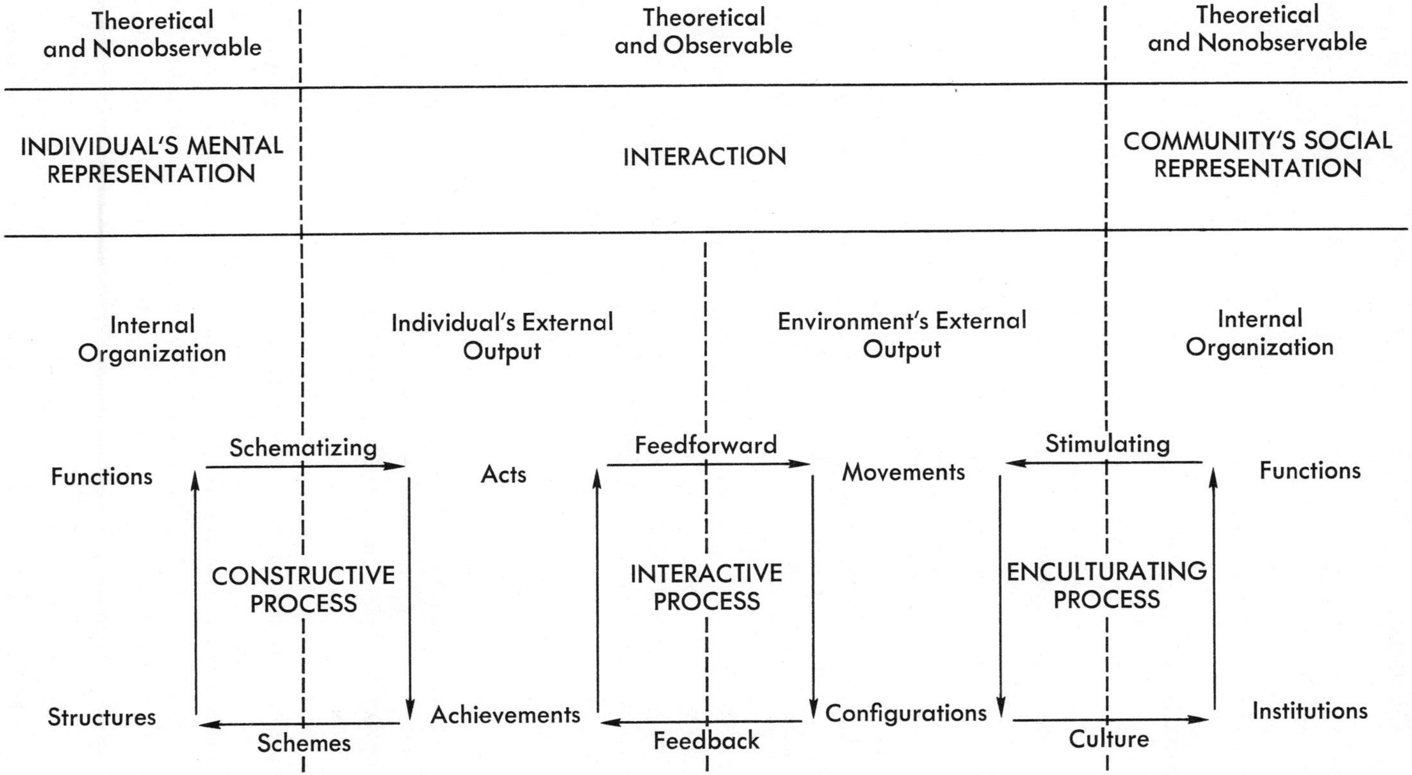

Figure 5.2 *A cross-sectional view of development*

between internal functions and external acts. These two theoretical constructs provide a conceptual basis that accounts for the so-called internalization and externalization of knowledge. They imply that from inception the child's cognitive acts and products are both internal (and not observable) and external (and observable). If our hypothesis that all cognitive phenomena are at once internal and external is correct, then the development of cognition cannot be studied by asking how the child internalizes external knowledge and how he externalizes internal knowledge. Instead the problem becomes one of understanding the communicative relationship between the internal and external forms of developing cognition. (For further discussion of the genetic relationship between internalization and externalization of mental operations, see Langer, 1964).

This, then, is the formal cross-sectional character of the constructive process of self-generative activity that must be elucidated in order to formulate a comprehensive theory of development. As Figure 5.2 suggests, the constructive process is only one of the three basic processes, to say nothing of the relations between them (for example, feedback and feedforward) that must be formalized and theoretically integrated for a full cross-sectional description and explanation of development. The limits of this book do not, however, permit an elaboration of the constructive process, let alone a discussion of all three processes and their functional relationships, for example, the role environmental external output plays in the content of behavioral achievements.

The Longitudinal Theoretical Method

A comprehensive longitudinal portrayal of development would require description and explanation of the evolving relations between all three processes—constructive, interactive, and enculturating. Again, such a treatment is beyond the scope of this book, and again only individual development and some aspects of the constructive process can be considered.

The most appropriate graphic model for the development of internal organization and external acts seems to be the inverted obtuse pyramid shown in Figure 5.3. In this diagram upwardly sloped arrows indicate the direction of normal development. As can be seen progress is always from one stage to the next (for the sake of convenience, we shall consider the first six substages as one stage). The functional structures of earlier stages are not lost with the development of later stages of organization, but are integrated into them. In accordance with the orthogenetic principle, they are changed or transformed. For example, the functional structures of sm_1 are transformed into sm_2, sm_3, sm_4, and finally sm_5, at the formal

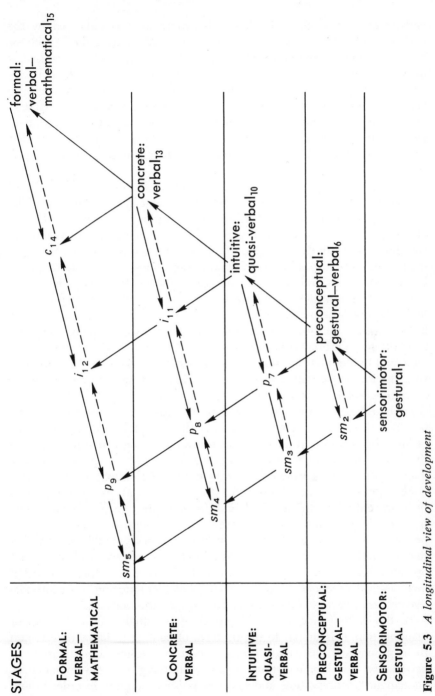

Figure 5.3 *A longitudinal view of development*

verbal-linguistic stage. This change is progressive, as indicated by the increment of the subscripts from one to five. This reflects the hypothesis that sensorimotor gestural activity is more sophisticated when it is used at the formal verbal-mathematical stage than when it is used at the concrete verbal stage. In turn, at the concrete verbal stage, sensorimotor gestural activity should be more sophisticated than at the previous stage, and so on. Consequently, progress is characterized not only by the movement from sm to p to i to c to f functional structures, but also by the fact that existing functional structures are transformed into higher forms at each stage.

Hierarchic integration (regulation and subordination), then, is always among the functional structures that are present at a given stage. The two basic characteristics of hierarchic integration are indicated by the downward sloping arrows of Figure 5.3. On the one hand, all functional structures maintain their relative developmental status in such a way that the highest structure subordinates and regulates lesser ones. On the other hand, functional structures are integrated in the form that they have reached at the specific stage of development, rather than in the form they had attained at a previous stage. It should be noted that even at the highest stage, sensorimotor gestural functional structures are developmentally more primitive than preconceptual gestural-verbal structures, as indicated by the fact that the highest sm structure has a smaller subscript than the lowest form of p structure. The same is true with respect to the other functional structures.

It should be obvious by now that operative relationships can only obtain between the functional structures that are present at a given stage of life. This means that microgenesis is always a progressive process from the lower to the higher functional structures that are present. In the diagram this process is indicated by the upwardly sloping *broken* arrows.

The consequent possibilities for theoretical analysis of progressive development are numerous. It should, for example, become possible to go beyond (1) the simplistic mechanical mirror notion that the growth of personal identity is merely the result of imitation of models, particularly parents, and reinforcement of it, as if imitation were a mechanism that operates in the same way at all ages, and (2) the more sophisticated but mythological psychoanalytic hypothesis that identification is an introjective process whereby copies of loved objects are interiorized.

To the degree that the development of personality is a problem of identification, it is similar to the problem of coming to know objects and their properties, particularly their causal properties. Investigation of personality development thus involves studying the development of permanence, conservation, and so on, of personal identity in order to find a coherent organization at each stage that is a progressive transformation of its precursor. The accommodatory function with its imitative component is only one important consideration. Even so, it is a very complex consideration because the type of imitation possible is determined by the cognitive competence at each stage and, in particular, by the schemes of action that the cognitive organization makes available. For example, it is impossible for the child to contruct hypothetico-deductive theories explicitly before the formal verbal stage. Consequently, it is impossible for him to imitate the ideological stance that he will be able increasingly to adopt (construct and imitate) when he becomes an adolescent.

The thesis is that the rules of cognitive functioning determine the type of schematizing activity, including accommodatory imitation, that is possible at each stage of development. Insofar as the process of identification involves imitation, its form (as distinguished from content on p. 160) develops in accordance with the progressively changing rules for imitative activity. Evidence for the assertion that the child's level of cognitive development informs (sets the limits to and the potentials for) the range of his imitative conduct is provided by a simple experiment (Kuhn & Langer, 1968). Three-year-old children do not usually perform the behavior they observe when they are told, "Look what I can do. . . . You can do anything you want." Four-year-olds treated similarly perform aspects of the model's behavior. Both three- and four-year-olds perform the observed behavior when they are told, "Look what I can do. . . . Do just exactly what I did." The difference, it seems, is that the three-year-olds have not yet developed the cognitive competence to decode the message implicit in the first instruction, that is, to perform the observed behavior. Both three- and four-year-olds understand the second, explicit instruction, and they perform accordingly. By four years, children develop the cognitive competence to understand an implicit instruction to accept behavior as a model. In passing, it should be noted that this cognitive developmental hypothesis accounts for many of the social imitation phenomena discussed in Chapter 3.

Even if one were to consider all aspects of the evolving rules that govern the accommodatory function, which also includes activities other than imitation, such as discrimination and rejection, the analysis would still be only partial and one-sided. In order to complete the analysis, it is necessary to consider the development of the assimilatory function from stage to stage and to recognize that the self is a special cognitive object with unique properties. Here, too, the rules governing assimilatory activity are determined by the cognitive organization. For example, the conception of oneself as an operator undergoes many transformations from (*a*) the initial sensorimotor gestural schemes of action in which the infant does not differentiate his own intentional efficacy from phenomenal causation to (*b*) formal linguistic mental operations in which the adult not only differentiates the two but establishes a hierarchy of values that functionally integrates personal intentions and capacities with external demands, controls, and causal powers.

The evolution of assimilatory and accommodatory schematizing, taken together, determines the formal aspects of particular developments, such as personal identity. The baby begins as an actor who does not differentiate (*a*) between himself and other objects, (*b*) between other objects, such as physical and social ones, and (*c*) within himself between subjective desires and objective capacities. His innate organization or preformed rules of operation determine the form of his initial schematizing activity. In turn, his activity results in the progressive evolution of the rules governing his assimilatory and accommodatory schematizing functions. A major consequence is progressive stages in the development of personal identity. The final or most mature stage should include the self as a consciously active operator that attributes the cognitive status of (*a*) a relatively subjective character, for example, internal, covert, psychological, spiritual, and ethical, to himself, and (*b*) a relatively objective substance, for example, external, overt, physical, material, and conventional, to other objects. The person also differentiates between other objects as to whether they are physical or social. More importantly, he differentiates within his own character between subjective wishes and objective abilities, and he hierarchically integrates all these aspects into a causal value system. For example, under certain conditions he may act according to his personal desires. In other situations he may distrust his personal assessment but not his "objective" analysis (which is still a personal or subjective construction but one that is usually consensually integrated with or accommodated to the assessment of others).

At this point it would be useful to highlight two basic and interactive features of this analysis. These features derive from the distinctions we have introduced between form and content and between origin and modification of psychological phenomena. Our thesis here is restricted to the origin of the form (it does not extend to modification of the content) of personal identity at each stage of development, which is determined by the person's interaction with his environment. The possible range of the form, but not the specific content, of the individual's interactions with his environment is determined at each stage by the schematizing competence he has developed.

Accordingly, we may hypothesize that, before the late sensorimotor gestural stage, the child can no more conceive of his own permanence than he can of the permanence of physical objects. Here we are still talking about a pragmatic conception that is restricted to presentational, here-and-now judgments until the end of the sensorimotor gestural stage, when the child's conceptions begin to be fully symbolic or representational judgments. Again, we may hypothesize that, before the intuitive quasi-verbal stage, the child can no more conceive of his own identity than he can of the identity of physical objects. And before the concrete verbal stage, he can no more conceive of his own conservation than he can of the conservation of physical objects.

Indirect evidence supporting the identity hypothesis comes from a study (Sigel, Saltz, & Roskind, 1967) on children's concept of "father." (Although the authors present their study as an investigation of conservation judgments their questions actually call for identity judgments, as defined in Chapter 4.) It was found that only 42 percent of five- and six-year-old children's judgments about matters such as "This father studied and became a doctor. Is he still a father?" were identity judgments. By comparison, 71 percent of the judgments of seven- and eight-year-olds were identity judgments. These judgments, of course, are about social objects other than oneself, and more direct evidence awaits application of this kind of method in questioning children about their own identity across personal transformations.

A thorough developmental analysis of personal identity is a major task that goes far beyond the present undertaking. The interested reader may refer to a significant attempt by Kohlberg (1966) to provide a developmental analysis of one important aspect of personal identity, namely, sex-role development. The general nature of Kohlberg's analysis is indicated by the major factors he considers in sex-role development:

> (1) The tendency to schematize interests and respond to new interests that are consistent with old ones. (2) The tendency to make value judgments consistent with a self-conceptual identity. (3) The tendency for prestige, competence, or goodness values to be closely and intrinsically associated with sex-role stereotypes, e.g., the association of masculinity with values of strength and power. (4) The tendency to view basic conformity to one's own role as moral, as part of conformity to a general sociomoral order. (5) The tendency to imitate or model persons who are valued because of prestige and competence, and who are perceived as like the self. (p. 111)

Recent psychoanalytic conceptions (particularly those of Erikson and Loevinger) of psychosexual, psychosocial, and ego development could well be integrated with this cross-sectional and longitudinal analysis of development. This consideration has been restricted to cognitive features because the best and the most empirical information available is on cognitive development.

Progress and Regress

The perspective presented here implies a certain view about progressive and regressive change. Developmental change is *progressive* when five criteria are met. First, it must lead to different general modes of action that change the significance of the organism's interaction with his environment. That is, the normative configuration of organismic action must constitute a new level. If, however, adaptation varies from moment to moment or is not conserved, the fluctuations are not general adaptations causing progressive development; they are simply particular, local adaptations. Therefore, the second criterion for progress is that the new norm of activity must be conserved in evolution. Changes must be hierarchically integrated so that coherence is maintained. That is, previously available systems of action must not be lost but subsumed and regulated by the new systems, while directed progress is elaborated: there must be a phylogenetic or ontogenetic augmentation of systems of action and an increase in the integrative and regulative role of the new level of action. In this way, organisms become more advanced and complex. Third, change is progressive only if new systems of action enable the organism to be more adaptive in his interactions with the environment. Fourth, change is progressive only if it leads to the formation of more advanced systems of functioning. In general, this means a qualitative advance in acts that is sometimes accompanied by a quantitative increment. Qualitative advances are said to occur whenever the organism progressively dominates his environment, that is, plays an increasingly large and active role in determining the nature of the organismic-environmental interactions. At the same time, of course, chance plays a progressively smaller role in determining change. The fifth and final criterion for progressive change, then, is a minimization of the role of chance; change is progressive if the organism increasingly acts to construct efficient means of adaptation and self-organization.

In accordance with these criteria, Figure 5.3 indicates that, except during the first stage, the individual operates at many levels during any given stage of his life. This means that in a given situation he need not be using the highest means available to him in order to show progressive development. The normal adult, for example, may have very primitive magical ideas about physical events. Piaget's findings of what he calls horizontal decalage indicate that the child need not use the highest, nor for that matter the same, means available to him when he is faced with different situations that can only be properly conceptualized in one way. For example, the child at the beginning of the concrete stage (at about six years of age) understands that a quantity of discontinuous objects, such as marbles, is conserved when the level they reach in one glass is different from the level they reach in another, differently shaped glass. The cognitive scheme of conservation that operates here is the same scheme that will enable him to understand that a continuous quantity, such as amount, weight, or volume, is also not changed by such manipulations. Yet the child typically does not understand conservation of amount for another year or two, weight conservation for about another two years, and volume conservation for another year or two.

If we distinguish between three major forms of acting, that is, acts of appreciation, comprehension, and production, then we can further recognize that an individual may operate at several levels during the same period of life. Consider artistic behavior. Most adults perform at a very primitive level when they are required to produce a painting. Yet some of these same adults have a relatively sophisticated understanding of painting. Even more have a fair appreciation that enables them to discriminate between an excellent and a poor work. In general, it appears that for most adults, appreciation of art outstrips comprehension, which in turn outstrips productivity.

Allied to the distinction in forms of acting is an important feature in the development of individual differences that we can only allude to here. At any but the first substage of development, there may be important individual differences as to which available system of action becomes the preferred or dominant mode. For interesting applications of this idea to perceptual development, see Wapner and Werner (1957) and Witkin *et al.* (1962), and to moral development, Turiel (in press).

Regression, like integration, is indicated by the downward sloping arrows in Figure 5.3. When higher functional structures disintegrate, the tendency is to use the next lowest functional structures available. The developmental direction of pathology and aging, then, is backward. But it is always backward to the forms of functional structures and actions that are present. It is never back to earlier, childhood forms of operation. This is true even in the severest form of regression where all but the lowest, the *sm*, seem to be partially dissolved. Thus, even the *sm* activity in the most regressed catatonic schizophrenia or senile dementia is different from that of the first two years of life. Regression does not mean that the senile or pathological individual operates in terms of the lowest functional structures or even of one configuration of functional structures. Moreover, it is necessary to remember that mental organization at any stage of development is composed of many functional structures that in turn are made up of numerous partial functional structures. It is highly likely that only the higher functional structures relevant to a delimited number of life situations have dedifferentiated and disintegrated, while the rest remain intact. Consequently, the pathological or aging person appears to be normal in most instances, and rightly so, because he is operating appropriately. His acts and achievements are primitive and therefore bizarre only in situations requiring functional structures that have disintegrated.

In sum, the direction of developmental change may be regressive as well as progressive. Following Hughlings Jackson's doctrine that the most advanced or developmentally highest mental processes are most susceptible to dissolution in psychopathology, Werner (1948, pp. 31–32) suggests that "many of the pathological phenomena can be attributed to breaking down of the subordinative regulative centers, thereby admitting genetically lower systems into independent activity."

Four characteristics become apparent as a consequence. First, advanced systems of acting may be dissolved so that hierarchic integration between systems breaks down. Correlatively, the boundary between systems is dedifferentiated and the systems fuse with each other; for example, conventional thought fuses with imagination. Werner argues that a comparative study of the formal but not contentual aspect of the behavior and mental operations of adults in pathological states and that of young children may provide important insight into the developmental principles governing progress and regress, their general commonality, and their specific differences. Second, just as primitive systems do not simply disappear with progressive development but are hierarchically integrated into the more complex organization that emerges, so aspects of higher systems of functioning are preserved when change is regressive:

> Just as any developmental stage preserves vestiges of the earlier stages from which it has emerged, so will any degeneration bear signs of the higher level from which it retrogressed. (Werner, 1948, p. 34)

Thus, not all the individual's behavior is marked by pathological disturbances due to regression. Third, the regenerative capacity is inversely related to the phylogenetic and ontogenetic level. The more advanced the individual's developmental status, the less he is capable of regenerating lost or impaired functional structures (von Bertalanffy, 1933). Fourth, in order for a new and higher organization of functional systems to be constructed, the old organization must be dissolved, and dissolution may often be accompanied by regressive behavioral manifestations until the new organization is well elaborated. Consequently, regression is not always pathological; it may actually serve progressive development.

Bibliography

Ach, N. *Ueber die Begriffsbildung*. Bamberg: Buchner, 1921.

Allport, F. H. *Social psychology*. Boston: Riverside Press, 1924.

Angyal, A. *Foundations for a science of personality*. New York: Commonwealth Fund, 1941.

Baldwin, J. M. *Genetic theory of reality*. New York: G. P. Putnam's Sons, 1915.

Bandura, A., & McDonald, F. J. Influence of social reinforcement and the behavior of models in shaping children's moral judgments. *Journal of Abnormal and Social Psychology*, 1963, **67,** 274–281.

Bandura, A., & Walters, R. *Adolescent aggression*. New York: Ronald Press, 1959.

Bandura, A., & Walters, R. *Social learning and personality development*. New York: Holt, Rinehart and Winston, 1963.

Berlyne, D. E. *Structure and direction in thinking*. New York: John Wiley & Sons, 1965.

Bertalanffy, L. von. *Modern theories of development*. London: Oxford University Press, 1933.

Bijou, S. W., & Baer, D. M. The laboratory-experimental study of child behavior. In P. H. Mussen (Ed.), *Handbook of research methods in child development*. New York: John Wiley & Sons, 1960.

Bijou, S. W., & Baer, D. M. *Child development*. Vol. 1. *A systematic and empirical theory*. New York: Appleton-Century-Crofts, 1961.

Block, J. Ego, identity, role variability and adjustment. *Journal of Consulting Psychology*, 1961, **25,** 376–383.

Bower, T. G. R. The visual world of infants. *Scientific American*, 1966, **215,** 80–97.

Breland, K., & Breland, M. The misbehavior of organisms. *American Psychologist*, 1961, **16,** 681–684.

Bühler, C. *Kindheit und Jugend*. Leipzig: Hirzel, 1928.

Cartwright, R. Effects of psychotherapy on self-consistency: A replication and extension. *Journal of Consulting Psychology*, 1961, **25,** 376–383.

Cassirer, E. *Philosophy of symbolic forms.* Vol. 1. *Language.* (1923) New Haven: Yale University Press, 1953.

Cassirer, E. *Philosophy of symbolic forms.* Vol. 2. *Mythical thought.* (1925) New Haven: Yale University Press, 1955.

Cassirer, E. *Philosophy of symbolic forms.* Vol. 3. *Phenomenology of knowledge.* (1929) New Haven: Yale University Press, 1957.

Cassirer, E. The concept of group and the theory of perception. *Philosophy and Phenomenological Research,* 1944, **5,** 1–35.

Erikson, E. H. Sex differences in the play configurations of preadolescents. *American Journal of Orthopsychiatry,* 1951, **21,** 667–692.

Erikson, E. H. Identity and the life cycle. *Psychological Issues,* 1959a, **1,** 18–164.

Erikson, E. H. *Young man Luther.* London: Faber and Faber, 1959b.

Erikson, E. H. *Childhood and society,* Ed. 2. New York: W. W. Norton, 1963.

Flavell, J., & Draguns, J. A microgenetic approach to perception and thought. *Psychological Bulletin,* 1957, **54,** 197–217.

Freud, A. *The ego and the mechanisms of defense.* New York: International Universities Press, 1946.

Freud, A. The mutual influences in the development of ego and id: Introduction to the discussion. *Psychoanalytic Study of the Child,* 1952, **7,** 42–50.

Freud, S. *Leonardo da Vinci: A study in psychosexuality.* (1910) New York: Random House, 1947.

Freud, S. Instincts and their vicissitudes. (1915) In *Collected papers,* Vol. XIV. London: Hogarth Press, 1958.

Freud, S. Mourning and melancholia. (1917) In *Collected papers,* Vol. XIV. London: Hogarth Press, 1957.

Freud, S. *The ego and the id.* (1923) London: Hogarth Press, 1950.

Freud, S. *Three contributions to the theory of sex.* New York: Nervous and Mental Disease Publishing Co., 1930.

Furth, H. G. *Thinking without language.* New York: Free Press, 1966.

Gesell, A. The ontogenesis of infant behavior. In L. Carmichael (Ed.), *Manual of child psychology.* New York: John Wiley & Sons, 1946. Pp. 335–373.

Goldstein, K. *The organism.* New York: American Book Co., 1939.

Goldstein, K., & Scheerer, M. Abstract and concrete behavior. *Psychological Monographs,* 1941, **53,** No. 2.

Goodnow, J. J. A test of milieu differences with some of Piaget's tasks. *Psychological Monographs,* 1962, **76** (36, Whole No. 555).

Greenfield, P. M. On culture and conservation. In J. S. Bruner, R. S. Olver, P. M. Greenfield *et al.* (Eds.), *Studies in cognitive growth.* New York: John Wiley & Sons, 1966.

Gurwitsch, A. *The field of consciousness.* Pittsburgh: Duquesne University Press, 1964.

Guthrie, E. R. Conditioning: A theory of learning in terms of stimulus, response, and association. *Yearbook of the National Society for the Study of Education,* 1942, **41** (II), 17–60.

Hartmann, H. Ego psychology and the problem of adaptation. (1939) New York: International Universities Press, 1958.

Hartmann, H., & Kris, E. The genetic approach to psychoanalysis. *Psychoanalytic Study of the Child,* 1945, **1,** 11–30.

Hartmann, H., Kris, E., & Loewenstein, R. M. Comments on the formation of psychic structure. *Psychoanalytic Study of the Child,* 1946, **2,** 11–38.

Heilburn, A. Conformity to masculinity-femininity stereotypes and ego identity in adolescents' reports. *Psychological Reports,* 1964, **14,** 351–357.

Hicks, D. J. Imitation and retention of film-mediated aggressive peer and adult models. *Journal of Personality and Social Psychology,* 1965, **2,** 97–100.

Hull, C. Quantitative aspects of the evolution of concepts. *Psychological Monographs,* 1920, **28** (1, Whole No. 123), 1–86.

Hull, C. Conditioning: Outline of a systematic theory of learning. *Yearbook of the National Society for the Study of Education,* 1942, **41** (II), 61–97.

Inhelder, B. Operational thought and symbolic imagery. *Monograph of the Society for Research in Child Development,* 1965, **30,** 4–18.

Inhelder, B., Bovet, M., Sinclair, H., & Smock, C. D. On cognitive development. *American Psychologist,* 1966, **21,** 160–164.

Inhelder, B., & Piaget, J. *The growth of logical thinking from childhood to adolescence.* New York: Basic Books, 1958.

Inhelder, B., & Piaget, J. *Early growth of logic in the child: Classification and seriation.* New York: Harper and Row, 1964.

Inhelder, B., and Sinclair, H. Learning cognitive structures. In P. H. Mussen, J. Langer, & M. Covington (Eds.), *New directions in developmental psychology.* New York: Holt, Rinehart & Winston, in press.

Jung, C. G. *Collected works.* Vol. 9, Part 1. *The archetypes and the collective unconscious.* New York: Pantheon Books, 1959.

Kagan, J. The concept of identification. *Psychological Review,* 1958, **65,** 296–305.

Kendler, H. H., & Kendler, T. S. Vertical and horizontal processes in problem solving. *Psychological Review,* 1962, **69,** 1–16.

Klein, M. *The psychoanalysis of children.* London: Hogarth Press, 1959.

Klein, M., & Riviere, J. *Love, hate and reparation.* (1937) London: Hogarth Press, 1953.

Kohlberg, L. A cognitive-developmental analysis of children's sex-role concepts and attitudes. In E. E. Maccoby (Ed.), *The development of sex differences.* Stanford, Calif.: Stanford University Press, 1966.

Kuhn, D., & Langer, J. Cognitive developmental determinants of imitation. Unpublished manuscript, University of California, 1968.

Langer, J. Implications of Piaget's talks for curriculum. *Journal of Research in Science Teaching,* 1964, **2,** 208–213.

Langer, J. Disequilibrium as a source of development. In P. H. Mussen, J. Langer, & M. Covington (Eds.), *New directions in developmental psychology.* New York: Holt, Rinehart & Winston, in press.

Loevinger, J. The meaning and measurement of ego development. *American Psychologist,* 1966, **21,** 195–206.

Lorenz, K. *Evolution and modification of behavior.* Chicago: University of Chicago Press, 1965.

Lovaas, O. I., Freitag, G., Kinder, M. I., Rubenstein, B. D., Schaeffer, B., & Simmons, J. Q. Establishment of social reinforcers in two schizophrenic children on the basis of food. *Journal of Experimental Child Psychology*, 1966, **4**, 109–125.

Luria, A. R. *The role of speech in the regulation of normal and abnormal behavior*. New York: Liveright, 1961.

Malinowski, B. *Sex and repression in savage society*. New York: Harcourt, Brace & World, 1927.

Markey, J. F. *The symbolic process*. London: Routledge & Kegan Paul, 1928.

Marx, M. H. The general nature of theory construction. In M. H. Marx (Ed.), *Theories in contemporary psychology*. New York: Macmillan, 1963.

Michotte, A. *The perception of causality*. New York: Basic Books, 1963.

Miller, N. E., & Dollard, J. *Social learning and imitation*. New Haven, Conn.: Yale University Press, 1941.

Mowrer, O. H. *Learning theory and personality dynamics*. New York: Ronald Press, 1950.

Oakden, E. C., & Sturt, M. The development of the knowledge of time in children. *British Journal of Psychology*, 1922, **12**, 309–336.

Pavlov, I. P. The scientific investigation of the psychical faculties or processes in the higher animals. *Science*, 1906, **24**, 613–619.

Pavlov, I. P. *Experimental psychology and other essays*. New York: Philosophical Library, 1957.

Piaget, J. *The language and thought of the child*. (1926) New York: Meridian Books, 1955.

Piaget, J. *The child's conception of physical causality*. (1927) London: Routledge & Kegan Paul, 1951.

Piaget, J. *The child's conception of the world*. London: Routledge & Kegan Paul, 1929.

Piaget, J. *The moral judgment of the child*. (1932) New York: Free Press, 1948.

Piaget, J. *The child's conception of number*. (1941) London: Routledge & Kegan Paul, 1952.

Piaget, J. *Psychology of intelligence*. New York: Harcourt, Brace & World, 1950.

Piaget, J. *Play, dreams and imitation in childhood*. New York: W. W. Norton, 1951.

Piaget, J. *The origins of intelligence in children*. New York: International Universities Press, 1952.

Piaget, J. *The construction of reality in the child*. New York: Basic Books, 1954.

Piaget, J. *Les mecanismes perceptifs*. Paris: Presses Universitaires de France, 1961.

Piaget, J. Psychology and philosophy. In B. B. Wolman (Ed.), *Scientific psychology*. New York: Basic Books, 1965.

Piaget, J. *Biologie et connaissance*. Paris: Gallimard, 1967.

Piaget, J., & Inhelder, B. *L'image mentale chez l'enfant*. Paris: Presses Universitaires de France, 1966.

Piaget, J., & Inhelder, B. *Memoire et intelligence*. Paris: Presses Universitaires de France, 1968.

Price-Williams, D. R. A study concerning concepts of conservation of quantities among primitive children. *Acta Psychologica,* 1961, **18,** 297–305.

Rapaport, D. Psychoanalysis as a developmental psychology. In B. Kaplan & S. Wapner (Eds.), *Perspectives in psychological theory: Essays in honor of Heinz Werner.* New York: International Universities Press, 1960.

Revesz, G. Experiments on animal space perception. *VIIth International Congress of Psychology, Proceedings and Papers,* Cambridge, Eng., 1924. Pp. 29–56.

Rheingold, H. L. The modification of social responsiveness in institutional babies. *Monograph of the Society for Research in Child Development,* 1956, **21** (2, Whole No. 63).

Rheingold, H. L., & Bayley, N. The later effects of an experimental modification of mothering. *Child Development,* 1959, **30,** 363–372.

Sears, R. R. Identification as a form of behavioral development. In D. B. Harris (Ed.), *The concept of development.* Minneapolis: University of Minnesota Press, 1957.

Sigel, I. E., Saltz, E., & Roskind, W. Variables determining concept conservation in children. *Journal of Experimental Psychology,* 1967, **74,** 471–475.

Skinner, B. F. *Science and human behavior.* New York: Macmillan, 1953.

Skinner, B. F. *Learning and behavior.* Carousel Films, 1959.

Spitz, R. Motherless infants. *Child Development,* 1949, **20,** 145–155.

Stern, C., & Stern, W. *Die Kindersprache.* Leipzig: Barth, 1928.

Thorndike, E. L. *Human nature and the social order.* New York: Macmillan, 1940.

Turiel, E. Developmental processes in the child's moral thinking. In P. H. Mussen, J. Langer, & M. Covington (Eds.), *New directions in developmental psychology.* New York: Holt, Rinehart & Winston, in press.

Uexküll, J. von. A stroll through the world of animals and men. In C. H. Schiller (Ed.), *Instinctive behavior.* (1934) New York: International Universities Press, 1957.

Vygotsky, L. S. *Thought and language.* (1934) Cambridge: Massachusetts Institute of Technology Press, 1962.

Vygotsky, L. S. Development of the higher mental functions. In A. Leontiev, A. R. Luria, & A. Smirnov (Eds.), *Psychological research in the U.S.S.R.,* Vol. 1. Moscow: Progress Publishers, 1966.

Wapner, S. An organismic-developmental approach to the study of perceptual and other cognitive operations. In C. Scheerer (Ed.), *Cognition.* New York: Harper and Row, 1964.

Wapner, S., & Werner, H. *Perceptual development.* Worcester, Mass.: Clark University Press, 1957.

Wapner, S., & Werner, H. An experimental approach to body perception from the organismic-developmental point of view. In S. Wapner & H. Werner (Eds.), *The body percept.* New York: Random House, 1965.

Warden, C. J., & Baar, J. The Mueller-Lyer illusion in the ring dove, *Turtor risorious. Journal of Comparative Psychology,* 1929, **9,** 275–292.

Watson, J. B. Psychology as the behaviorist views it. *Psychological Review,* 1913, **20,** 158–177.

Watson, J. B. The place of the conditioned reflex in psychology. *Psychological Review,* 1916, **23,** 89–116.

Watson, J. B., & Raynor, R. A. Conditioned emotional reactions. *Journal of Experimental Psychology,* 1920, **3,** 1–4.

Werner, H. *Comparative psychology of mental development.* New York: International Universities Press, 1948.

Werner, H. The concept of development from a comparative and organismic point of view. In D. B. Harris (Ed.), *The concept of development.* Minneapolis: University of Minnesota Press, 1957.

Werner, H., & Kaplan, B. *Symbol formation.* New York: John Wiley & Sons, 1963.

Werner, H., & Kaplan, E. The acquisition of word meanings: A developmental study. *Monograph of the Society for Research in Child Development,* 1952, **15** (1, Whole No. 51).

White, R. W. Competence and the psychosexual stages of development. In M. R. Jones (Ed.), *Nebraska Symposium on Motivation,* 1960. Lincoln: University of Nebraska Press.

White, S. H. A contemporary perspective on learning theory and its relation to education. Unpublished manuscript, Harvard University, 1967.

Whiting, J. W. M. Resource mediation and learning by identification. In I. Iscoe & W. Stevenson (Eds.), *Personality development in children.* Austin: University of Texas Press, 1960.

Witkin, H. A., Dyk, R. B., Faterson, H. F., Goodenough, D. R., & Karp, S. A. *Psychological differentiation.* New York: John Wiley & Sons, 1962.

Zaporozhets, A. V. The development of perception in the preschool child. *Monograph of the Society for Research in Child Development,* 1965, **30,** No. 2, 82–101.

Zazzo, R. The behavior of new-born anencephalics with various degrees of anencephaly. In J. M. Tanner & B. Inhelder (Eds.), *Discussions on child development,* Vol. 1. New York: International Universities Press, 1953.

Name Index

Subject Index